MW01278433

FROM THE STEEL CITY TO THE WHITE CITY

FROM THE

STEEL CITY

TO THE

WHITE CITY

WESTERN PENNSYLVANIA &
THE WORLD'S COLUMBIAN EXPOSITION

ZACHARY L. BRODT

UNIVERSITY OF PITTSBURGH PRESS

Published by the University of Pittsburgh Press, Pittsburgh, Pa., 15260
Copyright © 2023, University of Pittsburgh Press
All rights reserved
Manufactured in the United States of America
Printed on acid-free paper
10 9 8 7 6 5 4 3 2 1

Cataloging-in-Publication data is available from the Library of Congress

ISBN 13: 978-0-8229-4791-2
ISBN 10: 0-8229-4791-9

Cover Art: (*Top*) H. D. Nichols, and L. Prang and Company, "Chicago World's Fair 1893," 1893, Arts Department, Boston Public Library; (*bottom*) Schenley Park District, Pittsburgh, PA. University of Pittsburgh Historic Photographs, Archives and Special Collections, University of Pittsburgh Library System.
Cover Design: Joel W. Coggins

FOR COLBY AND REAGAN

Contents

Acknowledgments

I AM LUCKY to have deep academic and professional roots at the University of Pittsburgh, and this book is a product of everything Pitt has to offer. The idea for this project came to me over fifteen years ago when I was fortunate enough to have undergraduate classes with two professors who I later learned were both working to complete influential books—Edward Muller, *Before Renaissance: Planning in Pittsburgh, 1889–1943*, and Franklin Toker, *Pittsburgh: A New Portrait*. Both professors spoke about the Columbian Exposition as an omnipresent force that influenced not just Pittsburgh but the nation's identity, and they left me wanting to learn more. Their classes on Pittsburgh history and architecture have had a great impact on my career and for that I am eternally grateful.

As an archivist at the University of Pittsburgh, I have been fortunate to work with an incredibly knowledgeable and friendly group of colleagues that I am overjoyed to count among my friends. David Grinnell is the person best versed in Pittsburgh's archival record and was an invaluable resource for leads on where to find information and new avenues of research. Former fine arts librarian Kiana Jones pointed me to her research guide on world's fair resources at Pitt, which provided a quick overview of the material at my disposal. Kate Joranson, head of the Fine Arts Library, helped me track down images of artwork, including the missing *Modern Woman* mural. Judy Brink, former head of the Bevier Engineering Library, supplied articles that allowed me to better understand the language and science of electricity. Ashley Taylor's ability to provide constructive criticism, edits, and considerations after reading draft chapters was a remarkable asset in the early stages of this manuscript. Many of her comments and suggestions have enriched nearly every aspect of this book. Ed Galloway and Miriam Meislik also read early drafts of the manuscript and were eager to help me realize its publication.

As with any project that requires extensive use of primary sources, this book has relied on the kindness and expertise of several librarian and archivist colleagues. In particular, I would like to thank the helpful staff at the Chicago Historical Society, Art Institute of Chicago, Library of Congress, and the Senator John Heinz History Center, especially Matt Strauss, for allowing me to make quick, productive research visits to their archives. Julie Ludwig, an archivist at the Frick Collection in New York, also shared their most relevant material without my ever having to leave Pittsburgh. Everyone helped make my first extensive foray into the author's side of research a pleasurable experience.

Last, but certainly not least, I owe my most sincere thanks to my family. My wife Lauren's unwavering support and encouragement has been an immeasurable benefit to me during every aspect of researching and writing this book. Our daughters Colby and Reagan have also provided their own unique encouragement with every question about "Daddy's book" over the last several years. This book is for them.

FROM THE STEEL CITY TO THE WHITE CITY

Introduction

The Fair is wonderful—it is like a beautiful city in itself. . . . I feel as if I had only had a peep into Paradise.

—**Margaret Mitchell**

MARGARET MITCHELL, the daughter of a Western Pennsylvanian judge, struggled to describe the wonders she had just witnessed. In the last few days, she had seen enormous white buildings that appeared to be from ancient Greece or Rome, filled to the brim with natural and modern technological wonders. She encountered people from Egypt, Africa, Turkey, Germany, and Ireland, and even a Spanish princess. She also gazed upon the most impressive display of electricity the world had seen up to that time. Less than a week earlier she had boarded a westbound train with her husband, Kier, in their smoky hometown of Pittsburgh. Their destination, like millions of others during the spring and summer of 1893, was Chicago. They had made the journey to the shores of Lake Michigan to experience the World's Columbian Exposition.

While organizers of the 1893 World's Fair intended to commemorate the four hundredth anniversary of Christopher Columbus's discovery of the new world, the extravaganza became a celebration of the United States, particularly the progress it had made since the Civil War. Officially billed as an international exhibition, the fair offered the first previews of American technologies and scientific discoveries to foreigners and US citizens alike. At a time when the majority of the country still lived in rural areas, the world remained relatively small and so the world's fair was many visitors' first exposure to a variety of American regional cultures, not to mention cultures from across the globe. A trip to the exposition provided the first real indication for many Americans that technologies like electricity were on the verge of becoming household amenities. The fair also introduced many consumer products still in use today, including the first zipper, fiberglass, Quaker Oats, and Cream of Wheat.[1]

These exhibits were housed in what became the most visible and long-lasting influence of the Columbian Exposition—neoclassical architecture. Some of the country's greatest architects designed the fair's main exhibition halls in the familiar styles taught at the French architectural school the École des Beaux-Arts, providing a grand and beautiful environment for visitors to encounter the otherwise monstrous machinery that powered the Industrial Revolution.[2] The collection of fairground buildings paired with immaculate landscaping resulted in one of the finest examples of urban planning Americans had ever seen. At the conclusion of the fair, cities spent decades trying to replicate the look of the exposition, giving rise to the City Beautiful movement at the same moment when the urban population began to soar.[3]

Facilitated by advances in transportation, world's fairs became popular tourist attractions during the Victorian period, effectively bringing the entire world to a singular location. Much like another popular Victorian attraction, the department store, expositions used parades, art, and other promotions to attract visitors. Once inside, consumers examined the latest wares available for purchase, all meticulously classified.[4] Exhibitors and fairgoers also recognized that they could use the material culture on display as a means of organizing people. One could suddenly assert their social status by attending a world's fair, which promoted aspects of elite culture as the ideal, and purchasing items for use at home served as a constant reminder that they could afford such luxuries, particularly in the expanding middle class.[5]

In addition to establishing order within their own communities, intentionally or not, fair organizers also promoted the pervasive racism inherent in Victorian society. Planners gave precedence to the contributions of white exhibitors within exhibition halls, while pushing displays concerning nonwhite participants to the fairs' periphery. In Chicago, the Midway Plaisance, an area designated for amusement, contained such exhibits, thus insinuating that unfamiliar cultures were a source of entertainment and not worthy of the same intellectual consideration as the displays in the exposition buildings. Furthermore, because visitors and critics viewed world's fairs as exhibitions of science and learning, such denigrating exhibits seemed to provide authoritative justification for discrimination.[6] While organizers may have felt that living villages and amusements were less dignified, paying customers made it clear that they would rather enjoy the attractions of the Midway than peruse the dry informative exhibits in the exposition's shimmering halls. Ultimately, whether it was because of or in spite of racist depictions, people from all over the world flocked to see the utopian cities created at the world's fairs of the nineteenth century.

Overall, a world's fair serves as a microcosm of not what the host country is but rather what it aspires to be. It instills national pride and seeks to unite its citizens in a common goal. Furthermore, as a sign of their success, international exhibitions influence the very fabric of the nation, affecting its built environment, economy, and culture as the country moves toward realizing the aspirations on display. Using Western Pennsylvania as a case study, in this book I explore how these characteristics of one successful world's fair, the 1893 Columbian Exposition, developed locally by rallying civic pride to present an ideal view of Pittsburgh to the world and then incorporating elements of the fair to shape its future. Planners of future fairs, now called world expos, would be well served in considering how their exposition should exemplify the change they would like to see in their country, if not the world, while being mindful that the event will also reflect current cultural issues. Organizers will note that the planning and execution of a fair is only part of the journey, and that the final destination of widespread impact in the wake of a world expo only becomes clear decades later and is most evident at the local level.

Many across the country saw the 1893 Columbian Exposition as a chance for the United States to prove to the world that it was an industrial giant ready to become a global superpower. The nation's economy had shifted drastically since the Civil War, with a much greater emphasis placed on railroads and manufacturing, including iron and steel production. As a commercial center that had formerly served as a starting point for western expansion, Pittsburgh found itself as a major transportation hub during this period of extensive growth. Furthermore, natural resources such as petroleum and coal allowed Western Pennsylvania to become one of the largest iron- and steel-producing regions in the world. As a result, the road to the country's newfound success and power came directly through Pittsburgh, Pennsylvania.

Given its status as a focal point of the American economy, Western Pennsylvania was suddenly flooded with wealth. Manufacturers and entrepreneurs invested much of this money back into existing or speculative industries, fostering an environment of invention across the region. Better steelmaking processes meant bigger, more productive mills for men like Andrew Carnegie. Machines built to drive other industries began to generate a new form of power—electricity—through the innovation of George Westinghouse. Railroads expanded across the country to transport goods and ideas from coast to coast, traversing rivers, mountains, and borders. And through the success of such companies, an expanding middle class emerged in Pittsburgh, seeking ways to develop their own culture and carve out a place in the city to call their own.

In addition to economic and social developments, Pittsburgh companies, and to a lesser extent the city itself, also gained valuable experience in self-promotion. Like most white Victorians with disposable income, middle- and upper-class Western Pennsylvanians had developed a love for expositions. Dating back to the Civil War, Pittsburgh engaged in a cycle of local and international fairs and expositions that promoted the region's ever-developing resources and manufactured goods. In the process of planning exhibits and exhibitions, these organizers became adept at attracting fairgoers not only to their attractions but increasingly to the city where their products were made. As the nineteenth century drew to a close, it became clear that through their work the entirety of Pittsburgh was on display.

The Chicago fairgrounds provided a potentially lucrative opportunity for area companies to not only provide materials to construct buildings but also display for the world the variety of products being developed in Western Pennsylvania. It is true that the region's most famous contributions to the 1893 World's Fair, alternating current electricity and the Ferris wheel, had a lasting impact on the United States and the world, but that is only part of the story. The sum of Western Pennsylvania's exhibits in Chicago provided a snapshot of the area's industries, natural resources, and inventions, and successful exhibits at the fair launched local companies into the twentieth century, ensuring for the region a steady flow of work, money, and prestige. In addition, area lecturers at the exposition's often-overlooked World's Congress Auxiliary offered insight into Pittsburgh's sentiments and contributions to topics like women's rights, temperance, medicine, science, and religion. Taken together, Western Pennsylvania's representation at the Columbian Exposition was the first major step in demonstrating that Pittsburgh was more than simply America's crucible; it was, rather, a region of developing culture and innovation.

While displays were Western Pennsylvania's most apparent contributions to the fair, the area also sent thousands of tourists to Chicago where they were exposed to ideas, both in the fairgrounds and the city itself, which were then brought back home and implemented. Fairgoers were eager to travel from the Steel City to the White City to explore all they could, and then mold Pittsburgh in its image upon their return. Occurring at a time of relative prosperity in the region, lessons learned at the Columbian Exposition were readily adopted, particularly in the fields of urban planning, architecture, social reform, and leisure. Due to the region's economic success and the resulting expanded distribution of wealth, Pittsburgh, perhaps more than any other locality outside of the host city of Chicago, was in the best position to benefit from every opportunity the 1893 World's Fair had to offer. The region's citizens and industries proved eager to embrace the moment.

1

A Fair History of Pittsburgh

THE MORNING OF June 1, 1864, was hot and muggy, but the cities of Pittsburgh and Allegheny were abuzz with activity and anticipation. Months of planning were about to culminate in the ceremony scheduled for that afternoon, beginning with a parade. The mayors of both cities suspended all business between three and seven o'clock so that as many citizens as possible could attend the festivities and demonstrate their patriotism. The procession gathered at the Monongahela House and after four o'clock it began to march down Smithfield Street toward Fifth Avenue. From there the parade proceeded onto Market and Saint Clair Streets before crossing the suspension bridge to Allegheny, where it continued on Federal and Ohio Streets. In Allegheny's North Commons the group reached its final destination—the site of the Sanitary Fair.[1]

The United States Sanitary Commission formed in 1861 to support sick and wounded Union soldiers during the Civil War. Branches of the commission in cities throughout the country coordinated local fundraising initiatives and in autumn 1863 the Chicago branch held the first Sanitary Fair. This fundraising bazaar became the most popular and extravagant of the events held by several local branches. After attending Chicago's fair, Rachel W. McFadden and Mary

Ann Brunot, both members of the Pittsburgh Ladies' Branch, sought to bring a similar sanitary fair to Pittsburgh.[2] After their idea was rejected by Pittsburgh Branch president Thomas Bakewell, the Ladies' Branch took up the challenge of organizing the event, recruiting Brunot's husband, Felix, to serve as general chairman.[3] Felix Brunot used his network of friends and influence to convince the Pittsburgh Sanitary Commission to hold a fair, and on March 6, 1864, its leadership agreed. The commission decided that the fair would be held in June on the site of the old Allegheny City Hall. They also sorted area volunteers into committees to plan and organize the various exhibits and features of the fair. In addition to the formal work of Pittsburgh and Allegheny's more prominent citizens, local ethnic communities and churches supported the fair through donations of food and crafts.[4]

With just over two months to organize and build the Sanitary Fair, committee members sought out assistance from nearby communities. After the closure of the North Ohio Sanitary Fair in Cleveland on March 10, John W. Chalfant, James Park Jr., and Captain Charles W. Batchelor visited that city to purchase some of the buildings and fixtures for use at the Pittsburgh fairgrounds.[5] Once the trio secured the buildings, volunteer carpenters, committeemen, and other men with horses and wagons set off to Cleveland to dismantle the structures and load them onto railcars for the return trip to Pennsylvania, while another volunteer corps hauled the material from the Federal Street depot to the fairground site. Carpenters and laborers then donated their time to expand and erect the buildings in anticipation of the June 1 opening.[6] Meanwhile, the planning committee issued an address on April 15 to formally announce the Sanitary Fair and its purpose to raise money to support the work of the commission. To ensure the success of its event, the committee proclaimed, "We cordially invite the donations, contributions, aid and co-operation, not only of Allegheny City, Birmingham, Allegheny County and the State of Pennsylvania, but of Ohio, and all the States of the Republic."[7] The Pittsburgh Sanitary Fair would be a regional event in preparation as well as tourism and the sudden outpouring of support meant that exhibits began to arrive before the fair's buildings were completed and decorated.[8]

Chief Marshal General James S. Negley led the opening day parade, which included dignitaries like Pennsylvania governor Andrew Gregg Curtin. Local railroad administrator and former telegraph operator Andrew Carnegie, then overseeing Union military use of railways and telegraphs, marched in the group of assistants between local military and invited guests.[9] Also in the procession were the fair organizers, the mayors and councilmen from both cities, fire

Fig. 1. Monitor Hall contained models of the USS *Monitor*, the Confederate ship *Merrimac*, and cannon patterns from the Fort Pitt Works. In the background, the new Allegheny City Hall contained an art gallery and a museum called the Curiosity Shop. Harper Family Papers and Photographs, MSS 8, Detre Library and Archives, Senator John Heinz History Center.

companies, and bands.[10] Once they reached the fairgrounds, the participants entered Audience Hall for the opening ceremonies. Felix Brunot presided over the ceremony and Reverend William Preston from Saint Andrew's Episcopal Church delivered the invocation. After speeches by Governor Curtin and General Negley, the fair was officially declared open to visitors.[11]

Allegheny Commons contained several wooden buildings hastily constructed for the Sanitary Fair, including Audience Hall for concerts; Mechanics Hall to display locally produced machines, goods, and inventions; and Floral Hall, which included a Garden of Eden exhibit and miniature buildings in various international styles. The Ladies' Bazaar contained booths that displayed goods for sale and also included a Scotch Booth designed in that nation's traditional style. The Dining Hall included tables labeled for many of the area neighborhoods, towns, and counties so that members of the same community could come together to share a family-style meal for fifty cents. Farmers and other residents who could not afford to make monetary donations to the fair's cause contributed surplus meat and produce for the meals served there. Monitor Hall, the largest of the fair buildings, contained cannon patterns from the Fort Pitt Works, makers of the famous cast-iron Rodman guns, and samples of cannonballs. The building also housed a miniature lake containing models of the USS *Monitor*, the Confederate ship *Merrimac*, and several other smaller, less notable ships. Residents from outside the city made fresh evergreen wreaths that decorated these temporary buildings, giving their interiors a burst of color and the smell of Christmas, perhaps eliciting the giving mood that the holiday fosters.[12]

In addition to the wooden structures built for the fairgrounds, the Sanitary Fair also used Allegheny's new city hall, at the periphery of the Commons. The city council chambers hosted both an art gallery and a museum called the Old Curiosity Shop. Several local artists displayed their works in the gallery, which also included a collection of photographs.[13] More than 1,100 items were on display in the Curiosity Shop. Some of the more notable exhibits included the table used to write the Declaration of Independence, Continental money, and samples of clothing from various countries.[14]

The primary goal of the fair was to raise money, and its organizers collected donations in several ways. Admission to the many buildings, attractions, and evening entertainments ranged from twenty-five cents to one dollar.[15] In addition to the continual transactions at the bazaar, the final week of the fair included the sale of special items "such as autograph letters of well-known public characters, and photographs of persons and places of interest as well as curiosities and war relics, and good prices were obtained."[16] One such item was a letter signed by President Abraham Lincoln in which he specifically referenced the Pittsburgh Sanitary Fair. When the fair closed on June 18, it had raised over $320,000 for the Sanitary Commission. Although this was not the most money raised by a city's fair, the per capita donation of $3.47 proved that Western Pennsylvania was the most generous region in the country, and perhaps the most eager to attend an exhibition.[17]

While the noble patriotic cause of the Sanitary Commission was a strong factor in drawing residents to the fair, attendees' curiosity about the displays and entertainment was another likely influence. Upon the opening of the fairgrounds, the *Pittsburgh Gazette* proclaimed, "Never before in the history of Western Pennsylvania has an opportunity been presented to look upon so many, so rare and so exquisite attractions as will be exhibited in the various halls and booths of this Sanitary Fair."[18] In just eighteen days, the Pittsburgh Sanitary Fair had sparked a desire in Western Pennsylvanians to attend fairs, peruse their exhibits, and enjoy their entertainment. Furthermore, it provided valuable experience in organizing a large-scale public exhibition. Pittsburghers, like most white, middle- and upper-class Victorians, had developed a taste for the spectacular, and the era's obsession with great expositions would feed their craving through the rest of the nineteenth century.

———————

The Civil War had a significant impact on Western Pennsylvania. The successful application of railroads to move soldiers and supplies, thanks in part to Andrew Carnegie, demonstrated that this mode of transportation had a viable postwar future, especially for industrial and commercial centers like Pittsburgh. As networks of railroads began to radiate from cities throughout the country, regions that had been largely isolated from each other prior to the war were suddenly connected to more established cities in the East. While the railroads were able to quickly transport goods over long distances, they also created a sudden need for coal and rails and, perhaps more importantly, they spread news, ideas, and people. Trains transported newspapers and mail across regions in a matter of hours and across states in days, providing more robust accounts of events only minimally described via telegraph. Performers could also easily traverse the country, providing a more cohesive nationwide experience to theatergoers, circus attendees, and the like, thus helping to form a national cultural identity.[19] As a major transportation hub connecting the East Coast to the West, many of these people, goods, and information passed through Pittsburgh.

The proliferation of railroads in Western Pennsylvania also tied into the expansion of pre-existing industries, like oil. Edwin Drake drilled the first commercial oil well in Titusville, Pennsylvania, in 1859. The sudden supply of petroleum fed into the need for a better, cheaper fuel source than the whale fat then used for lighting, thus ensuring its early success.[20] As oilmen developed and improved drilling processes, there was a sudden demand for iron to manufacture the required boilers, engines, derricks, and piping, among other items. Once the oil was secured, it had to be sent to refineries, which used iron stills. Efficient transportation of oil was also necessary to meet increasing demands, and so companies laid rail lines to connect the oil fields to river transportation or established rail routes, requiring a greater supply of iron rails in the Pittsburgh region.

Iron production had been a part of Pittsburgh's economy for nearly a century before the Civil War, but the sudden demand for rails resulted in the tripling of the iron and steel workforce during the 1860s, with the amount of money invested in the metal industries increasing over 300 percent and product value rising over 500 percent.[21] It was during this period that Carnegie planted the seeds for his future steel empire with the consolidation of two companies to form the Union Iron Mills in 1865. That same year he also created the Keystone Bridge Company to design and build railroad bridges, placing orders for all its required iron with his Union mills. In 1870 he formed a company to manage his new blast furnaces, thus controlling the production of iron from raw materials to finished product. Advancing his enterprise even further, in 1875 Carnegie led the transition from iron to mass-produced steel in Allegheny County, and soon the entire country, with the opening of the Edgar Thomson Works in Braddock.

Other industries related to railroads, including the manufacture of locomotives, train components, and equipment, flourished in the region. These ventures, combined with the increased need for coal, resulted in an influx of wealth and people suddenly thrust upon Western Pennsylvania. Furthermore, the proliferation of railroads throughout the country allowed for cheaper and faster shipping of wares from already established industries like glass. In a little over a decade after the Sanitary Fair, Pittsburgh found an opportunity to showcase its growth at the first major world's fair hosted in the United States—the 1876 Centennial Exposition.

Held in Philadelphia to celebrate the centennial of the signing of the Declaration of Independence, the International Exhibition of Arts, Manufactures and Products of the Soil and Mine, also known as the 1876 World's Fair, comprised thirty thousand exhibits in buildings covering over 230 acres of the city's Fairmount Park.[22] Capitalizing on the experiences of the Civil War, many of the exposition's directors and officials had participated in planning large-scale events such as Philadelphia's Sanitary Fair or military mobilization, which made them well suited to organize a spectacle like the fair. While American fairs up to this point had focused on regional products and typically attracted a local audience, the Centennial Exposition featured exhibits from all over the country in an attempt to prove to the world that the American economy and government had fully recovered from the stresses of Reconstruction and were ready for business.[23] By the conclusion of the Centennial Exposition, ten million visitors from all over the globe had experienced the fair.

True to its name, much of the exposition was a celebration of America's natural resources and industry. While the fair included such groundbreaking inventions as Alexander Graham Bell's telephone and the Remington typewriter, the main attraction was the enormous Corliss steam engine. Standing forty-five feet high and connected to much of the machinery on the fairgrounds by over a mile of belts, the Corliss engine was the centerpiece of the opening day festivities on May 10, 1876, when US president Ulysses S. Grant and Brazilian emperor

Dom Pedro II pulled the levers to release the steam and start the machine.[24] The Centennial Exposition was the first international showcase of American innovation and manufacturing might, putting the country's burgeoning industry on display for the world.

The exhibits of Western Pennsylvanian companies and inventors demonstrated the beginnings of the shift from established industries like glass to growing interest and successes in railroads and iron and steel production. Traditional products of Western Pennsylvania were well represented at the Centennial Exposition, with *Frank Leslie's Illustrated Historical Register* of the fair proclaiming that "Pittsburg comes out stronger than any other section in the matter of glass, for which her manufacturers are celebrated. The fine glass of the O'Hara works is particularly beautiful."[25] In addition to glass, the fair also featured the work of craftsmen and manufacturers of agricultural machinery, indicating that while the city of Pittsburgh was urban the surrounding areas of Western Pennsylvania remained primarily rural.[26]

Highlighting new areas of focus, Porter, Bell and Company displayed narrow-gage locomotives and tenders. Other Pittsburgh companies exhibited components used by the rail industry, like railway springs.[27] Perhaps the most successful railroad-related Pittsburgh exhibit was from the Westinghouse Air Brake Company. George Westinghouse had moved to Pittsburgh from Schenectady, New York, in 1868 with an idea for a new, more effective train-braking mechanism using compressed air. After the first successful test of the Westinghouse brake, he was able to convince the Pennsylvania Railroad and several others of the value of the invention, giving him the backing he needed to establish the Westinghouse Air Brake Company.[28] After a business trip across the Atlantic to sell his brakes to railroads in England, Westinghouse was able to reach the entire world through his exhibit in Philadelphia. In addition to a variety of his revolutionary air brakes, Westinghouse also displayed air compressors and signaling devices.[29]

The growing and evolving metal industries of Western Pennsylvania were also on full display in Philadelphia. The Jones and Laughlin American Iron Works displayed samples of its iron products, including rails, and its pulleys and hangers were used to drive machine shop tools for the exposition. Iron tubing and pipes, as well as rolling mill rolls, were also exhibited as examples of the industry that would soon dominate the Pittsburgh region.[30] Overall, more than a dozen area companies exhibited iron and steel product samples in Philadelphia, signifying that this industry was the future of the region's economy.[31]

Foreshadowing his fast-approaching dominance of Western Pennsylvania,

the greatest displays of Pittsburgh's developing iron industry were the contributions made by the companies of Andrew Carnegie. Carnegie found himself on
the American Iron and Steel Association committee that organized the exhibits
of iron ore and products at the exposition and, not coincidentally, his companies exhibited their displays in the Main Building of the fair. These exhibits
included a model of the Lucy Furnace and samples of Union Iron Mills' wrought
iron products, including bars and beams.[32] While abstract samples were fine
to look at, examples of material used in real projects were more effective in
demonstrating the importance of Carnegie's mills. Union Iron brought some of
the wrought iron couplings used in the arches of the recently completed Eads
Bridge in St. Louis.[33] An even more impressive and immediate demonstration
of its product, though, was the wrought iron used by Keystone Bridge in the
structure of the exposition's Horticultural Building.[34]

While Pittsburgh's future tycoons Westinghouse and Carnegie were busy
exhibiting at the Centennial Exposition, another visited the fair seeking inspiration. H. J. Heinz was still recovering from his early venture into processed
and packaged foods, which had driven him to bankruptcy despite its success in
the market. Borrowing money from his cousin Frederick and brother John, he
founded the F. & J. Heinz Company in February 1876 and began the difficult
process of restarting his business and repairing his reputation.[35] While Heinz
took his family to visit the Philadelphia exposition, the company also benefited
from the trip. After reviewing the products exhibited in the Agricultural Hall
and all the types of new machinery available, including a canning machine,
he returned to Pittsburgh with a notebook full of ideas to further develop his
company. One such revelation was the potential and importance of advertising,
including the packaging and display of the products being sold.[36] Abundant, and
sometimes elaborate, advertising campaigns and the use of glass bottles to show
the purity of his products became a hallmark of Heinz as his company rocketed
to success throughout the remainder of the nineteenth century, and he had the
Centennial Exposition to credit for this inspiration. Having fallen in love with
the exposition and subscribing to the ideals and potential that fairs promised,
Heinz would spend the rest of his career exhibiting his products all over the
world and working to craft effective local exhibitions in Western Pennsylvania.

In addition to Heinz, over fifteen thousand Pittsburghers took advantage
of specially arranged excursions to Philadelphia to experience the Centennial
Exposition. One particularly large trip included two thousand area schoolchildren, their parents, and other interested citizens.[37] Facilitated by the spreading
rail network, waves of tourists flocked from the West to Philadelphia, meaning

that Pittsburghers could easily partake in the East Coast event and bring their experiences back home to share with others. Western Pennsylvanian exhibitors may have enjoyed an increase in business at the conclusion of the exposition, but more influential was the affirmation that exhibitions like the sanitary and world's fairs were a valuable source of information, advertisement, and recreation to be enjoyed by all who could afford admission. The task at hand, then, was to identify a means of reproducing the exposition idea in Pittsburgh.

———————

While people from all over the country worked to plan Philadelphia's world's fair, men in Pittsburgh and Allegheny were also striving to organize their own industrial exposition as a means of promoting local companies. In November 1874 the newly founded chamber of commerce created the Tradesmen's Industrial Institute to develop a fair and it settled on a site in Allegheny for its buildings.[38] Area businessmen funded the first exposition in 1875 to promote the region as an industrial and commercial powerhouse; however, the event appealed more to members of the working class and tradesmen than it did to entrepreneurs, financiers, and capitalists.[39] Nonetheless, organizers deemed the early expositions a success, drawing some now familiar names including exhibits of Heinz pickles, steel rails from the Edgar Thomson Works, iron from Sligo Mills and Crescent Tube, and other products.[40]

As the exposition strove to promote local industry, the manufacturers they wished to advertise were growing at a rapid pace. Carnegie aimed to have the most technologically advanced steel mill in the world when he constructed the Edgar Thomson Works, hiring the best men in the industry, including mill designer and Bessemer process patent owner Alexander Holley and inventor and mill supervisor William R. Jones. These men, along with Carnegie's willingness to implement the newest and most efficient machinery and methods, ensured that his mill would produce the best, most economically produced steel in the country. To guarantee that his product would sell, Carnegie capitalized on his friends still working for his former employer, the Pennsylvania Railroad. In exchange for the Pennsylvania's purchase of rails from the Edgar Thomson Works, Carnegie hired the company as the main transporter of their products throughout the country. By 1880, steel made up half of Allegheny County's total industry, and one-eighth of the nation's steel originated there. This output would become even greater in the ensuing decade with the addition of fully integrated mills in Homestead and Duquesne, as well as the conversion of American Iron's facility into Jones and Laughlin Steel's Pittsburgh Works.[41]

With such a dramatic rise in both locomotives in service and iron and steel production, Western Pennsylvania coal and coke also became a dire necessity. Bituminous coal mines in nearby Fayette and Westmoreland Counties suddenly became a significant part of Pittsburgh's economy. The demand for coal also drove support industries producing machinery, equipment, and other provisions along the rail routes connecting the coal towns to Pittsburgh.[42] In 1871 Judge Thomas Mellon provided a loan to a young bookkeeper named Henry Clay Frick so he could expand his new coke-processing company in the Connellsville region.[43] Frick's keen sense of business, as well as union-busting shrewdness toward his employees, allowed the company to flourish. Soon, his business prowess and products caught the eye of Carnegie, who invited Frick to join his steelmaking enterprise, Carnegie Brothers and Company, which he formed in 1881 to consolidate all of his existing interests under one company. By 1884 Allegheny, Westmoreland, Fayette, and Washington Counties mined 20 percent of the nation's coal, over 13 million tons. Frick also supplied much of the 5.5 million tons of coal that was converted to coke for regional consumption.[44]

The region's natural resources, location as a hub for both river and rail commerce, and good fortune to have the right entrepreneurs invest in up-and-coming industries, particularly steel, all amounted to a period of great prosperity and growth in Western Pennsylvania. In turn, this led to changes in local society as people moved both geographically out of the city and socially upward to the middle and upper classes. Because new mills moved outside of Pittsburgh's central business district to alternative locations with easy access to water and railways, towns consequently sprang up around them filled with millworkers and proprietors of ancillary services like stores and bars. While Carnegie located his massive works in towns outside of the city, other mills and factories along the Allegheny and Monongahela Rivers fell within the expanding boundaries of the cities of Pittsburgh and Allegheny. As noted by Joel Tarr, a result was that "from 1868 to 1900, the city grew in population from about fifty-five thousand to over three hundred thousand and increased its land area from 1.77 to over 28 square miles."[45]

Much of the increase in population during this time was the result of unskilled workers from central and eventually eastern Europe seeking employment in the Bessemer, and later open hearth, steel mills. While these new processes were highly mechanized and standardized, iron- and steelmaking methods of the early and mid-nineteenth century had traditionally relied on skilled workers of primarily English and German ancestry. The dependence of companies on skilled labor for production had resulted in a middle class of metalworkers who exercised a considerable amount of influence over the work-force. Among these Presbyterian ironmasters and other industrial elites little recreation was tolerated; however, the working class who served under these men enjoyed music, art, theater, and sports. By removing the influence of these skilled workmen, the shift from iron production to unskilled steel production, along with an increase in free time and disposable income, contributed to a cul-tural change that was more accepting of leisure activities and by 1890 the mid-dle class incorporated recreation into their lives.[46]

In order to fully include leisure in their way of life, this new middle class of managers, sales agents, and bookkeepers required neighborhoods conducive to such activities as music and reading clubs. As a location for these new res-idential oases, developers looked to Pittsburgh's newly acquired bucolic areas collectively known as the East End, separating their emerging community from the older neighborhoods closer to the Point. To further distinguish themselves from the working class, they also embraced material culture as a means of rein-forcing their status.[47] In particular, middle-class women benefited from their ability to purchase consumer goods such as washing machines, gas stoves, and other appliances, and to hire servants to use most of these conveniences. These amenities provided these women with the time that was necessary to become more involved in activities outside of the home, including social clubs, while working-class women lived in dirtier neighborhoods and thus spent even more time on housekeeping chores.[48]

The construction of these new middle-class communities required not only new homes but also improved and expanded infrastructure such as paved roads, water mains, and sewers.[49] The swift completion of these projects required both the allocation of municipal funds and compliance with local laws, and so the growing population of these neighborhoods conceded some of their political power to the city's Republican machine, led by Christopher Lyman Magee and William Flinn. Magee served as city treasurer during the 1870s and developed a relationship with many of the area's prominent businessmen. By appealing to influential men throughout Pittsburgh, he was able to gain considerable polit-ical power and could sway elections. To supplement his influence in the city of Pittsburgh, Magee partnered with Flinn, who had control over Allegheny County officials.[50]

To keep his power, Magee's men would grant small privileges that ben-efited the companies, industries, and personal lives of his supporters. These could run the gamut from the granting of railroad rights of way and the con-struction of new bridges to paving roads and running water lines in affluent neighborhoods.[51] While these projects benefited his supporters, they also lined the political boss's pockets. For example, Magee invested in traction, or street-car, companies to connect suburban expansion to the Golden Triangle. While on the surface this act aided his constituents, the increase in miles of streetcar lines also led to more fares and larger profits for his company. Not by accident, the construction company co-owned by Flinn became the contractor of choice for many of these public works projects.[52] As the cycle of increased power and expanded improvement projects continued to grow toward the end of the nine-teenth century, Pittsburgh's East End found itself in an opportune situation to incorporate any new advancement or national trend into the fabric of its contin-ually developing neighborhoods.

In addition to the upper class's desire to improve their own living conditions, Carnegie popularized the notion that they were also responsible for spending their money on programs that would benefit the lower classes. In his 1889 arti-cle "The Gospel of Wealth," Carnegie proposed that society could not trust the working class to invest their own money in improving their status, and so it was the duty of the rich to earn as much as they could so they would have more money to spend on the betterment of their employees. By promoting this way of thinking, Carnegie laid out a justification for his companies' aggressive pursuit of profits, as well as maintaining low wages for his employees. Serving as an example of his views, Carnegie began to build libraries in places of significance to his life, including his birthplace of Dunfermline, Scotland; his hometown of Allegheny; and Braddock, the location of his massive Edgar Thomson Works. Carnegie paid for the buildings, but he made the cities responsible for their maintenance. This arrangement reinforced his idea not only that the wealthy knew how to spend money better than workers, thus emphasizing social Dar-winist views of the era, but also that cities needed the upper class to guide municipal spending.[53] When civic leaders combined the principles of "The Gos-pel of Wealth" with an environment in Western Pennsylvania that nurtured public works projects, it became evident that Pittsburgh was on the cusp of a period of great urban development.

In the wake of the Centennial Exposition, it was clear that Western Pennsylva-nia had advanced beyond the agriculturally based county fairs that influenced the Sanitary Fair and the small-scale industrial fair efforts of the Tradesmen's Institute. In response to observations made in Philadelphia, a meeting was held on March 7, 1877, to reorganize the failing Allegheny County Tradesmen's

Industrial Institute, forming the Pittsburgh Exposition Society. The changes in leadership and organization were effective and the next several years' expositions proved to be a success. The Main Building of the exposition, built for the Tradesmen's exhibition, was six hundred feet long and housed the exhibits of merchants and companies from throughout the country, but primarily from Allegheny County. In the middle of the building stood a stage for musical performances.[54] By the early 1880s the exposition replaced many of its popular entertainments—such as horseraces, fireworks, and illegal gambling wheels—with more cultured lectures and displays, such as art galleries, that appealed more to the upper and middle classes.[55] Since admission to the exposition cost twenty-five cents for adults by 1883, many members of the working class simply could no longer afford to attend the festivities.[56]

In 1882, Pennsylvania's Agricultural Society decided to hold its annual fair in Allegheny County, and held a joint event with the Pittsburgh Exposition.[57] To accommodate the increase in exhibits, the Floral Hall and Machinery Hall were added to the Main Building, as was an expanded boiler house to provide power to the exhibitors. Floral Hall housed the displays of flowers and plants while Machinery Hall contained exhibits of engines, pumps, and other types of machinery from various industries. Additionally, there was a dining pavilion and, between the buildings and the Allegheny River, was the exposition grounds, which included a half-mile racetrack, a stockyard, and an athletic field that eventually served as the home of the professional baseball team that later became known as the Pirates.[58]

The following year tragedy struck the fairgrounds. At 1:45 on the morning of October 3, 1883, fire destroyed the exposition building. In addition to the structure, the goods and displays of dozens of exhibitors were a complete loss. While damages were estimated at over $375,000, the value of many historic artifacts and works of art on display was immeasurable.[59] At the time, the Pittsburgh Exposition was one of only six industrial expositions held in the United States, but with no building to house the displays and a bruised reputation, organizers were forced to put the fair on hiatus until they could regroup.[60]

On November 7, 1885, the Western Pennsylvania Exposition Society formed to pick up the pieces of the Pittsburgh Exposition. Among the new exposition directors was H. J. Heinz, a consistent exhibitor at the local exhibitions and an avid participant and award winner at fairs throughout the country. Heinz and the twelve other directors of the exposition society purchased six acres of land near Pittsburgh's Point as the site for its new buildings. At a cost of $450,000, the new grounds included three structures: the Main Building, Machinery

Hall, and Music Hall.[61] The society dedicated the facilities in May 1889 with a weeklong series of concerts. The first Western Pennsylvania Exposition opened on September 4; however, many exhibitors did not have their displays completely installed by opening day. While the location and name had changed, the exposition attractions were consistent with those previously hosted in Allegheny. Glass, brick, and tile production were popular exhibits, as were floral and art displays.[62]

One interesting difference, though, was that the Western Pennsylvania Exposition aimed to appeal to the working class in addition to the upper and middle classes. The society branded Saturdays as People's Days and admission to the exposition buildings was free to all. Along with the usual exhibits, concerts featured popular music that would appeal to the working class.[63] The exposition society hoped that these days would instill civic pride in the thousands of workers who lived in Pittsburgh so they might better understand and embrace their role in the growing metropolis and thus produce more goods for the local economy. Other evening performances featured music from the many ethnic groups represented in Western Pennsylvania. Members of those communities who could afford to pay admission to the concerts would do so, and regular exposition attendees would also take advantage of the opportunity to experience entertainment and music from different cultures.[64]

The persistence of organizers in continually retooling and rebuilding an exposition in the Pittsburgh area demonstrates that there was a real or perceived value in holding such events. Developing local industries like steel needed an outlet to advertise their products and the crowds at the exposition provided a ready audience. Concerts and art displays at exhibitions also allowed Pittsburgh to demonstrate that it was becoming a city of culture. With the successful return of the local exposition in 1889, Western Pennsylvania proved that it was among the increasing number of fair-loving industrial regions with a variety of exhibits to offer, many of which appealed to more than just a local audience. Furthermore, civic and business leaders gained valuable experience in organizing large-scale events and marketing their products, as well as their city. Pittsburgh had grown tremendously since the Centennial Exposition and only needed another opportunity to prove itself on the world stage. Fortunately, such an opportunity was close at hand.

2

Planning for the Exposition

IN 1889 the Exposition Universelle in Paris was held to celebrate the centennial of the French Revolution. Paris had become a regular host of world's fairs during the nineteenth century, always setting the bar higher for its successors. The 1889 Exposition featured the massive steel-and-glass Machinery Hall built of arched trusses typically found in bridge designs, as well as Gustave Eiffel's impressive tower. The iron structure, rising one thousand feet above the Champ de Mars, was the tallest in the world until 1930 and a financial success for Eiffel and his company's stockholders for years to come. The fair buildings contained exhibits from all over the world, most notably from South American countries, featuring examples of industrial products and machines, as well as museums and art exhibitions. The exposition also featured living displays including Javanese, Tahitian, and Senegalese villages, among others.[1]

The Exposition Universelle was a hit with the international cultural, scientific, and industrial communities; however, the United States did not make its usual effort to be well represented at the fair. Despite the shortage of American exhibits, there were several displays from Western Pennsylvania at the French world's fair, featuring both its established connections to the railroad industry and its rising participation in the field of electricity. H. K. Porter and Company exhibited the only American locomotive in Paris and the Pennsylvania Railroad brought samples of locomotive and railcar components. George Westinghouse, a name previously associated with railroad air brakes, displayed an automatic engine from the Westinghouse Machine Company powering a dynamo. After traveling the United States and setting up displays at local expositions for years, the H. J. Heinz Company exhibited, among other things, ketchup and award-winning pickle products. It was the start of that company's international following.[2]

While it had been only thirteen years since the Centennial Exposition in Philadelphia where the United States demonstrated its industrial and technological might, American industry—particularly in the realms of iron and steel—had advanced by leaps and bounds. The Exposition Universelle and the Eiffel Tower, however, reinforced the notion that France was leading the way in the production of those structural metals. Many businessmen in the United States agreed that they could not let this assertion stand and looked to the next opportunity to promote their country's ingenuity. Luckily, a major anniversary was a few short years away—one that would provide the perfect opportunity for another world's fair—the four hundredth anniversary of Christopher Columbus's first voyage to North America.

An international exhibition was the standard means for a nation to promote its advancements, but not everyone was convinced that the United States could pull off such an event. In an article for *Scribner's Magazine* evaluating the Paris Exposition, W. C. Brownell worried that the proposed American world's fair could not compare to its French counterpart. He elaborated, "I hope, however, it will be deemed neither supercilious nor unpatriotic if I suggest that, should the Exhibition of '92 as a spectacle possess the unity and excellence of the Paris Exposition, we shall certainly have cause for congratulation."[3] He identified three points of concern that Paris did not face but that a Columbian Exposition would need to overcome. The first was a suitable site on which to locate the fair. Secondly, Brownell believed that there was "no competent [American] organization, directed by a long and splendid tradition of aesthetic dignity and taste, to create and control the Exhibition of '92" when compared to the École des Beaux-Arts. Finally, he asserted that "the absence of any body of engineers, architects, sculptors, and decorators at all commensurate in numbers, solidarity, and aesthetic tradition, is the third, and perhaps the chief disadvantage."[4] The exposition's host city, and in fact the entire country, would need to overcome these obstacles if the fair were to be successful.

Brownell was correct in that the United States did not have a school analo-gous to the École des Beaux-Arts in Paris, which featured a demanding archi-tectural program; however, the École served as a surrogate institution to com-pensate for the lack of domestic architectural training and had begun to attract American architects seeking a more robust formal education. With intense training grounded in ancient and Renaissance architectural principles paired with competitions that required quick thinking yet well-conceived conceptual designs, the École was responsible for the education of some of the most influ-ential American architects in the latter half of the nineteenth century. Because study at the school was expensive, students had to come from wealthy families or secure sponsorship, which meant that École-trained architects were also some of the most socially connected designers in the country upon their return.[5] The shared experiences, training, and vernacular of these architects would play a cru-cial role in the design and successful completion of the exposition's fairgrounds.

American cities scrambled for support to host the proposed fair. Washing-ton, DC, and St. Louis were interested in the honor, but they never reached the status of being serious contenders. In the end, the decision came down to New York City, an established power, and the up-and-coming city of Chicago. To many, New York was the obvious first choice; it was the financial and cul-tural center of the country and Central Park would place the fairgrounds right in the heart of the city. On the other hand, Chicago had developed several great architects and engineers while rebuilding from the great fire in 1871 and had amassed a number of prosperous industrialists. This building expertise and cap-ital were necessary to successfully host the exposition. Also to its credit, some attributed the idea for using a world's fair to celebrate Columbus's first journey to the Americas to Dr. Charles W. Zaremba, a Chicago physician.[6]

One of Pittsburgh's most influential and affluent sons, Andrew Carnegie, threw his support behind New York's bid. During the summer of 1889 the *Pittsburg Dispatch* notified citizens that the New York City Chamber of Commerce committee working to secure the exposition had selected Carnegie, along with Grover Cleveland, J. P. Morgan, John D. Rockefeller, and Cornelius Vanderbilt, as members.[7] With such powerful men at the helm, the committee quickly attracted financial supporters. A small note in the *Dispatch* on Septem-ber 25 stated that New York had collected $20 million ($603 million in 2022) toward its bid, including $2 million ($60.3 million in 2022) from Carnegie. His decision to support his city of residence for the previous two decades was a low-risk, high-reward venture. While he did not serve on any of the bid's special planning committees like Rockefeller and Jay Gould, Carnegie had a vested

interest in their work. A successful bid would give Carnegie a chance to purchase stock in the fair, which, almost assuredly, would provide a substantial
profit. It would also give his companies the best chance at winning the steel
contracts for many of the fair's buildings. He implemented this same strategy
at Philadelphia's Centennial Exposition; in 1876 not only was Carnegie able to
convince the building committee to abandon its plans for wooden structures in
favor of iron, he also persuaded them to award one of the iron contracts to his
own mills.[8] His support for hosting the exposition would also provide Carnegie
a chance to build upon his relationships with the New York City elite as both
business contacts and social acquaintances.

The final selection of a host city was to be made by Congress and then
approved by President Benjamin Harrison. This meant that the winning location needed the support of politicians from across the country. Chicago's delegation began an aggressive public relations campaign. In addition to sending men
to Washington to appeal directly to politicians, organizers formed a committee
on national cooperation to create auxiliaries comprising Chicagoans originally
from elsewhere who could now rely on their contacts within their home state
to generate support for their bid to host the fair.[9] The campaign's widespread
boastful promotion would later lead to the urban legend that it earned Chicago
the nickname of "the Windy City" (the epithet appears to have originated in
the 1870s).

In October 1889 a contingent from Chicago visited Pittsburgh to lobby for
the city's support. During their stay, Judge William Bennett Cunningham of
Chicago's world's fair company delegation and formerly of New Castle, Pennsylvania, appealed to the similarities between the two cities:

> We do not forget that this city of Pittsburg has been like a mother to us. When
> our city was in ashes, and our people almost naked, Pittsburg was then our
> mother. In rebuilding the city, in furnishing material for its reconstruction,
> Pennsylvania has been like a father toward it. The great engine that distrib-
> utes water to all our homes was made here. The largest plate glass ornamenting
> our store fronts was made in Pittsburg, and in ten thousand ways Pittsburg and
> Pennsylvania have contributed to the building of Chicago. Nearly every promi-
> nent business house of Pittsburg has established a branch house in Chicago, for
> the purpose of reaching the great Western market. While Pittsburg assisted us
> by way of building up our city, we in turn furnish a market for all the produc-
> tions of your great manufactories. The interests of our people are the same.

In response, Pittsburgh mayor William McCallin offered to introduce the delegates to the Western Pennsylvania Exposition Society and local manufacturers, though he was noncommittal toward supporting Chicago as the host city.[10]

Deliberations finally came to the floor of Congress in early 1890. In the New York bid's statement to the Senate, their committee cited the city's successful celebration of the centennial anniversary of the ratification of the Constitution on April 30, 1889, as a demonstration of its ability to plan and execute a large-scale celebration. They provided a list of guaranteed subscriptions by individuals to fund the fair, totaling $5 million in contributions from Vanderbilt, Rockefeller, Morgan, and others. The list also included Carnegie's November 26, 1889, commitment to donating $25,000, not $2 million, to a New York fair. His name was misspelled in the listing, possibly representing the way those on the East Coast pronounce his name—"Carnagie."[11] The committee also noted that New York City would contribute an additional $10 million to the fair, bringing the total amount of promised funds to $15 million, as well as locations around Central Park and buildings for the exposition, including the soon-to-be-completed Metropolitan Art and Natural History Museums. They believed that access to the proposed sites by water and rail was unparalleled by any other city in the world and that improved infrastructure, like a nearly finished aqueduct, would make New York an attractive choice. That ten million Americans could visit the fair as a day trip was also promoted as a key to its financial success, with the committee citing the fact that three-fifths of visitors to the exposition in Paris came from its metropolitan area. Furthermore, foreign—primarily European— visitors arriving on the East Coast would have easy access to the site. Since the intention of the exposition was to demonstrate the country's industrial and intellectual might, the committee also proposed in their statement that undeveloped resources and ideas could "be brought best to the notice of the vast fund of wealth which exists in New York, and will be attracted to it from foreign countries."[12]

The Chicago bid provided a Midwestern spin on many of the same points offered by New York, focusing on the country's western expansion. While the city could not compare with New York's large population, it was a geographically central point in the United States. Thirty-eight railroads from across the nation terminated there and Chicago ranked first in the nation in waterway traffic. The Chicago delegates presented the fact that visitors from the Eastern Seaboard and Europe would need to travel beyond the Appalachian Mountains as a benefit that would give travelers the opportunity to see for themselves the impressive development of the American West. This meant likely stops in Pittsburgh, a main thoroughfare on the rail routes west to Chicago. The delegates also argued that the city of Chicago best typified the history of the United States; both the country and the city had risen from a frontier locale to a place of growing commercial, intellectual, and industrial achievement. Since Chicago was able to rebuild after the fire to become the foremost metropolis of the West, the committee asserted that the city had already demonstrated its planning acumen and ability to execute largescale projects. The committee was also able to gather $5 million in subscriptions to fund the fair.[13]

The New York delegation was confident. They had the money, the location, the reputation, and the involvement of many prominent Americans. Much of the country's industrial might, concentrated in the Northeast, backed its proposal. Cities in the West and Midwest threw their support primarily behind Chicago, while southern cities split their allegiance between St. Louis and Washington, DC. Pittsburgh was situated where geographic support for the proposed fair sites met, and its citizens had vested stakes in each location. The region relied on money from New York to fund its expanding industries. At the same time, exports moving from Pittsburgh to the West passed through Chicago and, as its visiting committee had indicated, the city itself had been a great consumer of Western Pennsylvania products. As the nation's capital, Washington, DC, was a logical symbolic choice to celebrate the four hundredth anniversary of Columbus's journey and would certainly be able to secure the land and money necessary to successfully complete the exposition. Lobbying for the sites began at the Capitol late in 1889 and the opportunity to select a city was rapidly approaching.

After much deliberation and dealing in Congress, the day of decision in the House of Representatives was at hand. Around noon on February 24, 1890, the representatives cast their first ballot to select a host city. John Dalzell, of Pennsylvania's 22nd District, representing Pittsburgh, and Charles C. Townsend, 25th District, representing Butler, Beaver, Mercer, and Lawrence Counties, both voted for Chicago on the first ballot, but the city was unable to earn the majority necessary to win the fair location. On the second ballot, Dalzell was able to convince Joseph W. Ray of Waynesburg, representing the 24th District, to also support Chicago after abstaining from the first vote. Sensing a shift on the second ballot, Pittsburgh representative Colonel Thomas M. Bayne of the 23rd District withdrew his support from the Washington, DC, bid and abstained. Seeing other representatives change allegiance from the Washington and St. Louis bids, Bayne voted for New York on the third ballot. It became clear that New York and Chicago were in a race to see which bid's supporters could sway southern representatives to its side and achieve the majority vote. On the eighth ballot Bayne changed his vote again, this time in support for Chicago, making him part of the swing that gave the city a majority of the ballots.[14]

The selection of Chicago to host the Columbian Exposition pleased the people of Pittsburgh. Initially, there was concern both locally and nationally that European visitors would be deterred by an additional day's railroad travel to an inland city; however, Pittsburghers now agreed that a Midwestern fair would be beneficial to Western Pennsylvania. In a *Pittsburg Dispatch* article about Chicago's selection, renowned local engineer Colonel James T. Andrews noted,

> Pittsburg is more famous abroad than any other city in America. It is safe to say that 75 percent of the foreign visitors will pass through Pittsburg, going or coming. Of that number thousands will stop here and examine the industrial wonders here to be seen. The choice of Chicago is, therefore, a great piece of good fortune for the city and her manufacturers have it in their power to make such an exhibit at Chicago as to fill the visitors to Chicago with genuine curiosity as to the workshop from which the exhibit comes which can only be gratified by personal inspection.[15]

Meanwhile, an editorial in the *Pittsburgh Press* touted the more immediate impact that the fair would have on the Pittsburgh economy, no matter the location. The author of the column confidently stated, "We should get the contract for much of the iron and glass that will be used in the exposition buildings, and doubtless will. There will be a very large quantity required, and the orders will naturally come to us, with the probability of giving an unusual impetus to trade in this vicinity."[16] What the author failed to take into account—or may not have known—is that Illinois Steel, in the Chicago area, was nipping at the heels of Pittsburgh's Carnegie Steel in terms of production.

President Harrison signed the bill to create the World's Columbian Commission on April 25, 1890, officially assigning the fair to Chicago and pushing back the opening to May 1893. This national commission served an administrative role and provided oversight for the World's Columbian Exposition Corporation, a private company composed of members of Chicago's elite and funded by individual stockholders. The national commission consisted of "two commissioners and two alternate commissioners from each state and territory and from the District of Columbia, and eight commissioners at large and eight alternates to be appointed by the President."[17] On June 26, 1890, President Harrison named prominent Pittsburgh Democratic lawyer William McClelland a commissioner for Pennsylvania and John W. Chalfant, the iron and railroad man who had helped secure Cleveland's Sanitary Fair buildings for his city, an alternate commissioner-at-large.

The act also required the commission to establish the Board of Lady Managers. The board consisted of two women from each state, territory, and Washington, DC, as well as nine Chicago women selected by the commission president. Each manager position was also assigned an alternate delegate to take her place if she were unable to serve. While membership in the board was fairly homogeneous, consisting of middle- and upper-class white women, the managers often came into conflict over their differing views on women's suffrage and equal rights as they addressed their duties.[18] The Board of Lady Managers served as the official channel between the commission and individual women or women's organizations, including all communication pertaining to applications to exhibit at the fair. The board also managed the Woman's Building, which was to exclusively display items produced or submitted by women from all over the world, as well as the construction of any other spaces for the sole use of women. Additionally, the board had the authority to appoint members to prize juries in cases where women had contributed to the eligible displays. For Pennsylvania, Mary E. McCandless, the daughter of former federal judge Wilson McCandless, who was active in several Pittsburgh women's organizations, served as a manager along with Harriet Anne Lucas of Philadelphia. McCandless was also appointed to the board's executive committee.[19] With McClelland, Chalfant, and McCandless involved at the highest level of the fair's organization Western Pennsylvania was sure to have a voice in the planning of the Columbian Exposition.

———————

Throughout 1890 Western Pennsylvanians followed the fair's progress in the newspapers. With so much of the local conversation tying Pittsburgh's economic success to the fate of the Columbian Exposition, many citizens felt invested in how things were developing in the Second City. The fact that the planning of the fair was steeped in controversy also ensured that the press would expend plenty of ink on that very subject. One topic of interest was the actual location of the fairgrounds in Chicago. In early July, the *Pittsburgh Post* reported the prospect of a dual site for the exposition, with locations on the lakefront near the city and in Jackson Park, further south. The author declared the dual site option undesirable. Editors also believed the subject of the fair's location to be a matter of competing business interests. On August 19 a journalist for the *Post* opined, "From the start the Chicago project has been little else than a big real estate speculation, and the right of one Chicagoan to get on the ground floor is just as valid as the right of another."[20] The notion that greed was driving the selection of the exposition site was echoed in an article reporting on Pittsburgh mayor Henry Gourley's visit to Chicago, which noted, "He thought the Chicago people were trying to use the proposed fair for personal profit."[21]

Despite these objections, several newspapers reported on September 26 that the dual-site plan was being adopted. The lakefront location in the heart of Chicago consisted of a sixty-acre strip between Lake Michigan and the city's business district. A seven-mile boulevard connected this location to Washington and Jackson Parks, the latter of which also boasted a lakefront space. These locations totaled over 1,000 acres compared to the 225 acres occupied at the Exposition Universelle in Paris.[22] At a November meeting of the national world's fair commission, just weeks before they were to present the location to President Harrison, they determined that a single site was preferable so that no groups of exhibits would be left out or considered to be at a less-desirable location.[23] After some debate, organizers and the committee agreed that the Jackson Park location, south of the business district, was preferable above all others. With the location settled, President Harrison could formally invite all the nations of the world to Chicago for the 1893 Columbian Exposition.

With the site now established, proposals for the fair's buildings began to appear in the local papers. With no official sketches to show so early in the planning process, the public's imagination ran wild with ideas. Newspapers published one example in August, when engineer John K. Hallock and architect Cyrus F. Dean, both of Erie, proposed a structure that included a dome with a radius of four hundred feet in honor of the four hundredth anniversary of Columbus's journey to the New World. The dome, designed to represent the Western Hemisphere of the globe with the route of Columbus's journey marked by a dotted line, capped a cruciform building 1,892 feet long and 1,492 feet wide, the numbers representing the appropriate years of celebration. The dome's construction would consist of a steel frame and wire mesh, which likely appealed to the people of the Steel City. Hallock and Dean also estimated that they could recover three-quarters of the cost of the building material in resale. This, along with projections that the number of admissions to the fair would be high, made the project an attractive idea and a worthy rival to the Eiffel Tower.[24]

On October 30, Chicago architects Daniel Burnham and John Root were officially selected to oversee the exposition's buildings and construction and, along with landscape architect Frederick Law Olmsted, settled on the idea of a court of honor comprising the fair's main exhibition halls surrounding a lagoon. While the Court of Honor would hug the shores of Lake Michigan, the Midway Plaisance, containing dozens of concessions that were initially intended to be a part of the fair's Anthropology Department, would stretch westward for about a mile. These attractions were meant to provide living exhibits of various cultures; however, over time, the Midway would evolve into a commercial center that mixed cultural displays with popular amusements.[25] In mid-December, Burnham traveled east, likely passing through Pittsburgh, to persuade several prominent architects to design the fair's buildings and appease the Northeast in the aftermath of New York's failed bid in the process. This trip resulted in Richard Morris Hunt, George B. Post, and the firm of McKim, Mead and White, all of New York, agreeing to participate. Two Boston architects, Charles Atwood and the firm of Peabody and Stearns, also signed on. Though Pittsburgh had few architects of renown at that time, several would rise to prominence in the decades following the fair by replicating the principles of Burnham and the exposition.

The addition of this cohort of eastern architects sparked outrage in Chicago, as the host city felt it was capable of providing its own architects to design the entire fairgrounds. It was Burnham's intention to ensure that the exposition reflected architecture of a national character instead of only Chicago, but eventually he bowed to his colleagues' pressure and included several Midwestern architects, including VanBrunt and Howe, of Kansas City, and Solon Spencer Beman, Henry Ives Cobb, William Jenney, and Louis Sullivan, of Chicago.[26] Later, another Boston architect, Sophia Hayden, would win the competition to design the fair's Woman's Building. With the construction of the fair officially in the hands of some of the most celebrated architects in America, everyone waited to see what great buildings would arise on the lakefront.

That following January, the architects decided to use the neoclassical style of the École des Beaux-Arts for all the Court of Honor buildings. They also established a uniform cornice height for the structures to instill a sense of uniformity. There was some popular debate concerning the role of architecture at the exposition, with many viewing it as an opportunity to promote emerging American or even experimental styles; however, because the fair had to appeal to a broad audience in order for it to be successful, the architects settled on a style that was already admired and accepted for its use in previous world's fairs, particularly the most recent one in Paris.[27] Later, Burnham decided to paint the court buildings in a single color, giving rise to the Columbian Exposition's most famous nickname: the White City.

Fig. 2. Depicted from atop the Administration Building, the White City's Court of Honor included several enormous Beaux Arts exhibit halls, including the Manufactures (left) and Agricultural (right) Buildings. H. D. Nichols, and L. Prang and Company, "Chicago World's Fair 1893," 1893, Arts Department, Boston Public Library.

Meanwhile, Burnham feared that organized labor might use the exposition to promote its efforts for a minimum wage and shorter workdays. He believed the short timeframe in which he had to build an entire city was not conducive to deliberations with labor unions, and so he attempted to bypass them when work finally began. On February II, I89I, the McArthur Brothers contracting firm hired fifty Italian immigrant workers to begin digging drainage ditches, but once union men learned of the group, they chased the crew away. A bemused *Pittsburgh Post* editorial pointed out the irony that the fair was established to honor "the memory and achievements of Christopher Columbus, an Italian," but "putting Italians at work on the Columbian temple at Jackson park—and they were the first laborers employed—and such hostility that they were discharged, after threats of a boycott and riot."[28] Sensing that he had to nip labor troubles in the bud early on, Burnham and other fair officials met with unions and agreed to their demands of an eight-hour day for fair construction workers at the end of February. Surely such a public victory for labor emboldened workers of all trades in Western Pennsylvania.

In addition to physical aspects of the exposition, Pittsburghers were also interested in its political influences and financial implications. There was concern that the world's fair was being manipulated to serve the interests of a variety of groups. The Democrat-leaning *Pittsburgh Post* reported in September that Republicans sought to politicize the national World's Columbian Commission by paying their men on staff exorbitant salaries, ranging from $5,000 to $15,000 per year. Secretary of the Treasury William Windom, himself a Republican, reviewed the national committee's finances for the fiscal year and determined that it would not have enough funds to function if its members were so compensated; however, he agreed to approve its suggested salaries with a warning that the committee spend its remaining money wisely.[29]

The threat of financial panic after the near collapse of London's leading banking house, Baring Brothers and Company, in late 1890 and 1891 had a sobering effect on the committee. The fair would need to expend an enormous amount of money, both to live up to the promise of being larger than the Paris Exposition and to justify travel to Chicago by potential tourists. In December, national commission vice-president Thomas Bryan, perhaps sensing the rising political tensions or potentially in an attempt to funnel more money back into the exposition itself, agreed to accept only half of his designated $12,000 salary. Bryan's official reason for turning down the money was ostensibly nobler. He explained that the newly established fair committees had cut back on the amount of time he needed to spend on exposition matters and since he did not need to focus all of his energy on its planning, he did not deserve all of the designated salary.[30]

Despite the seeming distance, their time as spectators watching the fair's progress hundreds of miles from Chicago was coming to an end and the period was quickly approaching when the people of Allegheny County, and all of Pennsylvania, would enter the fray. The Columbian Exposition was not just Chicago's enterprise; it was America's world's fair, and it was time for all the states to begin to consider how they would represent themselves in the exhibitions.

As the public continued to debate various aspects of the upcoming fair, some Pennsylvanians began to worry that the commonwealth had not taken initial steps to coordinate exhibits. In November the national commission sent a circular with its representatives from each state encouraging their legislatures to take up the matter of soliciting and organizing exhibits as soon as possible, as well as establishing a fund to defray their cost. Organizers intended for these exhibits to show the great strides the country had made in industry and innovation in addition to promoting the nation's abundant natural resources. To supplement the displays of individuals and companies in the exposition's Court of Honor buildings, many states also elected to erect their own buildings. These pavilions would showcase the resources of the states they represented, both in the materials used for their construction and in the displays found within them. Often the buildings contained references to their states' history that would appeal to their citizens, as they served as a home base for visitors and journalists from their respective states, offering a place for them to rest and converse with other fairgoers from their region. By the end of 1890, California, Texas, and Iowa were already preparing for their exhibits and there was a growing fear that the Keystone State was falling behind.[31]

In order for Pennsylvania to adequately display all it had to offer preparations needed to begin soon. An editorial in the January 6, 1891, *Pittsburgh Press* put this concern in print, proclaiming, "Our danger is that we may delay preparation for the proper representation of Pennsylvania until too late, and will awake to a realization of our mistake when it cannot be remedied." The author recommended "the organization of a commission to supervise the part which Pennsylvania shall take in this exposition, and that liberal appropriations be made for the erection of a suitable building, and for stimulating in every proper way a complete and satisfactory exhibit of all our industries."[32] By the beginning of summer that is exactly what would be in place.

Before Pennsylvania could convene a committee, Governor Robert E. Pattison needed to identify its leader. On June 8, 1891, Henry Clay Frick sent a telegram to Andrew Carnegie in London, informing him, "Governor asks are your plans such you would accept appointment head Worlds Fair Commission from Penna. Answer me."[33] Eleven days later Frick forwarded Carnegie's reply to Harrisburg: "Inform Governor deeply gratified. Impossible."[34] Several possible factors may have contributed to his decision to decline the governor's invitation. If he served as president of the committee, Carnegie would have been proclaiming his endorsement of Chicago as the exposition site. As a member of the New York City elite and supporter of its bid to host the fair, this could have been damaging to his social reputation, as their defeat to the upstart western city was still an open wound. The refusal to serve on the Democratic governor's committee may also have been a political maneuver by the stalwart Republican. Additionally, given that the committee would meet periodically throughout the next two years, any presidential duties would interfere with Carnegie's regular trips to Europe.

Despite Carnegie's refusal, Governor Pattison submitted the Act of Assembly forming the Board of World's Fair Managers of Pennsylvania on June 22, 1891.

The act stated that the board was "to provide for the collection, arrangement and display of the products of the State of Pennsylvania at the World's Columbian Exposition, in the year one thousand eight hundred and ninety-three, and to make an appropriation of three hundred thousand dollars therefor."[35] The board first convened in Harrisburg on July 1 and the governor, having abandoned his search to appoint a leader, served as president. Addressing the group, he was very clear about the importance of Pennsylvania and its board's charge in representing the Keystone State:

> Pennsylvania, occupying the position she does among the sister states, while probably in one instance overmatched in numbers, yet in all other respects the first in importance, should give to the Exposition in Chicago the very first and finest exhibition of any State in the Union. . . . This celebration should be upon a scale of magnificence not to be surpassed in the history of the nations of the world . . . it is within your power to make the exhibition of the natural resources, products and enterprise of the State of Pennsylvania a grand success at the Exposition to be held in Chicago in 1893. If it be a success, great benefits will result to this State and you will have the satisfaction of knowing that you have well performed your duty. If it be a failure, a corresponding condemnation will follow.[36]

Representatives for Western Pennsylvania at the initial meeting were James M. Guffey, Albert J. Barr, Alfred G. Roenigk, and Patrick Foley, all of Pittsburgh; Wallace W. Clendenin, of New Castle; George N. Riley, of McKeesport; and William Hasson, of Oil City. Pittsburgh's William H. Barnes was also named to the board but was not present at the first meeting. These men represented a cross-section of the Western Pennsylvania economy, including iron, steel, railroads, oil, finance, and commerce. They were also primarily Democrats, reflecting the incumbent party.[37]

In addition to those appointed specifically to the board, the governor named Pennsylvania national world's fair commissioner General William McClelland and Board of Lady Managers member Mary E. McCandless as ex officio members. The Board of World's Fair Managers of Pennsylvania then sorted its members into various committees to begin the task of organizing Pennsylvania's contributions to the fair. While Western Pennsylvanians participated in many of the committees, they were surprisingly absent from those pertaining to mines and minerals, railroads, and labor and innovation. Perhaps equally unexpected, there was Pittsburgh representation on committees relating to forestry and the arts.

At the second board meeting on August 13, it was announced that Barnes had withdrawn from service and the board members elected Pittsburgh's James B. Oliver, president of Oliver Iron and Steel, as his replacement. There was also an election for executive commissioner of the board at this meeting, won by Charles Wolfe of Lewisburg; however, a few hours after the meeting adjourned, Wolfe was dead, likely falling victim to the recurrence of an illness he had recently overcome. When the board next convened on September 10, it elected Benjamin Whitman, of Erie, as executive commissioner.

The board appointed a committee that included Hasson and McClelland to visit Chicago on September 1, 1891, to inspect the fairgrounds and the future site of the Pennsylvania State Building, the design for which the committee later decided would be a replica of Independence Hall. They reported on September 10 that "the position is most prominent, and the building to be erected thereon should correspond with it. Facing the grounds of the Art Gallery, it will be an object of great interest, and our State will be constantly on exhibition in the buildings we will there erect."[38] In addition, the board appointed General George Snowden, who had led National Guard forces into Pittsburgh to quell the 1877 railroad riots and would soon return in 1892 to diffuse tensions after the Battle of Homestead, to represent the Pennsylvania military at the National Committee on Ceremonies with McClelland. At the October board meeting, McCandless reported for the Committee on Horticulture and Floriculture that William Hamilton, an Allegheny City florist and member of the advisory board of the national commission, and C. C. Mellor, president of the Botanical Society of Pittsburgh, would participate in arranging the state's floral display, hinting that there was already more to Western Pennsylvania than choking black smoke and hills barren from mining.[39]

To support the work of the women's committee, the Board of World's Fair Managers of Pennsylvania authorized the creation of county women's auxiliary committees. In Allegheny County, the women's auxiliary committee comprised thirty-one women, with state board member McCandless as president. The committee also included Jennette Roenigk and Mary Barr, wives of state board members, as well as journalist Cara Reese and Margaret Magee Mitchell, the daughter of Judge Christopher Magee (not to be confused with his cousin, Pittsburgh's Republican boss Christopher Lyman Magee). The committee organized itself into several subcommittees and tasked them with securing exhibit materials relating to art, education, literature, moral reform, public health, science and invention, and social and economic science.[40]

In addition to establishing women's auxiliaries, the board also disbanded

its standing committees and agreed to establish new ones that better replicated the departmental arrangement of the Columbian Exposition exhibits and
buildings. Established at the November 12 meeting, the reorganized committee
membership better reflected Pittsburgh's strength and status as an industrial
and intellectual center. There was now Western Pennsylvania representation
on committees relating to horticulture; fish and fisheries; mines, mining, and
metallurgy; machinery; transportation; manufactures; electricity and electrical appliances; fine arts; liberal arts, which included education, engineering,
public works, architecture, music, and drama; and a committee that included
archaeology, ethnology, labor, and inventions. McCandless also remained on the
women's committee. The only committees without Western Pennsylvania members pertained to agriculture and forestry and livestock. Just after the board
assigned members to the new committees Oliver's resignation was announced
and they assigned his commitments to newly elected member Thomas Merritt,
of Reading.[41]

Earlier in November, Governor Pattison issued a plea to the citizens of Pennsylvania to support the efforts of the board and the state's exhibits at the world's
fair. This call reached Pittsburgh and the executive committee of the Pittsburgh
Chamber of Commerce decided at its November 16 meeting that they would
establish a committee to work with the state board to advocate for the interests of Western Pennsylvania at the exposition. On November 30 the executive
committee report introduced their World's Columbian Exposition Committee
to the entire chamber. The report argued that the committee should be formed
in response to the governor's call for "railroad companies, mining and manufacturing companies, education institutions, trade exchanges, labor organizations
etc. to assist in the way of exhibits of such inventions, mechanical contrivances,
agricultural or mineral products, scientific apparatuses, works of art etc. etc.,
which would be set forth to the state a representation of Pennsylvania, the second state in the Union in population and wealth."[42] There were some local fears
that potential exhibits from Pennsylvania's western city would be overlooked
in favor of its eastern metropolis, Philadelphia. To ensure that Pittsburgh and
Allegheny interests were well represented, the chamber of commerce's World's
Columbian Exposition Committee would disseminate communications from the
state board and arouse interest in local companies and organizations.

In addition to exhibits focused on individual companies, the committee also proposed to put the entire region on display. In describing the charge of the committee, it noted,

> Strangers from Europe, Asia, South America and Australia will come to this country in numbers never before witnessed, not merely tourists but business men and capitalists for the express purpose of noting our resources and we should be prepared to show them something in Chicago, which might be sufficient inducement to bring them to Pittsburgh where they can see for themselves that Western Pennsylvania with her [numerous] natural resources and unequaled development in many lines of manufacturing has entered the field to supply the world's demands in many commodities and that she contends with the marching growth of our foreign commerce to push her wares into many new markets.[43]

Not only would the fair be a chance to exhibit local industries, it would also provide an opportunity to lure foreign investors and businessmen into Pittsburgh itself in the hopes of attracting their interest and cash.

On December 14, 1891, the chamber elected the members of its World's Columbian Exposition Committee, with Colonel Thomas P. Roberts, the chief engineer of the Monongahela Navigation Company, who had previously spoken at length about the importance of such a committee, selected as chairman. The other members were leading men of Western Pennsylvania and the chamber of commerce, including William L. Scaife, H. K. Porter, and Alfred E. Hunt. These men represented local metal industries; coal, oil, and other natural resources; manufacturing interests; commerce; and finance.[44] Many of these committee members helped organize the city's reception and entertainment for pan-American delegates in November 1889, which included a small industrial exhibition and tours of local factories and mills. Their experience promoting Pittsburgh as a desirable economic partner, as well as a tourist attraction, would serve the committee well as they planned for the upcoming world's fair.[45]

In Harrisburg, days before the chamber's committee was established in Pittsburgh, Hasson moved to promote one of Western Pennsylvania's largest industries. He proposed that the state board form a special committee on petroleum and natural gas to advocate for a distinct space to display the products, machinery, and inventions associated with some of the region's most abundant and lucrative natural resources. The committee was approved and consisted of Hasson, Guffey, and Lewis Emery Jr., from Bradford. They pled with authorities in Chicago, pointing out that the 1889 Paris Exposition had an extensive oil exhibit even though the entirety of France did not produce a single barrel. In contrast, the United States produced over twenty-seven million barrels annually in the years leading up to 1892, over half of which was extracted from Pennsylvania and New York oil fields. Alas, the Chicago committee members would not concede to such an exhibit. They deemed a concentrated exhibit on such flammable products and the explosives used to extract them too dangerous a risk for the fairgrounds.

In January 1892, the state board's committee on manufactures set up an office in Pittsburgh for William Quinn to meet with all local manufacturers that planned to exhibit products at the Chicago exposition. Beginning on January 16, Quinn met with hundreds of business leaders; sent applications for exhibit space; distributed informational circulars to businesses and newspapers; met with the mayors of Pittsburgh, Allegheny, and McKeesport; and visited meetings of the chamber of commerce and several trade organizations. To support his work, Mayor Gourley asked the city's councils to establish a joint committee to confer with local manufacturers concerning the fair, noting, "Pittsburgh's importance as a great manufacturing center should be properly advertised at the Columbian Exposition, and there is no better way of doing this than by a full and complete exhibition of the products of our great industries."[46] Even with the help of the special committee, Quinn's task was an unenviable one, as he had every county in southwestern Pennsylvania in his purview. By March 1892, however, he could already show significant results, including the promise of an exhibit from the H. C. Frick Coke Company.

With less than a year until the opening ceremonies of the Columbian Exposition, the Chamber of Commerce of Pittsburgh was still drumming up interest from local businessmen to submit applications to exhibit at the fair. On May 27, 1892, they held a 180-seat dinner at the Duquesne Club, with many men of influence in attendance, including "bankers, wholesale merchants, manufacturers, insurance men, real estate men, oil and gas officials, and, in fact, a representation such as has never before been seen around a banquet table in this city."[47] The committee that planned the dinner was composed of several members of the chamber's World's Columbian Exposition Committee, including its chairman, Thomas Roberts; national Columbian Exposition alternate commissioner John Chalfant; and notable additions such as the Pennsylvania Railroad's Robert Pitcairn and Henry Clay Frick.

The committee created the banquet program to incite civic pride. Speakers recounted the history of various local industries and accomplishments of the Pittsburgh region, making their case for why it was among the greatest cities in the nation. That Chicago won the bid to host the world's fair by relentlessly promoting its successes and attributes was a wakeup call for those invested in Pittsburgh. For the first time since the announcement of the fair's host city, a tone of envy crept into the conversation. In reporting on the dinner, the *Post* lamented, "American cities inferior in population and resources have been made more widely known, to their great advantage. . . . We never acquired as a people the art of civic advertising, and were too much inclined to hide the light of our enterprise under a mantle of old-fogyism."[48]

In response to a toast to the city of Pittsburgh, Mayor Gourley was more direct in his remarks when he stated, "The most successful business men of the world are the greatest advertisers. What is true of individuals is true of cities. Chicago is an apt illustration of the truth of this statement. Its wonderful prosperity and growth proceed in a very large degree from the judicious use of wind. Every man, woman and child in Chicago has been taught to blow a horn." Relating the lessons of Chicago to his own city, Gourley issued a challenge to the men sitting before him in the Duquesne Club that night:

> We need a little of this kind of enterprise to keep our city and its wares before the people. Let us begin to advertise at the World's Exposition of 1893. Chicago will be the great Mecca around which the people of the civilized world will gather to examine the products and witness the achievements of all nations and of every clime. Let Pittsburgh be represented in order that we may show to all nations what this great home of labor is contributing to the multiplied movements that are lifting the world up to a higher plane and improving the condition of the human race.[49]

With the proper committees raising interest in exhibiting at the fair, both from the state of Pennsylvania and the region's chamber of commerce, Pittsburgh was primed to have an extensive showing in Chicago. Some local companies, such as Carnegie Steel and Westinghouse Electric, already had an international reputation and were being considered for major roles at the exposition. Gourley's speech had echoed the same sentiment area newspapers had made since Congress selected Chicago as host city—Pittsburgh would benefit greatly from the fair. He made his plea while in the room with the men who could dedicate the necessary capital to effectively promote their companies and drive the city to global prominence. Several of the businessmen in attendance would take him up on his challenge.

3

Coming Attractions

WHILE MANY of Pittsburgh's business leaders explored the various ways they could contribute to Western Pennsylvania's representation at the Columbian Exposition, other area companies and innovators had their sights set on a grander scale. Exhibits of local wares and industries would be important, but as the Chicago commissioners and planners were still sorting out the details of fair attractions, buildings, and utilities, companies in the Pittsburgh region saw their opportunity to incorporate, and thereby advertise, their products as some of the most memorable and influential aspects of the exposition.

One such business was the Keystone Bridge Company. At the conclusion of the 1889 Paris Exposition, it was clear the next world's fair must try to one-up Gustave Eiffel's tower. The tower immediately became the everlasting image of the Exposition Universelle and Chicago would need something even grander to put the 1893 World's Fair on the map. The simplest idea was to erect a structure even taller than Eiffel's and designs began to pour in throughout 1890; however, when construction for the Columbian Exposition began in January 1891 there was still no approved project.

In March 1891 newspapers such as the *Chicago Tribune* began to report rumors that a design managed by the Columbian Tower Company had gained approval from Daniel Burnham and his committee, making it the first reported plan to have support from fair officials. The article was full of details, even list- ing the name of the construction firm hired to build the tower with steel from Andrew Carnegie's Pittsburgh mills. A book published about the fair two years before it actually opened went so far as to describe the author's ascent to the top of the proposed tower and comments on the imaginary throngs enjoying the many attractions on its observation decks.[1] The June 20 issue of the *Chicago Tribune*, then, disappointed many future fairgoers when it announced that the exposition's ways and means committee had reopened negotiations with other tower companies, declaring that the Columbian Tower Company had not made enough progress.

By the summer of 1891 it was clear that any tower design accepted by the fair's committee would need to be temporary like the rest of the fairgrounds; funded privately due to the rising costs of buildings and other aspects of the fair; and erected in less than two years' time. These were all obstacles the Eiffel Tower had not been forced to overcome. Nevertheless, Eiffel himself reached out to William T. Baker, president of the exposition's board of directors, on August 4 with an offer to build Chicago a tower taller than the one he had constructed in Paris. Because time was of the essence and ideas were scarce, Baker agreed to entertain Eiffel's offer; however, the notion of America's fair featuring another tower built by a Frenchman irked many of the country's engineers. Once Eiffel's plan was shown to include only the design and not the money to pay for it, the ways and means committee quickly rejected his project, repeating the require- ment that all future proposals must include full funding.[2]

In October 1891 Chicago bridge builder George S. Morison presented the last credible plan to erect a tower at the Columbian Exposition. While earlier submissions had attempted to add ornamentation to Eiffel's design, Morison, for the sake of construction time and the temporary nature requested by the com- mittee, stripped nearly all of the decoration away, leaving something of a cross between the tower in Paris and an oil derrick. Modeled on the Eiffel Tower, Morison's design was an unprecedented 1,120-foot-tall structure with two platforms containing three-story buildings for restaurants and other accommo- dations, as well as incomparable views of the Columbian Exposition grounds and Chicago. The third and highest lookout would stand 900 feet above the fair and offer sweeping views of Lake Michigan and beyond. Because the tower needed to be built quickly and be profitable for its investors, Morison designed it with standard steel sizes in mind—seven thousand tons of it. This meant that

Fig. 3. Many articles pertaining to George Morison's Columbian Tower proposal depicted it rising above the White City and not outside the fairgrounds, as Carnegie's letter lamented. Photograph originally appeared in "The Columbian Tower," *Scientific American*, January 2, 1892, 9.

whatever company contracted with Morison for the tower project would not need to expend additional effort on casting, rolling, or pressing specialty pieces, thus reducing the overall cost. As a moneymaking venture, the tower would need to accommodate many people at once. Morison estimated that the tower could host more than twenty thousand visitors at a time on its three levels and incorporated eight elevators in his design to deliver them to their desired platforms. With admission rates from $0.50 to $1.50 depending on which level a person chose to visit, the tower would turn a profit if it operated at capacity for the entirety of the World's Fair.[3]

Carnegie's Keystone Bridge Company, in Pittsburgh, received word of Morison's plan and on October 12 representatives from Keystone and Carnegie, Phipps, and Company met to discuss the possibility of placing a bid to build the tower. They planned to have Carnegie, Phipps produce all the steel needed for the project. Keystone would then purchase the material and provide both the steel and the expertise to erect the tower, ensuring a profit for two Carnegie interests instead of one. They agreed to pursue the project provided that the American Tower Company, which was organized to oversee Morison's idea, consented to their financial terms.[4] A. L. Griffin, president of Keystone, authorized his chief engineer in Chicago, C. L. Strobel, to make a proposition to American Tower's McArthur Brothers Company and to submit the agreement to him for final approval.[5] Both parties moved quickly and McArthur Brothers and Keystone Bridge signed an agreement on October 15.

The Chicago press had all but given up on a tower for the upcoming world's fair after the failure of Eiffel's proposal and were eager to report on the newly signed agreement on October 17. Making note that Carnegie was the primary stockholder of the Keystone Bridge Company, many newspapers, including the *Pittsburgh Commercial Gazette*, proclaimed that "Carnegie's Tower" would be the tallest in the world. The mention of Carnegie's name, linking one of the country's most famous and wealthy men to the tower project in articles across the nation, set off a subsequent firestorm within Keystone Bridge and Carnegie, Phipps, and Company.

On October 19, the *Pittsburgh Post* reprinted a short but scathing editorial from the *New York World* blasting the proposed tower as a redundant imitation; the glorification of Carnegie, whose only claim to fame was getting rich by exploiting legal loopholes; and Chicago, a smoky, flat city unworthy of such a tower in the first place. This did not sit well with Carnegie, who saw this as a blow to his public persona. Officially, Carnegie claimed that he was skeptical of the business aspect of the tower and was not convinced there was money to be made in the project. His main sticking point was the fact that, by this time, any tower constructed would not be a part of the official fairgrounds. Carnegie told Morison that without a spot at the fair, the tower would be "a mere side show, like the Ohio fat woman, or the three-headed calf following Barnum's Circus." He feared people would reject the tower as a moneymaking scheme and advised Morison to deliver an ultimatum to the managers of the Columbian Exhibition: "No site, no Tower."[6] The same day the article was published in the *Post* Henry Clay Frick, acting in his capacity as the protector of the reputations of both Carnegie and his companies, sprang into action. He asked the company's attorney, Philander Knox, to interpret the agreement with McArthur Brothers so that Keystone could withdraw from the project.[7] Frick also chastised Griffin for signing the agreement.[8] Word of dissatisfaction reached Chicago and Strobel wrote to Frick to assure him that Keystone and Carnegie, Phipps were at minimal risk of liability being associated with such a large project, which he ensured would be successful.[9]

Griffin's company was the keystone to the entire enterprise and the very presence of a great tower, the proposed premier attraction, at the Columbian Exposition. Without the expertise and backing of Carnegie's steel mills and Keystone Bridge, the American Tower Company would likely fail to raise the money to complete the project before ever coming close to erecting a single beam, thus putting the fate of the entire fair in jeopardy. At the time, the tower was seen as the main attraction to the exposition, and without this draw, it was thought that the fair would be a financial disaster. Eager to smooth things over with Frick, Griffin offered his resignation as president of Keystone, asking only for a week to be able to fix his mistake.[10] On October 28, he wrote to McArthur Brothers to inform them that Keystone was backing out of the agreement because Carnegie's name was erroneously being used in newspaper articles to promote the tower scheme. Griffin claimed that Carnegie had no affiliation with Keystone other than that of a stockholder, albeit the majority holder by far.[11]

Attempting to salvage his project, Morison wrote directly to Frick on Halloween to express his regret that newspapers throughout the country used Carnegie's name to promote the project, but he also noted that Carnegie had willingly lent his name to other projects associated with his interests in the past, and his affiliation with Keystone was similar to his two limited liability organizations. Taking a stronger tone, Morison threatened Frick by indicating that if he backed out of his deal to build the tower it would show the world that contracts with Keystone were useless, thus resulting in fewer future contracts and endangering the company.[12] This was the exact opposite of Carnegie's hopes that the exposition would bolster his businesses, but his colleague played it cool. Frick's response on November 9 was a simple one, thanking Morison for his consideration of Keystone and citing his involvement in the project as their only reason for being interested, but also reiterating that the use of Carnegie's name was unacceptable.[13]

An audit of the American Tower Company proved Carnegie's stated concerns of bad business to be correct; mismanagement of solicited subscriptions left the company with no stockholders in early December. In response, the company planned to obtain subscriptions from prominent Chicago citizens to convince others to invest. Former Chicago mayor John A. Roche stated that if Carnegie would subscribe $50,000 then he could obtain subscriptions from four others for the same amount. Roche would then take the responsibility to raise the rest of the money. The company was convinced of the tower's success, giving it better odds than the Eiffel Tower because the United States had "double the population of France and . . . one much more inclined to spend their money freely."[14] On December 12, Carnegie sent his final word to members of American Tower and Keystone Bridge, definitively declining to attach his support to the project.[15] Although Frick had played his public relations role masterfully, Carnegie could not help but intervene while providing unsolicited advice to Morison in the process, particularly his "no site, no tower" ultimatum. This inability of Carnegie and Frick to work in concert would grow in the coming years, contributing to one of the most notorious moments in American labor history and the public collapse of their relationship.

News about the latest tower lagged behind Carnegie's refusal to support the American Tower Company and major journals, including *Scientific American* and *Iron Age*, began to report on the "approved" design.[16] The lack of outrage expressed by the press upon learning that the tower would not come to fruition is the ultimate evidence of the disappointment felt throughout the country. Rather than issuing a plea to continue the project, newspapers seem to have let the concept simply fade from the public's memory.

With the plan for a high tower behind them, the managers of the world's fair were again left wanting for some other way to upstage the 1889 Paris Exposition's Eiffel Tower. Burnham grew weary of reviewing failed tower designs and decided that Chicago's exposition must feature something different, something new. Early in 1892, Burnham expressed this desire at a meeting of the Saturday Afternoon Club. This group of engineers met periodically to discuss construction challenges associated with the fair, but this meeting also featured censuring and a challenge. Burnham rebuked American engineers for not coming up with a solution to the Eiffel problem and, furthermore, stated that another tower or something that was merely large would no longer be good enough. Fortunately, for Burnham, a thirty-three-year-old Pittsburgh-based engineer was in attendance.

George Washington Gale Ferris Jr. had built an impressive reputation in less than a decade. Born in Galesburg, Illinois, and raised in Nevada, Ferris graduated with a degree in civil engineering from Rensselaer Polytechnic Institute, the top private engineering school in the country, in 1881.[17] In 1885 he took a position with the Kentucky and Indiana Bridge Company to lead the testing of iron and steel they ordered from Pittsburgh's growing mills. During this time, Ferris became an authority on structural steel. Recognizing the need for a company specializing in steel inspection and quality control in Pittsburgh, Ferris capitalized on his experience and partnered with James C. Hallsted to found G. W. G. Ferris and Company, inspecting engineers, in 1886. Soon after the firm's founding they opened branch offices in New York City and Chicago, the latter a natural choice given that it was a hotbed of skyscraper construction.[18] The company won contracts to inspect the steel for the new Rand, McNally and Company building and Burnham's Rookery, which would soon house Ferris's branch office. These Chicago connections put Ferris in touch with many of the men who held influence concerning the Columbian Exposition and so, when the fair needed to hire someone to inspect the steel for its buildings, there was only one logical choice. Ferris's company would be responsible for inspecting the steel for much of the White City.[19]

Ferris listened intently as Burnham spoke to the Saturday Afternoon Club, taking inspiration from the speech. Later, he would describe a flash of an idea that hit him during a meal shortly after Burnham's talk, leading him to quickly sketch out the specifications on whatever paper happened to be nearby. The resulting drawings of a large observation wheel, which would rotate passengers several hundred feet above the crowds below, were so detailed and well considered that the final construction was nearly identical to the original idea; however, there was plenty of work to do before his vision could come to fruition. Ferris immediately returned to Pittsburgh and set his draftsmen to work creating scale drawings of the wheel. William F. Gronau, who became a partner in the firm when it was restructured in 1889, was put in charge of the work and responsible for calculating the stresses that would be put on the structure from its passengers, the wind, and its own steel frame. Computing the stresses of a large tension wheel had never been attempted before, and so Gronau had to devise the methods from scratch. He determined the exact amount of steel needed to support a wheel 250 feet in diameter, noting that if he added more steel for precautionary measures then the wheel would require even more steel to support the extra weight.[20] Once the idea proved to be viable, the next step was to pitch the wheel to Burnham and his committee.

In spring 1892, Ferris presented his wheel concept to the ways and means committee. They had denied a proposal for a much smaller observation wheel the previous September and, while Ferris's idea certainly met the criteria of being large and novel, the committee was not willing to risk approving the plans. Burnham was getting anxious. On March 4 he wrote to Harlow Higinbotham, chair of the ways and means committee, desperately asking for information about the status of the observation tower projects. Burnham stated that they had spent time on five different proposals, but none had been approved by the committee.[21] Now, Ferris's wheel idea had also been passed over. Understanding that the fair still lacked a premier attraction, Ferris continued to work on his design and in June he received a concession from the committee only to have it withdrawn the very next day. The committee's previous experience with winds from Lake Michigan blowing over the frames of fair buildings made its members fearful that the tall steel wheel would topple over in disaster. Even if Ferris could build it, some committee members and engineers doubted it would actually turn. If it did prove to be operational, others felt it would detract from the dignity of the exposition's White City.

Undeterred, Ferris doubled down on the wheel plan. On June 9 he incorporated the Ferris Wheel Company, which would "own, erect, construct, manufacture, lease, sell or operate bicycle wheels of the Ferris or other types for the purpose of observation or amusement." Capitalized at $600,000, the company would ensure that the wheel was not dependent on money from the exposition's coffers.[22] To lure investors to his cause, Ferris spent an additional $25,000 (over $750,000 in 2022) on more drawings and specifications. One key newcomer was Robert Hunt, a prominent Chicago engineer with ties to Ferris's inspection firm. Another was Andrew Onderdonk, an engineer known for contributing to the design of the Canadian Pacific Railway.[23] With endorsements from other well-respected engineers, more investors followed. While Ferris carefully planned his next moves, the ways and means committee denied another observation wheel proposal in July; however, the exposition dedication in October served as a reminder to the committee that time was running out.[24]

On November 14, Ferris incorporated the Pittsburgh Construction Company, founded "to build, construct or erect or manufacture bridges and buildings and to do a general contracting and building business." The actual purpose of the company was to erect the Ferris wheel should he secure a concession. Confident in his design and newly formed financial support system, Ferris again submitted his plans to the ways and means committee on November 29. While awaiting the committee's decision, Ferris contacted Luther V. Rice of St. Louis's Union Depot and Tunnel Company on December 12 to offer him the opportunity to serve as construction superintendent, operate the wheel during the fair, and eventually oversee its dismantling.[25] After just over two weeks of deliberation, the committee finally approved the Ferris wheel design for the Midway Plaisance on December 16, 1892. The proposed wheel was large and unique, and had financial backing, making it an attractive choice to the time-strapped group, but they still demonstrated some hesitation in accepting the plan. To insure their decision, the committee requested that Ferris post a $25,000 bond in case the project failed.

Ferris immediately set to work ordering the various pieces of his gigantic wheel. With many of the country's steel mills overwhelmed with orders, no single company could accommodate the entire workload so quickly and so Ferris capitalized on his intimate knowledge of the industry to carefully select a dozen companies to fill his requests. Pennsylvania companies produced several components of the wheel. Detroit Bridge and Iron Works fabricated the main wheel structure with steel supplied by Pittsburgh's Jones and Laughlin. The Keystone Bridge Company provided the two drive chains. McIntosh, Hemphill and Company, of Pittsburgh, supplied steel hubs and rolled plates. Bethlehem Iron Company forged the 142,031-pound axle. Westinghouse air brakes controlled the wheel. Pittsburgh's Samuel Diescher, who had previously developed the city's funicular, or inclined plane, railways designed the machinery and turning gear. In nearby Ohio, two 1,000-horsepower steam engines from William Todd and Company, of Youngstown, would power the wheel and the Walker Manufacturing Company, of Cleveland, furnished the cast sprocket plates.[26] All of these pieces formed a puzzle that had to fit perfectly together immediately. There was no time to wait for replacement parts if manufacturers did not construct any portion to specifications. All the work needed to be precise so it could be assembled in Chicago, and men from Ferris's inspection firm examined every piece to ensure accuracy.

Work at the wheel site began in January 1893 in near-zero-degree temperatures. The first step was to lay the concrete foundations for the 140-foot-tall support towers. This required workers to dig thirty-five-foot-deep holes into the frozen terrain. They used dynamite to blast through and loosen the three feet of solid earth for excavation. Once it was time to pour the foundations, workmen

Fig. 4. This view through the completed Ferris wheel shows the massive axle and web of spokes supporting and distributing the weight of the attraction. "Ferris Wheel, Chicago, Ill.," 2007678221, Prints and Photographs Division, Library of Congress.

used steam to prevent the concrete from freezing before it had time to set. Placed in the twenty-foot-deep concrete piers were the steel beams that would anchor the towers, and the entire wheel, to the earth.[27] The towers themselves were iron pyramids, with the side of each tower facing the wheel perpendicular to the ground while the outer face slanted inward, emphasizing the overall height of the attraction. The metal for Ferris's wheel arrived in Chicago on five trains of thirty cars each. Wooden scaffolding started to go up on March 20 and the erection of the towers began on March 29.[28]

Once workmen completed the towers, the most integral piece of the wheel, the forty-five-ton axle, the largest piece of iron forged at that time, was put in place. While in principle the wheel structurally functioned like that of a bicycle, since the Ferris wheel hung fifteen feet above the ground the axle bore the entirety of the weight, including the cars and passengers. On either side of the axle was a 12.5-ton hub on which thin spokes connecting to an inner rim were mounted, from a distance giving the appearance that the Ferris wheel was floating in the air, unattached to the towers on either side. Amazingly, it took workers only two hours to hoist the entire seventy-ton piece 140 feet into the air and fasten it to beams on the support towers.[29] The wheel itself comprised thirty-six identical wedges, which workers assembled on a timber form and then attached to the axle. They affixed the first panel directly beneath the axle and then assembly continued in either direction until the sides met at the apex, just as bridges are constructed from either end toward the center.[30] The great wheel was beginning to take shape, an early preview of just one of the many marvels that would greet fairgoers during their visit to the Chicago fair.

While Burnham fretted over selecting the signature attraction of the world's fair in early 1892, he had other pressing matters at hand. The dedication of the Columbian Exposition was scheduled for October, but the grounds and the buildings were nowhere near as complete as they should have been. Furthermore, promotors were already billing the fair as the largest display of electrical power the world had ever seen, but organizers had yet to determine the supplier of that electricity, let alone the type of electricity they would implement, as direct current (DC) and alternating current (AC) battled for dominance. Exposition managers were just beginning to think about the electrical component of the fair as the war of the currents reached a fever pitch. Their decision of DC or AC would be an invaluable victory for proponents of the winning side.

The battle to electrify the country was about five years old when organizers announced the bid to light the fair. It began in 1888 when Thomas Edison noticed that a Pittsburgh company was beginning to cut into his clientele. Edison's direct-current system had been the standard way of electrifying homes for nearly a decade, counting prominent citizens such as J. P. Morgan among its earliest adopters. Research into electricity advanced at a rapid pace and soon a new form of electricity began to encroach on Edison's market: alternating current. Whereas DC produces a constant voltage, AC alternates the flow of the charged particles that produce electricity. Because it could be transformed to a higher voltage and lower current than DC, AC could be distributed more efficiently over longer distances and then brought down to usable levels; however, the science and technology concerning the production and distribution of AC were comparatively new, and its application and practicality were initially met with skepticism.

Recently, though, a former Edison employee named Nikola Tesla had successfully developed a polyphase alternating current motor and power system, which used multiple electrical conductors set at specific intervals to maintain a constant voltage and thus more power. If properly implemented and promoted, polyphase motors would spell the end of Edison's electrical monopoly by demonstrating the practical application of AC. Tesla's polyphase motor drew the attention of several electrical engineers, and one, George Westinghouse, offered to purchase the patent from the scientist and invited him to further develop the idea in his Pittsburgh laboratory. After a frustrating year of clashing with the company's engineers about how to best operate his designs, Tesla returned to New York City dissatisfied with his progress, but with his valuable friendship with Westinghouse still intact.[31]

Edison was threatened by the Westinghouse-Tesla relationship and the AC system that would develop out of it. High-voltage AC could travel over long distances and be powered down for use in homes and businesses, whereas DC relied on power stations placed about every mile to transmit electricity to customers. Fewer stations meant lower costs, making Westinghouse the more attractive electricity supplier. Going on the offensive, Edison began to wage a publicity war against AC and its foremost advocate, specifically naming Westinghouse as the person who was risking innocent lives to sell his electricity.[32] Edison also staged several demonstrations in which he attempted to use AC to fatally electrocute animals, but when these demonstrations did not raise the appropriate outcry from the reporters in attendance, Edison financed another way to draw attention to the fatal current. On August 6, 1890, at Auburn State Prison, convicted murderer William Kemmler was strapped into an Edison-designed electric chair using Westinghouse products and AC. The first person to be subjected to the electric chair, he suffered through a gruesome eight-minute execution. Witnesses, including several newspaper reporters, were disgusted by the display, some to the point of becoming physically ill.[33] While Edison designed the demonstration to definitively verify that AC was deadly, it merely succeeded in proving that the current was lethal only when used at the extreme, effectively roasting a person alive. Nonetheless, AC became associated with the chair, electrocution, death, and, unfortunately, George Westinghouse.

The rapid success of the Edison and Westinghouse companies meant the firms were accumulating debt to meet the growing demand for their products, which became problematic when the outset of the November 1890 financial panic prompted creditors to come calling to collect from their companies. In the past, Edison had used the leading firm Drexel, Morgan and Company for financial security, while Westinghouse relied on stockholders, friends (often some of Pittsburgh's wealthiest citizens), and personal investment to meet his company's needs. His charisma and ability to excite others about his ideas and skills instilled confidence in potential investors, making it possible for Westinghouse to avoid relying on banks for capital.[34] This time, with a debt of about half a million dollars ($15.25 million in 2022), would require a more aggressive, and potentially humbling, campaign.

Westinghouse first doubled the amount of capital stock for the Westinghouse Electric and Manufacturing Company and invited several successful Pittsburgh bankers to save the company, but when they sought to wrest control away from Westinghouse he withdrew the invitation. Instead, Westinghouse took a page from Edison's book and traveled to New York to seek financial aid. While there he decided to merge two additional Westinghouse electric lighting companies—United States and Consolidated—into Westinghouse Electric and Manufacturing.[35] The friendship of Westinghouse and Tesla also proved to be valuable in preserving the company. Upon learning that the Pittsburgh firm was in real danger, Tesla ripped up his royalty contract, allowing Westinghouse to continue using his patents for an AC motor and system at no cost.[36] On July 15, 1891, the final pieces fell into place to eliminate the company's debt. These acts, along with some additional stock restructuring, allowed Westinghouse Electric to emerge from the financial crisis relatively unscathed and perhaps even stronger than before.

Meanwhile, Edison General Electric was also under duress. Edison had previously rebuffed the idea of a merger with another company, Thomson-Houston, not wanting to share control of his ideas with anyone; however, by this time, he owned only a small percentage of Edison GE stock. Unencumbered by the inventor's demands, company president Henry Villard contacted Thomson-Houston president Charles Coffin to discuss a merger that would not only resolve their current financial troubles but also reduce the number of expensive patent suits in the future.[37] Coffin and Villard brought in J. P. Morgan to broker the merger, which resulted in the formation of General Electric (GE) in early 1892. At its founding, Edison General Electric controlled three-quarters of the country's electrical business, but Thomson-Houston stockholders held the majority control of the new company and named Coffin the first GE president.[38] While

General Electric would not exist without his achievements, Edison's hands-off approach to managing his electric firm meant he now had no control over the direction and management of the company he had created. He had just fallen victim to Westinghouse's biggest fear; namely, being pushed out of his own business. Nevertheless, the company had achieved the same result—salvation. General Electric, however, was not above using its tenuous connection to Edison to further its own reputation and business. The war of the currents continued, with Westinghouse Electric and Manufacturing Company and alternating current on one side and General Electric and direct current on the other.

It was in these conditions, then, that Burnham and the Columbian Exposition sought out bids to electrify the fairgrounds in the spring of 1892. General Electric appeared to have the upper hand, as Edison had been supplying electricity to the Chicago construction site since October 1891. His electric plant powered fifty motors for various tools and machinery, not to mention arc lights to keep the site lit up for work during the night.[39] The fair paid Edison eleven dollars per light to electrify the construction site, but this time Edison was no longer in charge.[40] General Electric and company president Coffin now controlled Edison's patents, and with seemingly no other competitor to outbid his juggernaut the lighting of the exposition would not come cheap.

The first bidding in mid-March drew a line in the sand and showed the large electrical trust that they could not bully the fair commissioners. With Westinghouse preoccupied in Pittsburgh securing his company, General Electric initially bid $38.50 per arc light for six thousand lights and $15.78 per horsepower for the dynamos providing the electricity. Insulted by the clear price gouging proposed by the new electrical behemoth, the fair's commissioners decided to sign with smaller—and more importantly, cheaper—independent firms.[41] Next, companies were to submit bids for lighting the entire fair—ninety-two thousand incandescent lamps for a duration of six months—by April 2. General Electric bid $1.72 million ($52.5 million in 2022) for its DC system but, unexpectedly, an upstart Chicago company, South Side Machine and Metal Works, bid $625,600. It was of little surprise that the local firm prevailed in securing the contract given that there was more than a million-dollar difference between bids.[42] The question then became whether the unknown company could really deliver on its proposal.

Charles F. Locksteadt, of South Side Machine, knew his company would need help in fulfilling its contract and so he logically reached out to the only company that was not part of the General Electric conglomerate—Westinghouse Electric and Manufacturing. Locksteadt approached Westinghouse for assistance and

Westinghouse, feeling his company was now more financially stable, agreed.[43] The entrance of Westinghouse into the fray changed the tone of the electricity bid entirely. For General Electric, the fair was no longer just another contract to be won. It became a showdown between the young corporation and Westinghouse, its only remaining major competitor and threat. General Electric soon announced that it was slashing its previous bid to undercut South Side Metal and, sensing that a bidding war to electrify the cash-strapped fair was now a real possibility with Westinghouse in the mix, World's Columbian Exposition president Harlow Higinbotham announced that there would be one final round of bids in mid-May, less than one year before the fair's opening day.

In the weeks before the bid deadline, Westinghouse campaigned to win over the people of Chicago. The city was already disgusted by General Electric, seeing the company as the electricity trust that sought to play the fair for fools with its exorbitant bid. Chicagoans were also at odds with Edison over the amount of pollution his company's boilers produced in the Loop.[44] Even though he was all but removed from General Electric, the animosity surely transferred to the new company. The affable Westinghouse was their knight in shining armor, saving not only the exposition but also the entire city of Chicago from embarrassment. For his part, Westinghouse acknowledged this was an opportunity to build popular opinion concerning him, his company, and AC. Once he decided to bid on the fair job, he met with Ernest H. Heinrich, who had previously been an industrial reporter for Pittsburgh's *Chronicle Telegraph*, to capitalize on his connections in the Midwest. While Heinrich had no contacts to speak of, he did know Pittsburgh Associated Press staffer Colonel W. C. Connelly, who had connections to the Chicago press. Connelly and Heinrich traveled together and spent several days on a public relations tour for Westinghouse before the final bids were due.[45] As representatives from both companies trickled into Chicago in mid-May, Westinghouse accompanied his men to present their proposal while GE's Coffin did not make the trip, further substantiating the idea that Westinghouse was a man of the people. He had won the hearts of Chicago's citizenry; now he just needed to convince the fair committee.

On May 16, 1892, the committee on grounds and buildings met in the Rookery Building in downtown Chicago to hear the bids from General Electric and Westinghouse. General Electric held firm to its last offer for an all-DC system to light the fair and they also offered an all-AC system for nearly $100,000 less. By this point, they had no interest in making a profit and the bids were close to fulfilling the contract requirements at cost. Westinghouse countered with a bid for a combined AC/DC system and an all-AC system that was more than

$80,000 less than GE's AC proposal. Burnham favored the Westinghouse bid. It was the cheapest offer the committee had entertained throughout the entire process, and the previous greed of General Electric had left a bad taste in his mouth. However, the decision to award the contract to Westinghouse was not automatic. Others on the committee had ties to General Electric and would benefit from that company winning the contract, primarily from future jobs that would be earned through the publicity of lighting the exposition. There was also the matter of patent ownership, which proved to be a real obstacle in the field of electrical engineering. General Electric's vice-president, Captain Eugene Griffin, cautioned the committee that Westinghouse could not deliver on his bid because his lamps were currently under litigation for infringing on an Edison patent owned by his company.[46]

Burnham and his committee had to make a choice. The opening of the fair was quickly approaching, and they did not have the luxury of waiting for a lawsuit to play out in the courts. At the same time, they could not afford to overpay for such a large job as electrifying the fair. While relying on a questionable patent was a risk, paying extra to General Electric to ensure that it would not be an issue was not an option. After consulting with the exposition's lawyers, the committee agreed to award the contract to Westinghouse for his all-AC system. There was a proviso, however—the commissioners required Westinghouse to issue a $1 million bond ($30.5 million in 2022) guaranteeing the contract in the event the patent suit caused delays and prevented the completion of the job. Since Westinghouse had only recently secured his company, issuing a bond of this size was dangerous. Even if Westinghouse was successful, lighting the fair would not bring much immediate profit to his company. The allure of the publicity that would come from succeeding, though, was enough to win him over. Westinghouse agreed to the conditions and returned to Pittsburgh ready to work.

Westinghouse Electric and Manufacturing had several enormous obstacles to overcome if it were to complete the job on time. Engineers needed to design and build engines that were larger and worked harder than any previously constructed. To avoid relying on competitors, mainly General Electric, to supply the lamps required to fulfill the contract, Westinghouse and his men also needed to develop and manufacture a new type of bulb that did not infringe upon the GE-owned Edison patents. That Westinghouse had to accomplish all this work in Pittsburgh, and then transport and install it at the Chicago fairgrounds in less than a year, was an arduous task. That everyone expected it to successfully work by the fair's opening day in May was a nearly impossible challenge.

The engines required for the system were to be over four times the horse-power and run at over twice the revolutions per minute of typical Westinghouse machines. Westinghouse charged E. S. McClelland, his top draftsman at the machine shop, with designing a new engine that would drive a one-thousand-horsepower generator composed of two alternators using Tesla's polyphase system. This engine could accommodate ten thousand incandescent lamps. After only one night's work Westinghouse approved McClelland's plans and production began shortly thereafter.[47]

Generating the electricity was one thing, but lighting the fair was quite another. General Electric's Griffin had been correct in Chicago when he pointed out that Westinghouse did not hold the appropriate patents to follow through on his bid. General Electric possessed Edison's patent for an all-glass globe incandescent bulb, which was currently under litigation in federal courts, but in all likelihood would be upheld. This situation forced Westinghouse, then, to develop not only a new type of bulb that would not infringe on the patent but also one that he could manufacture quickly in order to meet his looming deadline. Recalling engineer Reginald Fessenden's patent that used silicon-iron and iron-nickel alloy wires, which Westinghouse had previously acquired from the Sawyer-Man Electric Company, he hit on a solution. Instead of relying on the one-piece bulb Edison had patented, he could manufacture a two-piece bulb that comprised a stopper containing the wiring that fit into the glass globe the way a cork fits into a bottle. The two pieces were then sealed with a cement to maintain a vacuum in the globe. The "stopper" lamps, as they came to be called, were not as efficient as Edison's bulbs because they could not maintain the vacuum for a long time, and so Westinghouse used Fessenden's iron filament instead of the expensive platinum that was required for a longer duration. Machines personally designed by Westinghouse could also manufacture the stopper lamps, which meant faster production. Westinghouse set up a glass factory in his Allegheny air brake works and soon bulb production was under way. Since Westinghouse took initiative instead of waiting on the outcome of the pending litigation, by the time the courts resolved the Edison patent suit on December 15, 1892, it was of little consequence to the completion of the fair contract.[48]

That did not mean GE would go quietly, though. A week later its lawyers filed a restraining order in the United States Circuit Court in Pittsburgh against Westinghouse Electric and Manufacturing to prevent them from using the stopper lamps, alleging that they were side-stepping an injunction against the Sawyer-Man lamp. By happenstance, Westinghouse and one of his attorneys were inadvertently tipped off about the suit by one of General Electric's lawyers during a chance encounter on a New York elevated train. Westinghouse was able to reach one of his Pittsburgh lawyers in time and so counsel was already waiting in the courtroom when GE's man arrived. When the case was heard after Christmas, Westinghouse lawyers were able to convince the judge that there was no infringement of the Edison patents by providing blueprints of the stopper lamp to illustrate its construction and operation. By settling the complaint quickly, Westinghouse and his lawyers prevented further injunctions from GE that would have cost the company valuable time and stopped him from completing his work in Chicago.[49]

In attempting to sabotage Westinghouse's lighting of the fair, General Electric failed to account for the inventor's acumen and personality. True to the Pittsburgh region's spirit of innovation, Westinghouse solved the lamp issue personally, relishing the challenge. While getting his hands dirty and expressing his pleasure in taking part in the process, Westinghouse's excitement became contagious throughout his workforce. E. E. Keller, manager of the company's Columbian Exposition work, noted years later that Westinghouse "had a sort of magnetic influence on the workmen . . . they seemed imbued with the idea that this was a game to beat an opponent who held all the aces, and that they were having a lot of fun doing it."[50] Opening day at the Columbian Exposition was five months away and there was still plenty of work to do, but the Westinghouse team reveled in the work and their victories. It was Westinghouse versus General Electric, the new electricity trust, and Pittsburgh was winning the battle.

―――――――――

The summer of 1892 was also significant to Pittsburgh's growing steel industry and its most notable company, Carnegie Steel. While Andrew Carnegie was away in Scotland, Frick was left to run the company and break the Amalgamated Association of Iron and Steel Workers, a union that had represented skilled workers at the Homestead mill for the last eleven years. After presenting several new contract proposals unfavorable to the union's negotiating committee, Frick locked out the workers and fenced in the mill. On July 6, three hundred Pinkerton detectives hired by Frick attempted to enter the mill grounds via the Monongahela River to secure the company's property, but they were met by a sea of townspeople. The ensuing firefight left ten dead and many more wounded. While newspapers around the world covered the battle from various viewpoints, the company continued the lockout until November, when the Amalgamated Association agreed to call off the strike and return to work, effectively demonstrating that unions could not compete against the growing juggernaut of unfettered corporations.

Throughout the summer and fall, many pro-labor newspapers cited the 1890 McKinley Tariff, which allowed the American steel industry to flourish, as a primary factor in the Homestead strike, with Carnegie put forth as the epitome of why Republican rule was detrimental to the working class. Carter Harrison, Chicago's Democratic mayoral candidate and publisher of the *Chicago Times*, used Carnegie's support of President Benjamin Harrison as part of his own ultimately successful campaign and a broader attempt to discredit the Republican Party. Overall, this sentiment provided a highly publicized reason for labor to vote Democrat in the 1892 presidential election, particularly in the Midwest, and so many considered President Harrison's failed reelection bid to be fallout from the Homestead strike.[51] The realization that any display by Carnegie Steel at the Columbian Exposition could be a potential site of outrage by friends of labor and wounded Republicans alike influenced Carnegie's actions toward the fair throughout the next year.

Meanwhile, as Westinghouse busied himself and his company in preparing to light the Columbian Exposition, committees in Chicago rushed to finish what they could before the October 1892 fair dedication ceremony. Initially they planned to hold the dedication on October 12, the official four hundredth anniversary of Columbus's discovery; however, perhaps in an effort to win over the citizens of New York City, which had already planned a weeklong celebration, organizers decided to push the dedication back to October 21. By moving the date, the fair commissioners allowed prospective attendees to attend the celebration in New York and still have enough time to travel to Chicago. They hoped to attract as many as possible to the fairgrounds so that visitors to the dedication would take back with them stories of the magnificence of the grounds and buildings, which would not be completely ready until May 1893 or possibly even later.

On October 20 a ten-mile-long procession of Chicago area civic groups marched through the city's business district. In addition to area ethnic organizations and other nonmilitary groups, the parade also included the state governors in attendance and their delegations. One Pittsburgh couple to make the trip to Chicago for the ceremonies was Judge Christopher Magee and his wife, Elizabeth Magee, a member of the Allegheny County Women's Auxiliary Committee. Elizabeth wrote their daughter, Margaret Mitchell, from the posh Palmer House hotel with her observations on the day's proceedings. Of the civic parade, she noted, "I was surprised at the short time it took to pass (only three hours)." The short duration, she speculated, was because ten thousand workers had dropped out at the last minute due to the presence of Pennsylvania governor Robert Pattison and chief justice of the Pennsylvania Supreme Court Edward Paxson. This was likely in response to the state's intervention in the Homestead steel strike in July, which had become a rallying cry for the labor movement. Magee did not mince words with her daughter, stating, "I for one was glad of it. . . . [I]f they would as greatly drop out of the country it would be a good thing." She also observed that Governor Roswell Flower was the only representative present from New York, indicating that there was still interest in lingering hostilities from the city that lost the bid to host the fair.[52]

The day of the dedication of the buildings began with a military parade to Jackson Park before attendees convened inside the cavernous Manufactures Building, the fair's largest exhibit hall, for the ceremony. The building was outfitted with a platform to accommodate 2,400 dignitaries, a stage for a chorus of over 5,000 singers, and a general viewing area to seat 100,000 guests. Because the Pennsylvania Board of World's Fair Manager's Horticulture Committee, led by Western Pennsylvania's William Hamilton, was already actively shipping plants to Chicago, the commonwealth was well represented during the dedication ceremonies. According to the committee's November report, "The decoration of the Manufacturer's Building for the dedication ceremonies was mainly the work of our Committee. The decoration of the main avenue on the stage was entirely from Pennsylvania."[53]

The *Pittsburg Dispatch* and *Commercial Gazette* took the opportunity to describe many of the exposition buildings in detail. There was some skepticism about whether the fairgrounds were truly as great as organizers had advertised and reporters were eager for their first opportunity to review the site for themselves. While the landscaping and buildings were incomplete and shipping crates were scattered throughout the grounds, articles about the fair in the wake of the dedicatory ceremonies were extraordinarily positive. In addition, the *Pittsburgh Press* published its first of many lists of local men and women who were in Chicago visiting the exposition. Several area newspapers also printed excerpts or complete transcriptions of several of the speeches made during the ceremonies, which meant readers in Western Pennsylvania were better informed than the tens of thousands in attendance at the festivities in Chicago—due to the large size of the crowd packed into the Manufactures Building and the lack of microphones, only those positioned close to the stage were able to hear the speakers.

Meanwhile, many cities throughout the country also held celebrations

honoring Christopher Columbus on October 21, and Pittsburgh was no excep-
tion. The sunny day drew tens of thousands to downtown Pittsburgh from that
city, Allegheny, and beyond. Decorations adorned many buildings in the Golden
Triangle, particularly on Fifth Avenue, Smithfield Street, Liberty Avenue, and
Grant Street, and stretched into Lawrenceville, the South Side, and the East
End. The main event was a thirty-thousand-participant parade, which the
Pittsburgh Press proclaimed as the biggest ever held in the city to that time.
The procession included veteran and active-duty soldiers, local industry representatives, bicyclists, marching bands, and various ethnic, fraternal, and
religious organizations. Breweries contributed several of the most memorable
floats, decked in red, blue, and white and Columbus reenactments. A brass band
preceded fifteen vehicles fielded by H. J. Heinz carrying paintings of his various
facilities.[54]

Once the Columbus celebrations ended, everyone involved looked ahead to
May and the official opening of the Columbian Exposition. Planners still had a
lot of work to do, both in Chicago and in Pennsylvania, but all involved were
optimistic that the fair would be a success. As workmen assembled the Ferris
wheel in early 1893, crews rushed around the fairgrounds completing the myriad buildings and exhibits. Opening day was quickly approaching, and while
the wheel would not be finished in time for the festivities, it would not be long
before the attraction would leave its mark on the exposition. Meanwhile, exhibits from all over the world began to pour into Jackson Park. The theory that
travelers from the East Coast and Europe would journey through Pittsburgh on
their way to exposition turned out to be true for the displays being transported
as well. Since many major railroads passed through Pittsburgh, Western Pennsylvanians had the opportunity to preview some of the wonders that would be
on display at the fair, building local anticipation for the main event.

On February 8, 1893, a 21-car train carrying most of the exhibit for Germany's Krupp Gun Company stopped at Union Station on its way to Chicago.
The materials were primarily in crates, but railroad employees were treated
to a view of an 18-foot-long rifle cannon and a piece of 14-inch-thick steel target that Krupp used during testing.[55] In addition to transporting the regular-
sized Krupp exhibits, the Pennsylvania Railroad was also tasked with moving
an enormous 122-ton cannon from Baltimore to Chicago. The special railcars
constructed in Altoona to move the ordnance, with swinging mounts for its 32
wheels and abnormally low load placement, were so impressive that they, too,
would be put on display at the exposition.[56] The 16.5-inch caliber Krupp gun
measured 48 feet long, making it the heaviest and longest cannon ever made

Fig. 5. The specially designed railcar used to transport the monstrous Krupp gun was so impressive that it was included in the Pennsylvania Railroad's fair exhibit. *Catalogue of the Exhibit of the Pennsylvania Railroad Company at the World's Columbian Exposition.*

up to that time. The gun fired 4-foot-long projectiles weighing over 1 ton each, requiring over 700 pounds of gunpowder for a single shot.[57] The steamship carrying the gun across the Atlantic Ocean arrived in Baltimore on March 19. Preparations were made to hoist the cannon out of the ship using hydraulic lifts at Sparrows Point, but complications delayed the extraction by weeks. After several false reports that the cannon would pass through the city in a few days, the *Commercial Gazette* announced on April 6, "The great Krupp gun has not kept its engagement with Pittsburgh this week, and in fact lies in the vessel which brought it to Baltimore."[58] Pittsburghers feared that a water route to Chicago via the Saint Lawrence River might be used instead of the railroads, robbing Western Pennsylvania of its chance to view the gun.

Finally, the cannon was removed from the ship and placed on the railcars. Because it was the largest freight shipment ever in the United States to that point, the train transporting the gun ran only during the day as a safety precaution. Furthermore, railroad officials required passing trains to stop until the special cars moved by in case any of the cargo had shifted. The Pittsburgh division of the route, with its steep grades and sharp curves, was deemed the most dangerous portion of the journey. On the evening of April 9, a train carrying smaller cannons removed from the same ship as the big gun stopped at the Pennsylvania Railroad's 28th Street yard in Pittsburgh on the Fort Wayne line. By then tales of the cannons had filled the newspapers and many came to see the German artillery, particularly the following morning when the departing train navigated a sharp turn over Liberty Avenue on its way to Allegheny. The two cannons that passed through the city were but a preview of the big gun, which was finally on its way across Pennsylvania.

On the evening of April 11, the monstrous Krupp cannon came to a stop in the yards behind Union Station near 13th Street, having traveled from Altoona at a speed of twelve miles per hour. From about 6:30 to 10:00 that night the railroad admitted people to see the massive gun. Despite objections from railroad staff, several men and boys went so far as to climb on the huge cannon and many in attendance signed their name on the gun and pieces of armor with chalk, while others carved their names on the wooden boxes protecting the breech and muzzle.[59] Older spectators, it was noted, made mental comparisons to Fort Pitt Foundry's Rodman cannon, the largest piece of ordnance produced in Pittsburgh during the Civil War. That gun measured less than half the weight and height of the massive Krupp gun, but its bore was three and a half inches wider. The next morning, when the gun entered Allegheny and stopped just past Federal Street, it was its citizens' turn to climb the gun until the special police of the Fort Wayne Railroad could clear them off. Good-natured, or perhaps curious, teachers in Allegheny declared a recess so that schoolchildren could watch the cannon as it passed by and made its way out of Western Pennsylvania.[60]

Shortly after the Krupp exhibit left Pittsburgh, another railroad attraction found its way into the city. One of the oldest locomotives in the country, the *John Bull*, passed through Western Pennsylvania on April 19. The engine was on its way to Chicago as part of the Pennsylvania Railroad's exhibit at the Columbian Exposition. The locomotive, built in 1839, pulled two early passenger cars and was followed by a more modern train outfitted with Pullman coaches. This, too, created interest in the Union Station rail yards, but the locomotive stayed for only a few hours before slowly moving on to its next stop.[61]

While the *John Bull* sat in Pittsburgh, preparations were under way to receive another exhibit on its voyage to Chicago. On April 26, officials from Philadelphia transporting the Liberty Bell were to spend a night in Pittsburgh on their way to the World's Fair. Whereas gatherings to view other passing exhibits were informal affairs, city and county officials met to make formal arrangements for the visiting relic. Pittsburgh mayor Bernard McKenna, members of both branches of city council, and other delegates met the travelers at East Brady before escorting the Philadelphia contingent into the city. The car carrying the Liberty Bell was run down the tracks on Liberty Avenue to Third Street so that everyone who wanted to view the historic symbol would have their chance. One hundred police officers were on duty to guard the bell from those wishing to touch or climb onto the already fragile artifact. A reception for the Philadelphia contingent was held in the city council chambers that night.

The train carrying the bell found some difficulty in crossing the state, meeting celebrations at nearly every town it passed. By the time the Liberty Bell reached Pittsburgh, it was two hours behind schedule, but that did not dampen the spirits of those waiting to greet it. Thousands turned out in the rain to get a glimpse of the bell. Those in attendance were treated to a fireworks display, too.[62] To ensure it remained on schedule the next day, the train left early in the morning after a rumor had already spread that the bell would be in Pittsburgh until three o'clock that afternoon. While many in Pittsburgh missed their opportunity to see the bell before it departed, large crowds gathered in Allegheny parks to cheer as the train made its way for Cleveland.[63]

Just as previous fairs had whetted the appetites of the region's boosters, these previews of fair attractions piqued the interest of potential visitors to Chicago in the upcoming summer. The *Press* noted that the excitement built up over the month of April was good publicity for the Columbian Exposition:

> It is well that this sentiment has been awakened, and the managers of the world's fair who are getting a valuable advertisement for the [Columbian Exposition] are to be commended for their skill in combining a shrewd business move with one of the most honorable and admirable emotions of human nature—that of patriotism. The German gun and the first train that ran over the Pennsylvania railroad are good cards, too, but it is to the credit of the people of the United States that there was no comparison between the calm interest felt in these private exhibits and the wild bursts of enthusiasm that greeted the historic bell as it made its way down Liberty street last evening.[64]

Beyond patriotism, Pittsburghers had reason to celebrate. When Chicago was declared the site of the world's fair, many prophesized that Western Pennsylvania would reap economic benefits due to the Midwestern location. So far, expectations that Pittsburgh would host many travelers were already being met and the Columbian Exposition had not yet officially opened. There was reason for optimism that the next six months would affect the city for years to come.

———————————

As opening day drew closer, an emerging national issue threatened to jeopardize the fair's success—a financial depression. Beginning in 1890, the United States had been engaged in an economic shift. At the start of the nineteenth century, three-quarters of the population worked in agriculture, but by its last decade that number had shrunk to 40 percent. As a result, 30 percent of the country's gross national product came from mining and manufacturing, but advances in agricultural techniques and equipment also maintained, and even enhanced, farm production. By mid-1892, however, these trends suddenly reversed. Building projects began to decline, thus reducing the demand for construction materials and investment opportunities. Overproduction and shifts in weather led to decreasing agricultural prices and output, leaving farmers unable to pay the mortgages they had incurred in previous, more productive years to expand their holdings. At the same time, the railroad industry realized that it, too, had overbuilt and so opportunities for further investment and construction on new roads were also in decline. In turn, these cutbacks trickled down to the iron and steel industry as demand for rails and structural metals decreased. Meanwhile, European investors were still reeling from the 1890 economic scare and sold their holdings in American companies. Taken together, this economic climate became known as the Panic of 1893.[65] Unbeknown to fair organizers, these conditions cast a shadow over the opening festivities of the exposition, but made themselves known just a few short days later when the stock market crashed. Whether it would have a significant impact on the fair had yet to be determined.

On May 1, 1893, the World's Columbian Exposition in Chicago's Jackson Park officially opened to paying customers. The day began with pomp and circumstance, as a parade marched through the Midway Plaisance on its way to the formal ceremonies in the White City's Court of Honor. Some of Pittsburgh's contributions to the fair would take center stage in the day's activities. As it made its way to the platform in front of the Administration Building, the procession passed beneath George Ferris's great wheel, which was still nearly two months away from its own opening ceremony. Sharing the stage with dignitaries such as President Grover Cleveland, Columbian Exposition president Harlow Higinbotham, director-general George Davis, director of works Daniel Burnham, president of the fair commission Thomas Palmer, and president of the Board of Lady Managers Bertha Palmer, was a table. Covered with an American flag, the table held a velvet pillow upon which sat a golden telegraph key, drawing the eyes of the attendees to the ceremony's altar.[66]

The telegraph key, when pressed, would send a signal to turn on George Westinghouse's machinery that would provide the electricity needed to bring the fairgrounds to life. After several speeches by others on the podium, President Cleveland had the honor of pressing the golden key. Speaking in the type of grandiose language that surrounded the exposition, the president proclaimed, "As by a touch the machinery that gives light to this vast Exposition is set in motion, so at the same instant let our hopes and aspirations awaken forces which in all time to come shall influence the welfare, the dignity, and the freedom of mankind."[67] As a choir sang George Frideric Handel's "Hallelujah Chorus," President Cleveland touched the key, sending the signal to Machinery Hall that would start the largest engine in the building. That the president of the United

States was brave enough to touch the key to complete the electrical circuit was itself a great victory for alternating current. The White House had installed electricity in 1891, but the president was not permitted to touch the switches for fear of electrocution, a fear no less an authority than Thomas Edison fed to the press.[68]

If the circuit was successful, Westinghouse's lights and all the other electrified features in the fairgrounds would come to life. If they failed, Westinghouse, Chicago, and the entire country would be embarrassed on a global stage. The crowd's roar stretched out from the platform as the realization that the president had pressed the key moved through the more than one hundred thousand people in attendance. A moment later, "the great pumps threw up tall streams of water from each of the two electric fountains, in full view of the throng. The Columbian fountain began to play, and at the same instant every flag was unfurled. Immediately the entire assemblage was kindled with enthusiasm, and amid their cheers, the whistle of the steamers upon the lake, and the booming of cannon, the World's Columbian Exposition was formally opened."[69] Westinghouse had accomplished the impossible—he successfully provided alternating current electricity to the entire Columbian Exposition in less than a year's time.

In its final form, the Westinghouse plant electrifying the fair consisted of one dozen two-phase alternating generators of one thousand horsepower each, the largest AC central station in the country at that time. Each generator weighed seventy-five tons and had a capacity of 15,000 stopper bulbs. Engineers divided the generators into groups driven by engines from Westinghouse and five other companies.[70] Westinghouse's contract to light the fairgrounds called for 92,000 lights; however, in order to compensate for the short lifespan of the stopper bulbs, his men installed 250,000. Of those, 180,000 bulbs were lit each night and the remaining 70,000 were backups to replace those that burned out.[71]

Seeing an opportunity to market AC and the capabilities of his Pittsburgh-based company to the world, Westinghouse took several measures to make sure electrifying the fair became a meticulous working advertisement. By connecting his generators to a variety of engines, Westinghouse demonstrated not only that alternating current was successful but also that engines from any company could power his machines. AC's reputation as the "executioner's current" still dogged Westinghouse and Tesla, so it was important that the power plant was on full display and that no accidents occurred in such a public venue. A marble switchboard in Machinery Hall stretching one hundred feet long and standing ten feet high controlled the electrification of the exposition in full view of passersby. The entire board could be controlled by one man, demonstrating its simplicity and demystifying the AC process for millions of skeptical visitors.[72] Westinghouse and Burnham took every precaution to ensure the safe transmittal of the current, and so electricity bolted to each building through wires in underground tunnels. Transformers with a two-hundred-light capacity then brought down the high-voltage current to a safe level and secondary wires encased in vitrified tile ducts distributed this electricity throughout the buildings. With the fair now electrified, Westinghouse's team turned its attention toward building its exhibit in the Electricity Building.

While reports from the dedication ceremony in October 1892 raved about the immense buildings and the wondrous fairgrounds, articles leading up to opening day the following May were not as glowing. The *Commercial Gazette* and *Pittsburgh Post*, in particular, were blunt in their description of the state of the exposition. In terms of exhibits, the *Post* ran the sensational front-page headline "Exhibits in Chaos, Conglomerate Confusion Characterizes Chicago's Big Show," but the article itself was complimentary of the fair's management, blaming the incomplete state on the delayed work of the exhibitors themselves.[73] A *Commercial Gazette* reporter sought out local companies to see how their exhibits were coming along, noting that "the Standard Manufacturing Company of Pittsburgh came to the front yesterday with a rush and tonight have almost completed work on the stands for its exhibit."[74] In addition to the incompleteness of several exhibits, rain had soaked the fair site and its unfinished roads. Upon reviewing the fairgrounds the day before the opening ceremonies, one reporter remarked, "There will be many thousands of people from a distance who will be sorely disappointed when they stand ankle deep in Jackson Park mud tomorrow morning to formally open the fair."[75]

The *Post* echoed the sentiments of many across the country when it proclaimed, "No one need hurry to the world's fair. They will save money, temper and comfort by postponing their visits until everything is in its place, the weather has settled and accommodations and rates adjusted to the public wants. The exhibits are yet in a state of disorder." They accurately advised, though, "All these defects will be cured in a few weeks," and predicted that "June and September promise to be the favorite months for taking in the exposition."[76] By the time the fair closed on October 30, 1893, over twenty-seven million visitors experienced the exhibits of the White City and state and national buildings, as well as the carnival-like atmosphere of the Midway Plaisance. It was the audience Western Pennsylvania had hoped for when Chicago won hosting honors three years earlier and the time had come to put the Pittsburgh region on display for the world.

4

Pittsburgh on Display

THE COLUMBIAN EXPOSITION proved to be the grandest world's fair to date, not only in terms of physical size but also in scope, supplementing the usual displays with areas designated for entertainment and intellectual discourse. Like most international exhibitions, exhibits at the 1893 World's Fair were to demonstrate the finest examples of natural resources, industrial products and machinery, and art from throughout the world. In Chicago, as in Philadelphia in 1876, emphasis was placed on the products and ingenuity of the United States. While the ultimate goal was to educate fairgoers, often displays served as advertisements of companies or individuals that would later result in sales. Organizers assigned every exhibit to a group or department and then a classification within that. These assignments served as the basis for where exhibitors would have their physical displays within the buildings of the exposition and also created the pools from which they were judged for awards. Unlike previous world's fairs, in which jurors evaluated exhibits against each other, at the Columbian Exposition they judged displays against ideal standards set forth by that group's awards committee.[1] The committees then presented each awardee with a bronze medal as well as a diploma stating their reason for winning the prize.[2]

Adjoining the exhibit halls of the Court of Honor, the Midway Plaisance marked the first time a world's fair had organized a space solely for the amusement of attendees. The various forms of entertainment found on the Midway represented not only developing technologies and the commercial culture they enabled but also an element of racial bias that influenced popular culture during the Victorian period. The White City displayed the achievements primarily of white men, a demographic most of the visitors were familiar with and a part of. Organizers separated the features of the Midway, particularly the living ethnological displays and exhibitions of cultural artifacts, from the more formal portion of the fair, thus subconsciously or intentionally reinforcing presumed white superiority.[3]

Along the mile-long stretch were street scenes reproduced from Constantinople, Cairo, and Vienna, while other "villages" replicated life in Algeria, China, Germany, Dutch East India, and Ireland. Promoters also hired the respective indigenous people to populate the Lapland, South Sea Island, Dahomey, and American Indian villages. The inclusion of nonwhite people was meant to demonstrate that these races were evolutionarily inferior when compared to the exhibits on the other side of the Intramural Railroad tracks. Organizers of the exposition created this experience of cultural disparity for fairgoers in order to reinforce the racist belief system that influenced both political and popular American culture.[4] Even though fairgoers looked down on many of these people, certain aspects of their cultures captivated them. For example, performances by the belly dancer Little Egypt in the Streets of Cairo Midway exhibit scandalized and tantalized Americans throughout the summer of 1893.

Among the Midway's amusements, fairgoers could attend an Ottoman version of Buffalo Bill's Wild West Show or view panoramas of the Alps and the Kīlauea volcano. There was a rollercoaster called the Barre Sliding Railway and another railway made of ice. Examples of gold mining camps, glass factories, and worker housing could be found among models of the Eiffel Tower and Saint Peter's Cathedral. Animal exhibits were also featured, including a California ostrich farm and a trained animal show. In addition, there were opportunities for visitors to encounter technologies like the camera obscura, stereopticon, tachyscope, and an electric theatre that presented a realistic depiction of the natural changes that occur during a full day in the Alps.[5] Towering above them all was the great Ferris wheel. Anyone who paid admission to the Columbian Exposition, primarily from the growing middle class, had some disposable income to spend on amusements and many of the attractions on the Plaisance required an additional fee. However, after payment of that fee, the Midway exhibits exposed a new class of Americans to experiences that had previously been available to only a select few.

In addition to the exhibits of the White City and the raucous atmosphere of the Midway Plaisance, a third arm of the Columbian Exposition, the World's Congress Auxiliary, was located in Chicago's commercial center. Events associated with the congress were primarily located in the new Art Institute of Chicago building, to which the fair's directors contributed one-third of the construction costs with the understanding that the building, with its two large auditoriums, would be ready by the beginning of the exposition. The congress's motto was "Not things, but men," and it promoted the presentation of ideas and research instead of manufactured products and other physical items. The congress was composed of twenty departments organized into 225 divisions focused on specific topics. By the end of the fair, the congress held 1,283 sessions presenting about six thousand speeches and papers by nearly four thousand individual speakers from almost one hundred countries.[6] About seven hundred thousand people attended the sessions and while debate was not permitted during the event, journalists from throughout the world reported on the presentations in newspapers and journals, where responses were also printed.[7]

It was understood by most fairgoers that Pittsburgh was an industrial powerhouse, but when presented with all the region had to offer in the fields of science, technology, and social issues for the first time, many attendees left the fair with a greater appreciation of its citizens. The exhibits, and even more explicitly the papers presented at the various meetings of the World's Congress, offered a glimpse of the innovation and culture that lay beneath the murky smoke of the Steel City. When considered together, the representation of Western Pennsylvania at the Columbian Exposition not only provided a snapshot of the region's contemporary economy (with the notable exception of the area's largest steel companies) but also hinted at areas of future growth and influence at the dawn of the twentieth century.

––––––––––

The Pennsylvania Board of World's Fair Managers put together an exhibit for most of the departments to feature the products of the state as a whole, but many companies and individuals registered their own private exhibit space to highlight their offerings to the millions of attendees. Not only did they plan to sell products in Chicago, several of these companies also hoped to lure tourists to visit their works and perhaps make an even larger investment in their business. The Columbian Exposition exhibits from Western Pennsylvania demonstrated the wealth of natural resources and industries that could be found in the Pittsburgh region (see appendix). There were samples of various minerals, crops of all kinds, machinery, manufactured goods, and more, all meticulously sorted into their proper groups. These displays featured industrial products of Pittsburgh just as the city was on the cusp of its greatest period of population growth to provide a workforce for its developing steel mills, but they also included agrarian contributions from the surrounding rural areas.

Unsurprisingly, Pennsylvania's strongest contribution to the exhibits at the fair was found in the displays concerning mining and mineral resources. Eastern Pennsylvania promoted its coal deposits through exhibits that included an impressive obelisk of anthracite samples, but the state exhibit also included many examples of bituminous coal from the Pittsburgh region. Western Pennsylvania's oil industry, which was on the brink of losing its prominence thanks to new finds in the south-central United States, was also featured, most prominently by the Eclipse Lubricating Oil Works, of Franklin. With crude, refined, and lubricating oil samples displayed in glass bottles with a golden Pennsylvania coat of arms, the Pennsylvania state catalog described the exhibit as "the most elegant display of petroleum products ever made."[8]

The Oil Well Supply Company of Pittsburgh displayed items within its own building just south of Machinery Hall. Inside, the company displayed a variety of well-drilling tools and machinery, such as portable engines and boilers, tongs, and tubing. There were also working models of drilling rigs. In addition to oil, the display also featured several items pertaining to natural gas drilling, including meters, valves, and gas tanks. Western Pennsylvania's extensive displays in the mines and machinery departments demonstrated that the region relied on not only manpower to extract natural resources but also machines to drive efficiency and ancillary industries to provide the hardware and machinery necessary to complete their work.[9]

The Pittsburgh region also exhibited iron ore samples, including several from Carnegie Steel Company, which was, surprisingly, its only contribution to the exposition's displays. The state exhibit included many examples of clay, limestone, and sand-related products that were indicative of many of Pittsburgh's industries. As had been the case at several previous expositions, Western Pennsylvania companies displayed glass products, but in fewer numbers, indicating Pittsburgh's first industry had given way to iron and steel production. As a result, samples of fire clay used to make bricks for lining blast furnaces,

Bessemer converters, cupolas, and coke ovens were more prominently featured. Many exhibits of sandstone also appear to point to an extensive building boom.[10]

While various raw materials were on display, there was not much participation by Western Pennsylvania companies concerning metallurgy of iron and steel. Smaller local companies won awards for their exhibits, but larger companies, like Jones and Laughlin Steel Company and Carnegie Steel Company, were noticeably absent. Since both companies had successfully participated in the country's last world's fair, it is curious that they failed to show in Chicago; however, the companies and the industry had both grown immensely since 1876 and they may have used the fair as an opportunity to size up their competition without tipping their own hand and possibly giving away trade secrets.

In the case of Carnegie Steel specifically, there are several additional reasons why Andrew Carnegie would wish to dodge exhibiting at the Columbian Exposition. One of the most widely held theories is that he feared some sort of response against the company in the wake of the 1892 strike at his Homestead Steel Works. Worries about a possible anarchist or labor-related demonstration had cast a shadow over the fair from its very beginnings as the 1886 Haymarket riot was still fresh in the memories of many who served on the exposition's committees. Furthermore, Alexander Berkman, Henry Clay Frick's failed assassin in the days after the Battle of Homestead, had been inspired by the accused Haymarket conspirators, which indicated that the nation's anarchists were capable of inciting violent acts against capitalists. While these are valid reasons for Carnegie to not endorse an exhibit at the fair, they lose some of their strength when it is considered that Frick continued to pursue a large display for the Frick Coke Company even after the strike ended. Of the two tycoons, Frick was arguably more visible during the Homestead struggle since he oversaw the mill at the time and was responsible for hiring the Pinkerton detectives to secure the works. Furthermore, while Carnegie suffered some damage to his reputation, Frick was physically harmed during the conflict.

Instead, then, it is likely Carnegie had personal motives for distancing himself from the fair. It was clear from the outset that he felt the exposition, no matter its location, would be a prime source of contracts for his burgeoning steel mills. By aligning himself with the New York bid to host the 1893 World's Fair, Carnegie positioned his companies to be first in line to supply the structural steel for the buildings in the event's most likely destination. When New York lost the bid, Carnegie quickly commanded his companies to buy stock in the Chicago fair. In May 1890 he instructed Frick to buy $20,000 in fair stock as an investment, believing it would help persuade the fair's commissioners to award them steel contracts later.[11] When the company failed to secure any of the major building contracts, Carnegie recoiled from the fair altogether, declining to serve on the Pennsylvania Board of World's Fair Managers and influencing the withdrawal of his company from the exposition's tower project. His frustrations emerged in a December 1891 letter to Frick while lamenting the performance of their chief engineer in Chicago, C. L. Strobel. "It is provoking to think that being a Chicago engineer, he has allowed the Mechanics' Art Building contract to go to Philadelphia. Our contribution to the Fair would have given us a preference and a chance to take the work at the others bid, if our interests had been in the hands of a business man."[12] Carnegie was bitter that his scheme had failed and so he sought to deflect responsibility. Furthermore, his personal feelings toward the exposition factored into his actions concerning the fair until after its conclusion and renowned success.

Perhaps unaware of Carnegie's animosity toward the Columbian Exposition, Frick had initially intended to erect an exhibit for Carnegie Steel, assigning the responsibility to Strobel in December 1891. On August 12, 1892, Frick, still recovering from Berkman's assassination attempt, signed off on the design of the display, which was created by a hired decorative artist, and submitted the proposal to Carnegie for approval. Carnegie dismissed the plan in September 1892 as being "too Frenchy," and while the display was never built, his criticisms provide a glimpse of what it may have included. The proposal included chains hung from the ceiling and twisted steel columns for decoration. Also included in the plan was an arch made of samples of Carnegie Steel's various products. Carnegie's main concern was that the proposal was too pretentious and did not emphasize the strength and solidity of their products. Still reeling from the onslaught of negative publicity from the Homestead strike, Carnegie was gruff in his reply that "rather than have such a spread-eagle thing, I should vote to have no exhibit at all."[13]

Planning for the exhibit continued until January 28 when Frick informed his sales agent in Chicago that there would be no grand Carnegie Steel display.[14] When canceling the plans, Frick explained that he felt all along that an exhibit would not be worth the money, but that he wanted Carnegie's consent before abandoning the booth; however, his animosity toward Carnegie only grew as the "retired" steel baron continued to quash his plans for the company. Moreover, Carnegie's dismissal of the proposed Frick-approved artist-designed exhibit likely struck a critical chord with Frick, who considered himself a connoisseur of art in addition to a titan of industry. The cracks in their relationship were beginning to show and their business partnership would not last the close of the decade.

Despite his stated concurrence with Carnegie's decision that an exhibit at the fair would be a waste of resources, Frick did value the exposition enough to invest considerable time and money into a display for the H. C. Frick Coke Company. On February 1, 1892, Frick Coke general manager Thomas Lynch wrote to Frick suggesting that their exhibit include samples of coal and coke, as well as the "whole Standard plant in miniature."[15] Frick readily agreed, stating, "I am anxious that the exhibit should be most attractive and am willing that you should expend all the money necessary to make it so. . . . [T]he largest Coke company in the world should avail themselves of the opportunity to make the most artistic and instructive display."[16] The working model of the Standard mine, including the shaft, engine, and boiler houses, larry track, a section of coke ovens, and a few blocks of worker housing cost over $3,000 (over $92,000 in 2022) to build. Another working model, this time of the steel head frame, tipple, and engine house of the Leisenring No. 2 mine, cost an additional $2,400.[17] In November, fair organizers offered Frick space outside of the Mines Building on which he could construct a standalone pavilion to feature his company, but with the opening of the fair only months away, he declined the opportunity and stuck to his original plans.

The Frick Coke models were an overwhelming success, winning an exposition award. The *Black Diamond* coal trade journal declared, "One of the grandest, most complete in every detail, hence very interesting and instructive, exhibits to be found at the Exposition, an exhibit that attracts great attention, is that of the H.C. Frick Coke Co., installed in the East gallery of the Mining Building, a few steps south of the center stairway. It is a magnificent display, showing *en miniature*, in actual operation, the process of manufacturing, as also the mechanical handling of coke in every stage."[18] The *Connellsville Courier* proclaimed, "The Frick exhibit was one of the main features of the gallery, dividing the honors with the Standard Oil Company's exhibit."[19]

Behind the Standard model was the model of Leisenring No. 2, which used an electric motor to operate its machinery. Five model cars demonstrated all their parts and were filled with coke. There was also a pyramid constructed of coke and samples of many Frick Coke products in glass bins. In addition to promoting his company, Frick also touted the superiority of the coal they were mining. The *Black Diamond* reported, "The Frick Company at great expense have made surveys of the entire Connellsville region. These surveys were made

Fig. 6. The H. C. Frick Coke Company miniature of the Standard Mine at the 1893
   World's Fair was so successful that it was repurposed for the 1894 Western Pennsylvania Exposition. Western Pennsylvania Exposition Society, *Sixth Annual Exposition 1894*, University of Pittsburgh Library System.

by their own engineers and from them have been constructed one of the finest
relief maps it has ever been our pleasure to examine."[20] In addition, they produced and distributed a pamphlet, *Connellsville Coke*, which provided a history of the region's development.

   In contrast to the well-established Frick Coke Company, a relatively new
Pittsburgh company that would go on to become a global competitor also exhibited in the Mines Building. In 1889 the Pittsburgh Reduction Company (later
the Aluminum Company of America, or ALCOA) was funded by a loan from
Mellon Bank to expand on its production of aluminum. The only commercial
aluminum producer to display at the Columbian Exposition, the Pittsburgh
Reduction Company booth included "a working model of an extraction pot,"
hundreds of pounds of aluminum "in all shapes and worked in every way, a
fine set of aluminum alloys, and several cases of manufactured goods made
from their metal by various American firms."[21] Not only did the exhibit promote its products, it also demonstrated how the company used electricity in a

modernized process to create aluminum at a cheaper cost than older methods. This innovative use of new technologies led the chief of the Columbian Exposition's Department of Electricity, J. P. Barrett, to include a description of the Pittsburgh Reduction exhibit in that department's published history.

Another industry represented at the exposition was transportation, and Pittsburgh's relationship to the railroads was evident in the exhibits displayed by Western Pennsylvania firms. While over a quarter of the domestic railroad exhibitors came from Chicago-area companies, the Pittsburgh region's fifteen exhibits drastically outnumbered those from larger cities such as Philadelphia, Boston, Baltimore, and Cleveland. The Pittsburgh Locomotive Works and H. K. Porter exhibited samples of the various locomotives they built to the specific needs of companies in several industries.[22] The Pennsylvania Railroad, which had large operations in Altoona, constructed its own building at the fair in which it displayed refrigerator, stock, freight, and passenger cars in addition to its custom-built Krupp gun cars.[23] Other Western Pennsylvania companies provided samples of railcar parts, including Westinghouse air brakes, which had been a popular attraction at the 1876 Centennial Exhibition.[24] Additionally, Westinghouse won an award for an exhibit of electric street railway equipment displayed in the Electricity Building. Such street railways and trolleys would have a great influence on the development and expansion of Pittsburgh in the near future.

Western Pennsylvania was also represented at congresses related to the transportation of commercial goods. At the International Congress on Water Transportation, Thomas P. Roberts, chief engineer of Pittsburgh's Monongahela Navigation Company and the chair of the Pittsburgh Chamber of Commerce's world's fair committee, served on the congress's advisory committee representing the United States, demonstrating the national status held by him and Western Pennsylvania. In addition, G. H. Anderson and J. F. Dravo were delegates for the chamber of commerce, indicating their interest in promoting the benefits of doing business in Pittsburgh. Roberts presented a paper on a projected canal that would connect Lake Erie to the Ohio River, explaining that Pittsburgh's status as one of the country's busiest commercial hubs necessitated such a waterway.[25] Dravo supported the project, further explaining that the difficulties associated with building a lock-and-dam system on the Ohio River were negligible because the result would be year-round inland navigation on a waterway connecting the Great Lakes to the Gulf of Mexico. Needless to say, the completion of the proposed canal would have resulted in a financial boom for Western Pennsylvania.[26]

Given its status as a commercial center and transportation hub, one would expect Pittsburgh to have had abundant representation at the World's Railway Commerce Congress, but that was not the case. Representatives of Midwestern railroad companies and the federal government provided the majority of speakers and presented papers. While Western Pennsylvanian speakers did not dominate the stage, the contributions of Pittsburgh to the railroad industry could not be ignored. In a talk about advances in railroad safety, Arthur W. Soper of New York proclaimed,

> Not merely the United States but the whole world can afford to honor men like George Westinghouse, who has made his continuous automatic air brake a mechanical and commercial success, and thereby enhanced the safety and comfort of the traveling public. . . . George Westinghouse, however, could not have met such success in the introduction of his air brake had not the liberal minded, advanced and appreciative men of the Pennsylvania railroad . . . perceived the merit of this invention, realized its necessity for the future, and aided in its being universally adopted by the railroads of this country and of the world. The cooperation of these people led to the introduction of the air brake on the whole Pennsylvania system and naturally on all the lines with which the Pennsylvania system exchanged business, and has resulted in saving of life and property that cannot be estimated.[27]

So, even though Pittsburgh did not have many delegates at the congress, the contributions to railroad travel by Western Pennsylvanians were omnipresent. Furthermore, the conversation about Pittsburgh as a commercial center proved that Western Pennsylvania continued to play an integral role in the transportation of goods to and from the blossoming American West.

All of this industry in Western Pennsylvania required an extensive workforce; however, the region's workers were not directly represented at the exposition's labor congress. Even though the last few years had been marked with labor unrest, Chicagoans Henry Demarest Lloyd and Jane Addams held the congress in one of the most agitated cities in the country, counting some of the most influential labor leaders of the nineteenth century among its attendees, including Samuel Gompers of the American Federation of Labor, Terence V. Powderly of the Knights of Labor, and Eugene V. Debs of the American Railway Union. Hamlin Garland, a writer who would pen an 1894 essay on the fallout of the 1892 Homestead strike for *McClure's Magazine*, was also in attendance, gaining insight into the plight of workers. While the congress followed the same format as the others, including talks on working conditions, wages, legislation, and other topics, on August 30 sessions were canceled and attendees joined the throngs of unemployed demonstrating along the lakefront. Despite its incorporation of traditional demonstration speeches and the constant fear that labor activists would ruin the success of the world's fair, the event remained peaceful. The congress strategically closed on September 4 and many attendees joined the Labor Day parade in Chicago's Loop.[28]

The proliferation of exhibits pertaining to Western Pennsylvania's industries reinforced that Pittsburgh was a manufacturing powerhouse, complemented by ancillary fields such as transportation that shipped products throughout the country, via both water and rail. These displays evidenced that the region was dominated by the influence of wealthy capitalists exploiting both the area's minerals and its population for mass production. The lack of Pittsburgh representation at events relating to labor further demonstrates these circumstances, as the previous year's defeat of the union at Homestead rippled throughout organized labor in Western Pennsylvania. There was no doubt that these exhibits were product-oriented, pushing the workforce, and much of the region's population, to the periphery. Manufacturing played an integral role in Pittsburgh, but those seeking to truly learn about the city and its inhabitants would need to look beyond the representation of its industries.

***

While natural resources certainly played a major role in the success of Western Pennsylvania industries, they also contributed to products from the region's soil and rivers. The Pennsylvania Fish Commission had an impressive exhibit in the western annex of the Fisheries Building, led by its former president John Gay, of Greensburg. Pennsylvania was able to transport a large exhibit across the country thanks to the special railcar, the *Susquehanna*, that it used to distribute fish throughout the state and to Chicago for the fair. Completed in June 1892, the olive-green car measured sixty-four feet long and, at capacity, the *Susquehanna* could hold up to eighty-four ten-gallon fish containers.[29] Workmen then placed the cans inside water tanks running the length of the car. The background of the fish on exhibit was not listed in the Pennsylvania state catalog or the fair directory, though, and so it is impossible to know the origin of the species on display.

The farmlands near Pittsburgh were also tasked with feeding and supporting the region's growing population. While stockyards were a noticeable presence in East Liberty, there was no representation of Western Pennsylvania livestock in Chicago. In fact, there were only four livestock exhibits from

Pennsylvania at the fair, all from the eastern side of the state.[30] This was likely due to the cost and complications of transporting cattle for exhibit in a city widely known for its extensive stockyards and slaughterhouses and not because of deficiencies in Pittsburgh's companies. Instead, the strongest showing in the region's exhibits featuring products manufactured by machines and by hand were leather goods, which had industrial uses in addition to clothing its growing workforce.[31]

Western Pennsylvania did have several noteworthy displays relating to agriculture. While Pittsburgh had a reputation as an industrial and commercial center, much of the surrounding lands were used for farming, which was well represented in Chicago. Included in the state exhibit were examples of Western Pennsylvania rye, wheat, corn, and oats, as well as products from livestock like wool and dairy items. To supplement the region's contributions to the Pennsylvania display, the private exhibits in this department all came from Pittsburgh companies that used these crops to produce food and drinks that were in high demand. These products included biscuits and crackers from the United States Baking Company and, unsurprisingly to those familiar with the area's history from a century prior, whiskey from several distilleries.[32] The present and future of Pittsburgh may have been found in furnaces and mines, but elements of its past were still an active and essential part of the region's economy.

The most popular agricultural exhibit from Western Pennsylvania was that of the H. J. Heinz Company. Since the Centennial Exhibition, H. J. Heinz had regularly displayed his products at regional, national, and international fairs, winning awards at many stops along the way. At the 1889 Paris Exposition, Heinz was awarded the first medal ever given to an American pickler, establishing his company on an international scale. The Heinz exhibit in Chicago had the largest floor space of all the food and beer exhibits in the Agricultural Building and was made of polished, hand-carved oak. At each corner of the pavilion was a pagoda staffed by a woman who spoke one of four languages: English, French, Spanish, or German. A fifth woman was responsible for a registry book, encouraging legitimate visitors to sign their names and discouraging "giddy young girls and [wily] boys" from doing so.[33] At the center of the exhibit, behind the counters, was an enormous pyramid of glass jars containing Heinz products. Above the pyramid, resting on two columns, was an electrified sign with "H. J. Heinz Co." spelled out in lightbulbs. Visitors could view some of Heinz's collection of art and antiques, and sample Heinz pickles, relishes, and preserves. Despite all these features, however, the exhibit had difficulty attracting customers. While organizers gave the foreign and state exhibits

Fig. 7. The Heinz booth in the Agricultural Building featured a pyramid made of the
company's products, an electric sign, and pagodas at each corner staffed by women
who spoke English, German, Spanish, or French. H. J. Heinz Company Photographs, MSP 57, Detre Library and Archives, Senator John Heinz History Center.

precedence on the first floor of the Agricultural Building, they stationed Heinz
and the other American food manufacturers on the gallery level, with forty-four
stairs separating their exhibits from weary fairgoers.

When Heinz visited the fair with his family in June, he noticed that his
exhibit was not attracting visitors because of its location. Heinz, who had a
sixth sense for advertising, arrived at a solution to draw more customers. He
printed tags that the bearer could redeem at the Heinz exhibit in the Agricultural Building to receive a free souvenir. Boys distributed the cards throughout
the grounds and they were also available at a second, more conveniently located
Heinz exhibit in the Horticulture Building. The souvenir was "a green gutta-
percha pickle one and one quarter inches long, bearing the name Heinz and
equipped with a hook to serve as a charm on a watch chain."[34] His plan worked
almost immediately. By mid-July his exhibit manager reported that while most
other buildings saw about six thousand people per day, the Agricultural Building hosted somewhere between seven and eight thousand. Of those visitors, four

Fig. 8. The Westinghouse exhibit in the Electricity Building included booths on either
side of General Electric's Tower of Light, as well as a portrait of Christopher
Columbus made of lightbulbs. George Westinghouse Museum Collection, MSS
920, Detre Library and Archives, Senator John Heinz History Center.

to five thousand visited the Heinz booth each day to sample products on tooth-
picks and crackers and receive their free pickle charm.[35] Suddenly the exhibit
had become so popular that guards had to regulate the crowds until workmen
could reinforce the floor. Even after these precautions, the *New York Times*
reported at the conclusion of the exposition that workers discovered the floor
was sagging in the place where the Heinz display had stood.[36]

Thanks in part to the promotion, the Heinz display won several awards
for its products, including pure malt vinegar, evaporated horseradish, and
preserved sweet pickles, and gave away one million pickle charms during the
exposition. The trinkets, which Heinz had distributed at factory tours as early
as 1889, earned an international reputation at the fair. The charm scheme also
invited great animosity from the foreign exhibitors located on the first floor of
the Agricultural Building. Heinz's exhibit manager wrote to him, "The galleries are having more patronage as it is becoming known that from here goods
are being sampled. Scarcely any exhibitors doing so on the ground floor."[37] Just

as visitors had overlooked Heinz's exhibit at the beginning of the exposition, people passed by the exhibits on the first floor to climb the stairs to receive their souvenir. The foreign exhibitors complained to exposition officials that Heinz's tactics constituted unfair competitive practices, but to no avail. Their supply of products on display simply could not rival the lure of free food and a souvenir. As for the other American exhibitors in the gallery who also benefited from the crowds that Heinz's marketing acumen brought to their booths, they held a dinner in Heinz's honor and presented him with an inscribed loving cup.[38]

Western Pennsylvania had several other successful exhibits in the Horticulture Building in addition to the small Heinz booth distributing pickle charm coupons. William Hamilton, superintendent of Allegheny Parks, was responsible for the Pennsylvania state exhibit, which was given a prominent role around the artificial mountain in the dome of the building. This display featured palms and other exotic plants with contributions from Allegheny Parks and Charles Clark and Captain Jacob J. Vandergrift, both of Pittsburgh.[39] The presence of such striking greenery from the Steel City indicated that there was some group of individuals who were eager to carve out their own Eden near the smokestacks casting shadows over the region. Furthermore, contributions by officials like Hamilton hinted that civic leaders were willing to invest in the expertise necessary to beautify their city.

———————

In addition to exhibits that presented the fruits of physical labor, Western Pennsylvanians took the opportunity provided by a global stage to demonstrate that it was also a region of intellect, which manifested in various expressions including scientific achievement and social reform. What most fairgoers knew of Pittsburgh came from descriptions and lithographs found in national magazines like *Harper's Weekly*, which often focused on physical descriptions of the city, posh developing neighborhoods, and violent acts pitting rowdy workforces against their employers and law enforcement. To counter such popular impressions of the region, these exposition displays and lectures showed the world that Pittsburgh was more than America's workshop; it was a city where people lived, learned, thought, and thrived.

One of the most public examples of Pittsburgh being forward-thinking was its role in continuing developments in the field of electricity. The Phoenix Glass Company won awards for its display of electrolier globes and shades and the Standard Underground Cable Company provided samples of its static arresters; however, when it came to electrical innovation and products in Western

Pennsylvania, there was only one company of real impact—Westinghouse Electric and Manufacturing. While the entire exposition served as George Westinghouse's exhibit of alternating current and his company's ability to make it readily available to the masses, the Westinghouse company also set up a large traditional display.

The Westinghouse exhibit covered fifteen thousand square feet on the first floor of the Electricity Building and displayed a standard Westinghouse alternating current lighting apparatus, as well as advances in applied electricity. A model power plant using the Tesla polyphase system was attached to a receiving station by a thirty-foot-long high-tension transmission circuit, demonstrating how alternating current is produced, transmitted, and transformed to safe voltages across long distances. Westinghouse also demonstrated its lighting efforts in the form of a mural containing a portrait of Christopher Columbus that covered the wall above the building's south gallery. Westinghouse stopper bulbs outlined all the mural's decorative work and lettering, supplied with electricity from the fair's main power station.[40] To promote its work in electrifying the fairgrounds, Westinghouse hung a simple sign at its exhibit announcing, "All Exposition Buildings are lighted by our system. See the great plant in Machinery Hall."[41] Taken together, exhibit items pertaining to electric production, meters, transportation, and lighting demonstrated not only the breadth of the company's interests in the electric industry but also its mastery of these fields as many of the display pieces won awards.

In addition to the work of the Westinghouse Electric and Manufacturing Company, the exhibit also provided space for the work and demonstrations of Nikola Tesla. The Westinghouse exhibit, including the lighting of the exposition buildings, relied heavily on Tesla's work with alternating current and the company had previously purchased the rights to his patents. Tesla himself conducted many demonstrations at the exhibit, harkening back to the days when he would demonstrate the powers of alternating current to crowds of electrical engineers. He used AC to rapidly spin metal eggs and copper balls and then smoothly reversed their rotation at set intervals. Tesla also demonstrated his first disruptive discharge coil and doused himself in glowing electricity, an experiment he used to thrill visitors such as Samuel Clemens in his laboratory in New York City.[42] While there was much to see in the exhibits of the Electricity Department, those who were well versed in matters of electricity realized they were looking into the future when observing Tesla's exhibits and Westinghouse's fully functioning AC system based on his research.

At the fair's Electrical Engineering Congress, the display of Tesla's ideas by the Westinghouse Electric and Manufacturing Company was a popular subject. The discussion began when Charles F. Scott, of Pittsburgh, gave a talk titled "Exhibit of Tesla Polyphase System at the World's Fair." The following discussion touched on many aspects of Tesla's system as demonstrated by the Westinghouse display. While commenting on the transmission of electrical power, Westinghouse employee A. B. Stillwell used the opportunity to touch on the purpose of the polyphase motor display, explaining that "in preparing this exhibit of the Westinghouse Company we have not shown small machines. It is no exhibit of toys or models or drawings. We have simply shown what we believe to be the best development of the polyphase system." Stillwell then went on the attack against direct current, which he classified as merely a partial solution to the problem of transmitting electricity over substantial distances. When describing the Westinghouse-Tesla motors he explained, "We have here a system which performs all kinds of service over a single transmission circuit, and from a single [polyphase] generator."[43]

While Tesla allowed others to debate the merits and possibilities of his polyphase motors, he prepared to take the stage for his own presentation. Tesla's inventions and breakthroughs had affected the success of the entire Columbian Exposition by allowing Westinghouse to light the fairgrounds at a reasonable cost and displays of his work offered a glimpse into the electrical future. This, however, was the chance for Tesla to speak directly to his peers. Most of the electrical congress was held at the Art Institute building in downtown Chicago, but his presentation was held inside the more prominent Agricultural Hall. Tesla was a renowned showman, famous for his ability to set himself aglow in electric light, so his name and reputation were placed front and center in the White City. At his talk on the evening of August 25, Tesla addressed his fellow electrical scientists by introducing two machines he had built to aid in their research. He presented his mechanical and electrical oscillators, which would allow for greater precision in experiments using alternating current. While the two machines were simple in design, he had changed the face of electrical research yet again.[44]

Meanwhile, Westinghouse's primary competitor, General Electric, attempted to use its exhibit in the Electricity Building to repair its reputation after losing the bid to light the fairgrounds. Even though the formation of GE just a year before had quietly pushed Thomas Edison out of the new corporation, Charles Coffin and GE exploited their ties to Edison and his status as the father of electricity to improve their own image. They erected an eighty-foot-tall column on a round Greek pavilion topped with an eight-foot Edison

Fig. 9. Tesla's display contained samples of equipment pertaining to his work, including his famous Egg of Columbus, which demonstrated the rotating magnetic field of alternating current. On the wall behind the exhibit was a sign that read "All Exposition Buildings are Lighted by Our System See the Great Plant in Machinery Hall." Westinghouse Electric Corporation Photographs, MSP 424, Detre Library and Archives, Senator John Heinz History Center.

lightbulb weighing half a ton as a monument to the inventor and General Electric. The Tower of Light, as it was called, was located at a major nexus of the building and directly adjacent to the Westinghouse exhibits. GE also provided a large searchlight that lit up the night sky from atop the White City's colonnade. Perhaps finally coming to terms with the superiority of alternating current, GE also displayed its own AC system. Overall, the GE exhibit was more recognizable and memorable for most visitors, but in terms of electrical engineering it was no match for Westinghouse's impressive demonstration of lighting the entire exposition.

On the Midway Plaisance, George Washington Gale Ferris Jr.'s wheel provided another feat of Pittsburgh-based engineering. By the time people began to descend on the fairgrounds in May much of the wheel's steel skeleton was in place, and by the first week of June workers disassembled the timber scaffold surrounding the spectacle. Once cleared of obstructions, the real test of the wheel—the first turn—could commence. On the evening of June 9 steam poured into the engines and the Ferris wheel began to slowly rotate. The first turn was under way. When the wheel was about one-eighth of the way around, Westinghouse air brakes activated the steel bands to stop it and a loud screech filled the Midway, attracting the gaze of passersby during the otherwise unceremonious trial run. After the initial state of panic, William Gronau, the engineer responsible for calculating the stresses on the wheel's structure, realized that the sound was just rust scraping off the bands as everything came to a halt. The first brake test was successful, and the wheel began turning once again. This time another noise alarmed the gathering crowd. It was the sound of loose bolts, nuts, and tools raining down through the web of the wheel's steel rods as they fell from where workers had left them throughout the assembly process.[45] Once the forgotten items had all settled, however, the wheel turned almost silently. After twenty minutes, the first revolution of the Ferris wheel was complete. Luther V. Rice, who was overseeing the wheel's construction, sent a telegram to Ferris in Pittsburgh congratulating him on the successful test. Foreshadowing the wheel's eventual renown, Rice noted that the "Midway is wildly enthusiastic."[46]

Ferris sent his response to Chicago the next morning. After quickly congratulating Rice, he got right down to business. He requested that Rice "rush the putting on of cars working day and night. If you can't put the cars on at night babbitt the car bearings at night so as to keep ahead."[47] Every day the wheel was not open for business cost Ferris and the Columbian Exposition money, so it was imperative that the workers mount the cars onto the wheel as quickly as possible. As described in the *Official Guide to the Midway Plaisance*, the wheel supported thirty-six pendulum cars, framed of iron and clad in wood. The cars measured twenty-seven feet long by thirteen feet wide by nine feet high, with five plate glass windows on each side. Each car could hold forty people and one conductor to operate the doors.[48] The wheel was designed so that the bottom six cars could empty and refill with passengers from platforms on either side. This meant the ride would stop six times during the course of a complete revolution to receive new riders.

By June 11, six cars were hung on the Ferris wheel and the next major test was quickly implemented. Since an observation wheel of this size had never been built, there was no way to know how a ride on the great wheel would affect its passengers. Someone would need to volunteer to make the inaugural revolution. Gronau, Ferris's wife Margaret, and a few others agreed to take the first trip as a sign of good faith to the public that the new attraction was safe. They boarded a car and their journey 250 feet into the air commenced. Only a few moments later the wheel stopped. Visitors on the Midway, having wit-nessed a few people enter a car, scrambled to board the next car on the wheel and the engineer stopped the ride to let them on and prevent injury. Soon visi-tors filled the cars and the twenty-minute trip around the wheel was completed. Fairgoers continued to ride the wheel until dusk, when Rice threatened to leave the cars suspended in the air all night if they would not disembark.[49]

This test, too, proved successful. Some riders expected to experience the sensation of falling to some degree during their car's descent, but to their dis-appointment this feeling never materialized. "On the contrary," noted one guidebook, "if one were to go around with closed eyes there would be no knowl-edge whatever that the wheel was in motion. The sensation is never disagree-able, but always delightful. There is not the slightest suggestion of dizziness or sea sickness, and even the most timid lose all fear after the wheel has moved around but a few feet."[50] For riders, though, a fear of and exposure to this new experience revealed their very base emotions, ones they witnessed and admon-ished in the "less evolved" cultures they observed along the Midway. By tak-ing a trip around the wheel, visitors became a part of the attractions on the Plaisance.

The following day Rice sent a message to Ferris in Pittsburgh to inform him of the success. He also referenced the eagerness of the fairgoers: "People are wild to ride on [the] wheel and extra forces of guards [are] required to keep them out."[51] By June 15, thirty cars were hung and journalists were offered a ride on the great wheel at six o'clock that evening in anticipation of the opening cer-emony on June 21. At the ceremony, George and Margaret Ferris and Chicago mayor Carter Harrison rode the wheel's first official revolution, which began with Ferris blowing a gold whistle, harkening back to the exposition's opening ceremony and President Cleveland pushing the golden telegraph key to start the electric current.[52] The first paying customers then lined up for their turn on the Ferris wheel, which had a capacity of 1,400 riders, until it was finally shut down at eleven o'clock that night.

At 250 feet in the air, the wheel offered unparalleled views of the fair-grounds, and as one's car descended, it presented the entire White City to the rider. As one guidebook explained, "If the day view is beautiful, at night it is like a vision of fairyland. The myriad lights in the Fair grounds and city seem like so many stars enlarged and dropped from the skies."[53] The Ferris wheel did have some competition on the Midway when it came to aerial views of the

Fig. 10. As fairgoers passed beneath the Ferris wheel, men worked through mid-July
to attach the cars of the giant attraction so it could be opened to the public and
begin making money for both the Columbian Exposition and George Washington
Gale Ferris Jr. "World's Fair, the great ferris wheel, 280 feet high, Chicago, Ill.,"
2006680016, Prints and Photographs Division, Library of Congress.

fairgrounds. There was also a captive balloon, but limitations in the number of
riders and the $2.50 rate kept many visitors away. In addition, the balloon was
simply not as safe as the wheel. On July 9 a violent storm shredded the balloon
to pieces, whereas the great wheel remained unscathed. Rice had explained
before the storm that the two large towers could withstand gusts of one hundred miles per hour and "that if struck by lightning it would absorb and dissi-
pate the thunderbolt so that it would not be felt."[54] The July storm had proved
that the Ferris wheel, despite appearing flimsy, was indeed very sturdy, scoring
another victory for Pittsburgh's engineering prowess.

By the end of the Columbian Exposition, nearly 1.5 million tickets for a twenty-minute ride on the Ferris wheel had been sold. The cost for a ride, fifty cents, equaled that of admission to the Columbian Exposition itself.[55] The onset of financial panic, incomplete exhibits, and poor press coverage throughout the East Coast were frequently cited as factors for low attendance in the early weeks of the fair; however, many pointed to the wheel as the reason for improved exposition attendance once it opened to visitors.[56] The novelty of the great wheel attracted fairgoers throughout the duration of the fair, to both the delight and the chagrin of Daniel Burnham and the World's Columbian Exposition Corporation. As author Erik Larson noted, "Had the Exposition Company stood by its original June 1892 concession rather than waiting until nearly six months later, the wheel would have been ready for the fair's May 1 opening. Not only did the exposition lose its 50 percent share of the wheel's revenue for those fifty-one days—it lost the boost in overall admission that the wheel likely would have generated and that Burnham so desperately wanted."[57] While the attraction had been a great financial and engineering risk, George Washington Gale Ferris Jr. had achieved the desired effect. He had out-Eiffeled Eiffel and, furthermore, he had used his experiences and connections in Western Pennsylvania to make his dream a reality.

The Liberal Arts Building hosted a variety of exhibits relating to nonindustrial innovations and advancements in science, public works, education, and civic organizations, among other things. While these displays played an integral role in sharing the discoveries and work being done in Western Pennsylvania, many of these areas were also supplemented by participation in congresses at the world's fair. For example, the Ferris wheel and Westinghouse's exhibits each demonstrated engineering achievements; however, the Engineering Department of the World's Congress Auxiliary counted three Pittsburghers among its members: former president of the American Society of Engineers Maximillian J. Becker; metallurgist and Pittsburgh Reduction Company founder Alfred E. Hunt; and American Society of Civil Engineers president William P. Shinn. Not only were Western Pennsylvanians sharing their successes, they were also being recognized as some of the nation's engineering leaders.

In addition to the previously discussed Electrical Engineering Congress, another conference held under the auspices of the engineering congress pertained to aerial navigation. Again, a scientist who spent time in Western Pennsylvania was the most discussed subject at the event. This time it was Samuel Pierpont Langley, secretary of the Smithsonian Institution and former director of the Western University of Pennsylvania's Allegheny Observatory. Langley first presented some of the research he conducted at Allegheny Observatory in a paper titled "The Internal Work of the Wind." In addition to this paper, speakers throughout the entire conference referenced Langley's research pertaining to flight. The calculations of Langley and others made a significant impact on the legitimacy of aerial navigation and the idea of flight by a heavier-than-air craft. As recounted by Columbian Exposition historian Hubert Howe Bancroft, "It was shown that aerial navigation could now be classed among the science . . . [and] that a speed of 60 to 80 miles would eventually be attained with flying machines propelled, like birds, by self-developed energy."[58]

In addition to his research on flight, Langley was also a member of the advisory council for the Congress on Astronomy, part of the Department on Science and Philosophy. John Brashear, an Allegheny Observatory faculty member, displayed some of his telescopes, and observatory director James E. Keeler presented observations he had previously made at Lick Observatory, outside of San Jose, in a paper at the congress titled "The Wave-Lengths of the Two Brightest Lines in the Spectrum of the Nebulae," which aimed to standardize measurements of the chief and second spectral lines when observing nebulae.[59] Meanwhile, Langley's brother John, who had taught in the civil and mechanical engineering department of the Western University of Pennsylvania in the 1870s, read a paper during the Congress of Chemists that addressed the "works and aims of the committee on international standards as to the composition of steel."[60] The many contributions of Pittsburghers to engineering and scientific congresses demonstrated that Western Pennsylvania was a hotbed of scientific experimentation and achievement. The willingness to seek out efficiency was at the core of the region's economic success, and developments in production methods and design were rooted in discoveries like the ones presented at the world's fair; however, the presence of research in astronomy and other noncommercial fields also showed that Western Pennsylvania supported a culture that promoted doing science for science's sake.

Another example of congress participation supplementing physical exhibits was the field of medicine. Meadville's Carroll Aluminum Manufacturing Company showcased its aluminum dental instruments in the Manufactures and Liberal Arts Building; however, various medical conferences better demonstrated the growing acumen of Pittsburgh's doctors, which would later blossom as an economic driver after the deindustrialization of the region in the late twentieth century. At the dental congress, W. H. Fundenburgh of Pittsburgh served on the registration committee and J. A. Libbey was secretary of the Pennsylvania state conference committee. During the congress, Pittsburgh dentist J. G. Templeton commented on the effective use of a cocaine solution as a local anesthetic during oral surgery.[61]

At the World's Congress of Homoeopathic Physicians and Surgeons, Dr. James H. McClelland of Pittsburgh was a central figure. A renowned physician and president of the Pennsylvania State Board of Health, McClelland had been on staff at Pittsburgh's Homeopathic Hospital since it opened its doors in 1868 and was an integral part of its administration. As president of the American Institute of Homoeopathy, the oldest national medical association in the United States, McClelland served on the advisory council with Pittsburgh doctor John C. Burgher and was an honorary vice-president of the congress. During his address at the opening of the conference, McClelland spoke to the importance of the work that was about to begin. "This Congress, let me suggest, stands for more than a report upon the medical sciences in general, great and important as they are. It stands for a reformation in the science of therapeutics more far reaching and important than any of ancient or modern times."[62] Later, drawing on his experience at the Homeopathic Hospital, McClelland offered commentary on papers about advances in homeopathic surgery and the role of homeopathic physicians in matters of public health.

Millie Chapman, of Pittsburgh, served on the committee appointed by the American Institute of Homoeopathy and the women's committee. She also delivered a paper titled "Pre-natal Medication," which promoted the idea that physically and mentally healthy parents make healthy children and advocated for the treatment and medication of maladies beginning at the birth of the prospective parents to ensure the best health for their future children. Overall, her paper was well received by those in attendance. Another Allegheny doctor, L. H. Willard, shared his experience treating victims of steel mill accidents and advocated for quick action to complete necessary surgical procedures to avoid complications and possible shock.[63] The presence of these physicians and their participation in the congress suggests that a robust Pittsburgh medical community was emerging and contributing to the greater understanding of medicine throughout the country.

In other cases, exhibits were the only example of Pittsburgh achievements in a particular field. The most abundant contributions from Western Pennsylvania to the Manufactures and Liberal Arts Building were the exhibits regarding education in the region. Pittsburgh and Allegheny public schools displayed work from students of every year.[64] The Western University of Pennsylvania, the oldest and largest university in the Pittsburgh area, was one of the few

Fig. 11. The Western University of Pennsylvania exhibit included samples of student and faculty work, as well as photographs of the university's buildings, alumni, and professors. *Catalogue of the Exhibits of the State of Pennsylvania and of Pennsylvanians at the World's Columbian Exposition.*

Pennsylvania higher education institutions to exhibit at the exposition. On September 29, 1892, its board of trustees appointed Brashear, William J. Sawyer, and Western Pennsylvania Medical College dean James B. Murdoch to a committee to oversee the development of the school's exhibit. On the last day of 1892, fair organizers granted the university two hundred square feet of exhibit space located at the southwest corner of the gallery level of the Manufactures and Liberal Arts Building, overlooking the exhibits below.[65] Also in December, the university's chancellor, William J. Holland, began contacting alumni and former faculty, chancellors, and trustees to request their photographs for inclusion in the exhibit.

On March 22, 1893, the Board of World's Fair Managers of Pennsylvania notified Holland that the university and local public schools should ship their exhibits to Chicago in the same car as quickly as possible. Displays from across the country were pouring into Jackson Park and the board warned Holland that the increased traffic could delay the unpacking of the crates. Holland and C. B. Connelley, the superintendent of Western University of Pennsylvania's engineering shops, traveled to Chicago to assemble the exhibit. In a letter to his parents on May 5, Holland predicted that he and Connelley would complete the university's exhibit on May 9 and that it would be one of the first college exhibits installed at the fair.[66] In addition to the photos submitted by alumni and faculty, the exhibit also included photographs of university buildings and laboratories, as well as examples of student work in engineering, chemistry, carpentry, and machine work. Faculty contributions included samples of Langley's research at the Allegheny Observatory, specimens from the Smith Cabinet of minerals and animals, and mathematical models by mechanical engineering professor Reid T. Stewart.[67]

As part of the Catholic school exhibit, the Pittsburgh diocese displayed student work from three colleges, Pittsburgh Catholic College of the Holy Ghost (now Duquesne University), Saint Vincent College and Saint Fidelis College; seven academies; and parish schools from twenty-four municipalities, including Pittsburgh and Allegheny.[68] The presence of so many local Catholic displays at the 1893 World's Fair, and the election of Pittsburgh's first Catholic mayor that same year, indicated that Catholics were becoming a force in the traditionally Protestant-dominated region; however, Western Pennsylvania's religious variety was better represented at the most anticipated and discussed portion of the World's Congress Auxiliary—the World's Religious Congresses, or Parliament of Religions.

Today considered the first organized interfaith gathering in the world, attendees of the Religious Congresses represented religions from all over the world in conferences held at the Art Institute from August 27 to October 15. Given the diversity of people in Western Pennsylvania in the 1890s, it is no surprise that Pittsburgh-area religious leaders were active participants in various meetings in Chicago; however, their role in the congresses was not as prominent as those from other industrial cities like Cleveland and Cincinnati. Despite the variety of religions present in Pittsburgh, many denominations, particularly those practiced by the city's immigrants, did not hold meetings at the fair and the conversation for those denominations that did meet was carried by leaders from more populous cities like New York, Chicago, and Philadelphia.

Representing the region's Protestant faiths, Reverend Ambrose M. Schmidt of Pittsburgh served as chairman of the Congress of the Reformed Church and Reverend William Rupp of the Pittsburgh Synod presented the conference's greeting and gave its first address, titled "The Reformed Church and Her Creed."[69] Meadville's Reverend David H. Wheeler was part of the panel "Methodism in Relation to Social Problems" at the Methodist Episcopal Church Congress and Bishop Benjamin Tucker Tanner, originally from Pittsburgh, presented a paper titled "What Are the Demands of the Hour, Both in our Ministry and in Our Church?" at the African Methodist Episcopal Congress.[70]

Meanwhile, at the Columbian Catholic Congress, Reverend John T. Murphy, of the College of the Holy Ghost, presented a report on Catholic high schools.[71]

Western Pennsylvania Jewish leaders were also active in Chicago. At the Jewish Denominational Congress, Rabbi David L. Mayer gave the invocation for the August 27 evening session, titled "The Fundamental Doctrine of Judaism."[72] At the separate Jewish Women's Congress, Pauline Hanauer Rosenberg, of Allegheny, gave an address titled "Influence of the Discovery of America on the Jews." In her speech, Rosenberg pointed to the European colonization of America, and the establishment of the United States in particular, as a turning point for Jewish people who could finally flee persecution and seek acceptance in the New World. It is there, she remarked, that Jewish Americans were able to flourish in their own cultural institutions as well as in the greater American society. On September 6 Rosenberg served as the honorary presiding officer of the morning session, which, in addition to her speech, proved her to be a national leader within the American Jewish community.[73]

In matters of social reform, Western Pennsylvania was better represented in its congress participation than in displays. Western Penitentiary showed a model cell house, cellblocks, and samples of prison work, but at the International Congress of Charities and Corrections Warden Edward S. Wright spoke about Western Penitentiary's use of the Bertillon system of registering prisoners, a method that had been implemented in the United States just a few years prior. This involved "measuring the anatomy at every conceivable place, taking all scars and marks on the body, photographing the prisoner and noting all peculiarities with which he is affected. Warden Wright's address brought forth great applause, and it was commented upon by various wardens of the 66 penitentiaries of which this country boasts." Other attendees of the conference included Charles G. Donnell of the Allegheny County Poorhouse, in Pittsburgh; Gusky's Orphan's Home Ladies Auxiliary president Mrs. S. L. Fleishman; and the secretary of the National Prison Association, Reverend John L. Milligan, of Allegheny.[74] The Pittsburgh region's representation at the congress was comparable to larger cities like Philadelphia, and its inclusion of reports and speakers in the program indicate that Western Pennsylvania was at the forefront of charitable work and prisoner management.

Beginning on June 5, the Congress on Temperance brought together representatives from organizations from all over the country, including several with ties to Western Pennsylvania. Their participation provides a cross-section of the temperance movement in the Pittsburgh region and insight into the involvement of people from various backgrounds and religions. Waynesburg College president Alfred Brasher Miller attended with the Pennsylvania Synod of the Cumberland Presbyterian Church, and Ellen M. Watson and Mrs. B. C. Christy of Pittsburgh visited with the Pennsylvania Woman's Christian Temperance Alliance. Other delegates included T. H. Boyle, of Uniontown, with the Supreme Council of the Royal Templars of Temperance; W. H. Brown, of New Brighton, with the General Conference of the African Methodist Episcopal Church; and Presbyterian minister W. B. Carr, of Latrobe.[75]

Several Pittsburghers also delivered speeches at the Congress on Temperance, demonstrating the region's leadership in the temperance movement. Speakers included chancellor of the Catholic Diocese of Pittsburgh Reverend Regis Canevin and Francis Murphy, who recruited tens of thousands of Western Pennsylvanians to pledge temperance while he was headquartered in the First Methodist Protestant Church and later millions nationally.[76] Reverend Wilbur F. Crafts, a Pittsburgh Presbyterian minister who would go on to serve as a lobbyist for the constitutional amendment to enact Prohibition, submitted a paper titled "Sunday Closing of Saloons"; however, when organizers decided to open the Columbian Exposition on Sundays he refused to attend in protest. Instead, the congress referenced his paper in title only and published it in full in its proceedings. Crafts's paper offered insight into how temperance organizations might promote their cause in mill towns across Western Pennsylvania. Appealing to the growing interest in labor concerns, Crafts argued that workers should support Sunday closings to provide a day of rest to overworked barkeeps and to ensure a ready workforce on Monday. In industries where pay was reliant on output, unimpaired workers generated more product and thus made more money for all involved. He also suggested that places that enforced Sunday closures saw a drop in crime. Lastly, speaking directly to his primary audience, Crafts stated that Prohibitionists should support Sunday closures because eliminating sales on that one day curtailed one-fourth of drinking, a satisfactory start to their cause. What he failed to explicitly address was the fact that Sunday prohibition, much like sabbatarianism, would further restrict the ability of many workers to enjoy their one day of rest as they pleased.[77]

At the Congress of Women speakers gave addresses on various aspects of womanhood and the difficulties women faced, with the hope that by presenting conditions as they existed their presentations could provide a basis for future improvements.[78] Feminist pioneers Julia Ward Howe, Susan B. Anthony, and Elizabeth Cady Stanton were highlights at the congress and women from all over the country participated as speakers. The inclusion of several Western Pennsylvanians at the congress was on par with similar industrial cities like

Cleveland and Cincinnati, and their speeches demonstrated the varying views of feminism found in the Pittsburgh region.

One such woman, Cara Reese, was a journalist for the *Pittsburgh Commercial Gazette*. From 1884, she wrote "Cara's Column," which consisted of society articles for women readers and later provided much of the paper's coverage on the progress of the Allegheny County Women's Auxiliary for the Columbian Exposition. In her speech, titled "We, the Women," Reese addressed the development of two types of women—homemakers and wage earners—and the animosity they had for each other. Reese explained that years of suffering had driven women to the pursuit of money, which would bring the wage-earning woman closer to equality with men. She also warned that equality would come at the cost of the loss of femininity, stating, "Knowledge at first startling soon becomes commonplace, womanly reserve wears away, feminine graces vanish, the cold practical atmosphere in time dulls the sensitive nature, and the woman worker becomes a money-making, fame-seeking machine; an ingrate, often forgetful of friends and favors; a cold, selfish, calculating automatum, and above all chronic discontent."[79] To combat the current disconnect of the homemaker and wage earner, Reese encouraged them to care for and sympathize with each other so they could succeed and be happy together in the future.

While Reese argued that women had had change thrust upon them, forcing them to enter the workforce, another Western Pennsylvania reporter, Mary Temple Bayard, of the *Pittsburg Dispatch* and *Philadelphia Times*, suggested that women were more proactive in their pursuit of equality. In her speech "Women in Journalism," Bayard stated bluntly that male and female journalists were equals, each achieving success based on the quality of their work. This equality, she argued, was a shining example of what women were fighting for, pointing out that "journalism is at least the profession where the sexes receive the same remuneration for the same work equally well done. Surely the whole duty to our sex has been discharged when this is true."[80] Bayard argued that journalism required women to shed their conventionality in order to acquire this workplace equality, but "those who have weathered the discouragements readily declare the game to be well worth the candle."[81] In her eyes, women could not expect change without a willingness to stray from the established norms, but the gains made through adaptation were worth the effort.

The Congress of Women was a great success, and, throughout the entirety of the World's Congress Auxiliary, women constituted the majority of participants. In Board of Lady Managers president Bertha Palmer's closing address, she reflected on the impact the work of the congress and women's auxiliary had on visitors, stating, "It was the proudest moment of my life when I was told last Saturday, with a heartfelt hand-shake, and with accents of deepest sincerity, by one of our visitors, that seeing me had given her more pleasure than anything at the fair, except the Ferris wheel."[82] While Palmer's work was much appreciated, nothing could escape the shadow of the Pittsburgher Ferris's great attraction.

Although Western Pennsylvanians represented the region at many of the congresses, there were also some notable omissions. At the Congress of Bankers and Financiers, much conversation was provided by New Yorkers about the ongoing financial panic and the merits of a gold, silver, or hybrid monetary standard. Pittsburgh, however, was surprisingly absent from the list of speakers despite the fact that the Mellon family was long entrenched in venture capitalism and left their fingerprints all over the successful companies of Western Pennsylvania. S. Davis Page, of Philadelphia, presented a report on the history of banking and resources in Pennsylvania at the request of Governor Robert Pattison, but he gave only a passing mention to Pittsburgh's banks.[83]

The surprising absence of one particular Pittsburgher in Chicago is also of interest. During the week of August 14, the Universal Peace Congress convened as part of the World's Congress Auxiliary; however, despite his keen interest in this cause, one that would consume much of his later life, Andrew Carnegie was thousands of miles away during these meetings. This was not for a lack of invitation. On February 27, 1892, Charles H. Howard had contacted Carnegie with a request that he serve on the advisory council of the Peace and Arbitration Congress. In this capacity, he would never need to convene with other members, but they could seek Carnegie's guidance regarding submitted proposals. Ironically, Howard's letter seems to indicate that the committee was more interested in using Carnegie's name and reputation to promote its work, the very same arrangement Carnegie had condemned just months prior in connection to the Columbian Tower.[84] In March 1893, Carnegie received confirmation of his appointment to the council from Howard and World's Congress Auxiliary president Charles C. Bonney. Letters from W. T. Stead, editor of the *Review of Reviews*, indicate that he expected Carnegie's participation at the congress to promote the idea of reuniting Britain, Canada, and the United States in a Federation of the Race.[85] In July 1893, Benjamin Trueblood, secretary of the Peace and Arbitration Congress, sent an invitation for Carnegie to attend and present a paper at the meeting, but Carnegie declined to travel to Chicago for the conference.[86] Even in his absence, though, Carnegie's interest was present throughout the event. He sent greetings to the congress from Europe and he was referenced in several papers regarding international peace efforts.[87]

The contributions of Western Pennsylvanians to exhibits and congresses relating to technical skill served as an overt example of the type of experimentation and creation that was happening in Pittsburgh, demonstrating that the region not only manufactured massive amounts of product but could also use them effectively. This glimpse into the achievements of individual scientists and engineers placed a greater emphasis on the people behind the inventions, unlike the manufacturing exhibits, which focused on processes and outputs. Additionally, talks relating to social issues like temperance reflect the sentiments and priorities of various groups of Pittsburghers. This shift in perspective from capitalists treating the region as a machine to progressives considering it as a community, or network of communities, would be instrumental in the coming decades as social reform efforts and cultural development became more prevalent.

———————

Perhaps even more surprising than the innovations demonstrated in both exhibits and congresses, Western Pennsylvanians also contributed examples of art that spoke to a developing culture that many visitors attributed to older, grander metropolises like Philadelphia and New York City and not an industrial center like Pittsburgh. When the Pennsylvania Board of World's Fair Managers' Committee on Fine Arts established advisory committees for the various classes of art solicited by the Chicago fair, Pittsburgh artists Joseph Ryan Woodwell and John Wesley Beatty served on the painting committee, and Alfred S. Wall and George Hetzel were alternates. As expected, Philadelphia, which was home to the Pennsylvania Academy of the Fine Arts, dominated the state's artistic contributions to the exposition; however, several active Western Pennsylvanian artists provided some notable offerings. For example, Pittsburgh's Thomas Shields Clarke won an award for his oil paintings *A Fool's Fool*, *The Night Market in Morocco*, *Portrait of Madame d' E*, *A Gondola Girl*, and a drawing for a stained-glass window titled *Morning, Noon and Night*.

Woodwell displayed a series of landscape paintings depicting Magnolia, Massachusetts. His daughter, Johanna, contributed an oil painting and a watercolor portrait. Hetzel exhibited two paintings, *Wood Scene* and *Study from Nature*, while Alfred Bryan Wall, the son of alternate member Alfred S. Wall, submitted his painting *Across the Meadows*. Pittsburgh artists David B.

Walkley and Martha Goldman and Allegheny's Ida Joy Didler also displayed paintings. Philadelphia architect Charles Z. Klauder showed five drawings at the fair. While he had no connection to Western Pennsylvania at the time, over thirty years later he would design the University of Pittsburgh's Cathedral of Learning, Heinz Memorial Chapel, and Stephen Foster Memorial.[88]

In addition to the official exposition departments, the state board also arranged for contributions from artists and craftspeople from throughout the state to fill the Pennsylvania building; however, the eastern side of Pennsylvania dominated the displays. The few items with ties to the Pittsburgh area were some local newspapers and two books available to visitors in the Women's Parlor: Nellie Bly's *Around the World in 72 Days* and Mary O'Hara Darlington's *Fort Pitt*. The omission of contributions from Western Pennsylvania inside the replica of Philadelphia's Independence Hall was just another instance in a greater rivalry between the two halves of the state that presented itself during the exposition. However, in an effort to counter the perception that Philadelphia was the only noteworthy city in the state, the Pittsburgh Chamber of Commerce distributed its pamphlet *Guide to All Points of Interest in and about Pittsburgh* to fairgoers. The publication sought to attract potential tourists to the Steel City by promoting its "picturesque views" and various recommended rail and river excursions throughout the city and region.[89] Whereas local companies hoped to attract business to Western Pennsylvania through their exposition displays and factory visits by fair travelers, the chamber's guide took a different approach, instead promoting the beauty and sites of the region to appeal to leisure tourists.

The last group of displays containing contributions from Western Pennsylvania was the Woman's Building. While men or male-dominated companies contributed the majority of exhibits throughout the rest of the exposition, women from all over the country designed and completed all these exhibits, including the building containing them, but only some of these displays were included and judged as part of the established exposition departments. Art was a major component of the Woman's Building and several works had ties to Western Pennsylvania, highlighting a popular leisure activity of the region's middle- and upper-class women. Bessie Young, of the Pittsburgh School of Design, contributed a stained-glass piece titled *Three Leaded Windows with Pennsylvania Coat of Arms*. Eurilda Q. Loomis France, a painter born in Pittsburgh, displayed her oil painting *Preoccupation*. Another painter, Mary Cassatt, who was born in Allegheny, displayed a pastel work titled *The Young Mother* and two etchings, *Mother and Child* and *Woman and Parrot*.[90]

While Cassatt had left Allegheny at a young age and spent her formative years in Philadelphia, including her studies at the Pennsylvania Academy of the Fine Arts, a commission from a Pittsburgh Catholic bishop to reproduce two paintings in Italy rekindled her love of art and was the impetus for what became an internationally renowned career. In an effort to make more money for her pending trip to Europe, Cassatt traveled to Chicago to sell some of her paintings, but the Great Fire of 1871 destroyed the artwork.[91] This event portended the contentious fate for her most notable work to be displayed in Chicago, the mural *Modern Woman*, which hung in a tympanum in the Woman's Building during the Columbian Exposition.

In 1892 Palmer and art exhibition organizer Sarah Hallowell visited Cassatt in Paris to convince her to paint a mural for the Woman's Building, stressing its significance to the perception of all women.[92] It had been previously decided that the tympanums at either side of the building would depict the evolution of women from their traditional roles to modern women, reflecting the popular obsession with Darwin's theory of evolution during the late Victorian period. Palmer selected Mary Fairchild MacMonnies, a classical painter and the wife of sculptor Frederick MacMonnies, who created the Court of Honor's Columbian Fountain, to paint the *Primitive Woman* mural. Her classical style and motifs were suited to portray the traditional roles of women, but the *Modern Woman* mural needed a modern artist.

Mary Cassatt was the best-known American woman active in the up and coming impressionist movement. Hiring Cassatt for the Chicago mural, though, was a risk. Her use of bold colors and modern subject matter flew in the face of traditional painting practices. American audiences were not used to this type of brightly colored art and, with little communication from Palmer and MacMonnies on how the murals should tie into the rest of the interior or each other, the mural was sure to stand out in the cavernous building. Cassatt had also never painted a mural before and, in general, impressionists frowned upon murals and other decorative arts. This, however, played into Cassatt's personality. She relished the challenges associated with trying an unexplored medium and, perhaps even more so, she enjoyed overcoming the criticism of her fellow impressionists.[93] Cassatt decided to accept the invitation and was paid $3,000 for her work, the same as her male peers at the exposition.

The mural canvas was twelve feet high by fifty-eight feet wide. In order to paint such an enormous piece, Cassatt relied on an idea previously implemented by Claude Monet. She built a large studio behind her summer home and had a trench dug inside. Cassatt then used a system of pulleys to move the canvas up

Fig. 12. Mary Cassatt's *Modern Woman* mural depicting woman's pursuit of fame, knowledge, and recreation hung above the crowds inside the Woman's Building. Hubert Howe Bancroft, *The Book of the Fair: An Historical and Descriptive Presentation of the World's Science, Art, and Industry, as Viewed through the Columbian Exposition at Chicago in 1893.*

and down so she could reach the entirety of the work from the ground rather than climbing up a ladder or scaffold.[94] While the mural was big, the space inside the Woman's Building was even bigger, and so Cassatt did not concern herself with matching the styles of her mural with that of MacMonnies. In fact, she used the opportunity as a rebuke of the classical style she knew her counterpart would employ in the *Primitive Woman* mural.[95] As the opening of the fair drew closer, Palmer suggested that the muralists make changes to their works so they could be more in sync, but they were so radically different that the alterations did not help.

Cassatt used a large, deeply colored decorative border to divide her mural into three panels, which contained smaller-than-life-size figures. The borders and open space around the figures made it difficult for viewers to see, much less analyze, the content and message of the work. The bright colors of impressionist painting exploded from the plain walls of the building's interior, indicative of Cassatt's unwillingness to conform, her lack of experience with the relationship between murals and their surroundings, or perhaps both.[96] The panel scenes were set in the countryside, away from woman's traditional home-dominated tasks, and depicted young women to show that Cassatt's vision was of the near-future generation. Furthermore, Cassatt pushed her common theme of mothers and children to the boundaries of the mural, indicating that while motherhood was still a part of being a woman, it was not their central purpose.[97]

The left panel of the mural depicted girls chasing fame—a type of ambition that flew in the face of contemporary norms—while being chased themselves by ducks. The ducks represented the uncomfortable position women would face, as well as the squawks of criticism that would impede their progress.[98] The center panel showed women picking apples from a tree, plucking the fruits of knowledge. This refers to the influx of women into higher education; however, Cassatt biographer Nancy Mowll Mathews argues that "the seriousness of Cassatt's woman conveys her belief in the burden that education brings with it: the responsibility to go forth with that education and make one's own way in the world as a professional woman."[99] The right panel demonstrated women's pursuit of recreation: the arts, music, and dance. In all, Cassatt's mural is her ideal world, where women are able to happily study and enjoy their creative interests to contribute more fully to human culture.[100]

The language writers used to evaluate the Woman's Building blended art criticism with Victorian values. The fact that statues and other representations of Columbia, a goddess-like figure representing the spirit of Christopher Columbus, dotted the fairgrounds meant that Cassatt's mural was virtually surrounded by depictions of the ideal Victorian woman, making *Modern Woman* stand out that much more. While *Modern Woman* was more groundbreaking than its counterpart, critics were quick to point out its failures as a mural— mainly that it drew attention to itself rather than complementing the building and surroundings. Complaints about Cassatt's color scheme specifically were typical of anti-impressionists of the time.

Not only was Cassatt's work compared to traditional painting but Cassatt, too, was held up to the social standards of the very female archetype her mural sought to overcome.[101] Critics charged that her mural was not feminine enough, attributing this quality to Cassatt's own unladylike character. They argued that Cassatt was asserting her vision of what femininity was evolving into. As explained by Wanda Corn, "In the forceful style of her mural, Cassatt acted out her new womanhood and profoundly challenged the boundaries of acceptable behavior for women of her social class. What rankled the critics was how she told her stories. . . . In personally declaring independence from the conventions of aesthetic harmony, she raised her painterly voice, so to speak, pushing herself and her mural into visitors' awareness and eliciting charges from the press that she was cynical, sarcastic, and aggressive."[102] Cassatt resented the attacks on her mural and womanhood and decided not to make the trip to Chicago to visit the Columbian Exposition. Despite the notoriety her painting earned during its time in the Woman's Building, shortly after the fair the mural went missing and to date has not been found.[103]

By the close of the fair, it was evident that Western Pennsylvania was not only active in manufacturing, agriculture, and extracting natural resources but exceptionally skilled at doing so. Throughout the buildings of the White City, Western Pennsylvania demonstrated the variety that made it one of the most productive and multifaceted areas in the nation. Exhibits by Western Pennsylvania companies, organizations, and citizens won nearly 150 total awards at the exposition, reinforcing the region's status as an economic powerhouse and drawing attention to its burgeoning educational institutions and new industries, like electrical equipment. Established companies like Carnegie Steel failed to make a substantial showing at the exposition and went on to continued prosperity, but others, like H. J. Heinz Company, rode their newfound fame from the fair to achieve global success.

On the other hand, the World's Congress Auxiliary accomplished what the exhibits of the Columbian Exposition often could not—the meetings highlighted the intellectual and socially conscious activities of Western Pennsylvanians. Technologies and advancements associated with electricity and transportation were certainly on display at the fairgrounds, but during the congress's meetings speakers presented the science behind those machines, often with an eye toward future advances. Participation in the conferences relating to temperance and the women's movement also demonstrated Pittsburgh's place as a center of social and cultural change. As the congress progressed, it became clear that there was more to Western Pennsylvania than coal, oil, glass, and steel. The people of Pittsburgh proved to be just as valuable a resource as the minerals and ore they plucked from the earth.

5

"A Peep into Paradise"

AS DEMONSTRATED BY the success of Western Pennsylvanian exhibits at the Chicago Fair and the engagement of participants in the World's Congress Auxiliary, the Columbian Exposition occurred at exactly the right time to showcase not only Pittsburgh's expanding industrial and technological might but also its developing sense of civic responsibilities and activities. As noted by historian Francis Couvares, in Pittsburgh "technological revolution, work reorganization, massive immigration, and the restructuring of urban space all occurred simultaneously . . . and transformed the character of everyday experience at work, at home, and in the streets of the city."[1] In addition to the increased production and success of a variety of area industries, shifts in both the composition and the structure of the workforce further developed an entire class of people who could afford to pour their time and money into efforts to improve their city. Given this increase in available personal resources, the fair opened at just the moment when the society developing around Pittsburgh's changing economic climate could best take advantage of what the exposition had to offer.

Unsurprisingly, the rise of steel was a driving factor in the evolution of Pittsburgh's economic and social spheres. This industry bred a culture of innovation, encouraging the constant development of technology to make mills more efficient and, therefore, more lucrative. Production had traditionally relied on skilled workers who could wield their power over mill owners to dictate working conditions; however, the implementation of the Bessemer steelmaking process relieved companies of their need for these craftsmen. With a new work-force that consisted primarily of unskilled, often immigrant, employees who could be easily replaced, owners regained control over their operations, as evi-denced by the company's victory in the 1892 Homestead steel strike. They also realized they could maximize profits by managing each step in the steelmaking process by building fully integrated mills. Andrew Carnegie's Edgar Thomson Steel Works, in Braddock, led the way as the first fully integrated mill in south-western Pennsylvania, but by 1890 mills like it became the dominant industrial employer in the region.[2]

By necessity, managers compartmentalized fully integrated mills into departments overseeing the many aspects of production, sales, bookkeeping, and other duties. Drawing from his experience working for the Pennsylvania Railroad during that company's rapid expansion, Carnegie adapted its idea of networks of middle managers to coordinate work for his steel mills.[3] As Car-negie's companies acquired more mills and other companies began to notice how his facilities were administered, the railroad managerial system became the standard. This, in turn, created an increase in the number of white-collar workers in the Pittsburgh area whose needs and desires supported storeowners, service providers, and others required to meet their demands.[4] Together, these groups created an influx of families into the region's middle class.

As southern and eastern European immigrants began to settle into the older, more populated inner-city neighborhoods on the periphery of the developing Central Business District to take advantage of the unskilled labor opportunities within the region, middle- and upper-class families moved to the suburbs, par-ticularly Pittsburgh's developing East End district.[5] This movement into newly cleared areas or farmland allowed the middle class to create an environment, including housing, infrastructure, and institutions, that best suited the ideal life they wanted to live. One of the aspects of middle-class life this relocation addressed was increased leisure time. Previously, Pittsburgh's upper class had not had local access to cultured amusement, like museums, or clubs relating to art and literature. The relocation of many of these families to the East End pro-vided a climate that promoted parties, clubs, and other elements of elite cul-ture. By 1890 the middle class had incorporated recreation into their lives with music, theater, and reading organizations.[6]

In addition to the development of recreational opportunities within the sub-urbs, the white-collar Central Business District at the Point also became the playground for those who worked downtown. Theaters were a primary source of amusement. The *Pittsburgh Press* reported in June 1893, "The [1892–1893 theater] season has been one of the most successful, if not actually the most successful that Pittsburgh has ever known," a testament to the middle class's desire for entertainment.[7] In the early autumn each year, the Western Penn-sylvania Exposition became a source of amusement for members of the region's more affluent classes. While musical performances and other forms of "high cul-ture" were one feature of the Western Pennsylvania Exposition, the eight-week event also promoted local companies and the work of the Pittsburgh Chamber of Commerce.[8] Exposure to the spectacle of this regional exposition prepared middle-class families for the wonders awaiting them at Chicago's World's Fair.

Even though the Columbian Exposition was hundreds of miles away from Pittsburgh, local middle-class families were well equipped to make the jour-ney. White-collar workers received regular leave and holiday and vacation time that, coupled with their increased discretionary income and improved transportation modes like Pullman sleeper railroad cars, made extended long-distance summer travel a middle class staple. Furthermore, these families, like many others across the country, saw a trip to the fair as a necessary component of the culture they were striving to develop. If they wanted to successfully par-ticipate in society events, families would need to be able to convincingly discuss their experiences at the exposition.[9] To reinforce their stories, the *Commercial Gazette* and *Press* printed almost daily lists of Western Pennsylvanians who attended the fair in Chicago. Over six thousand families, nearly all from the middle and upper classes, asserted their status by signing the registration book at the Pennsylvania State Building and were subsequently reported by the local press.[10]

Capitalizing on the fact that the fair was not only a place to see but also a place to be seen, area department stores initiated marketing campaigns that used pending visits to Chicago as a means of selling the latest fashions. An April 1893 advertisement for Campbell and Dick, the self-proclaimed "People's Store for the World's Fair," warned customers that they should purchase all their travel necessities at home because "they may fleece you when you get there." Hand-bags, umbrellas, and traveling suits were some of the items they promoted to potential vacationers. On opening day of the exposition, Joseph Horne Company advertised its collection of purses that they assured customers were "made espe-cially for us, on large orders, to meet the big demand incidental to the World's

Fair Travel." Boggs & Buhl, Solomon and Ruben, and Kaufmann's department stores also used the fair to draw in customers.[11] Playing on the insecurities of families striving toward the middle-class ideal of a trip to the fair, area stores strategically used the Columbian Exposition to sell new, refined clothing and accessories to those who needed to look their best during this opportunity to display their status to the rest of the community.

Visiting the fair was such a priority for some that families dealt quickly with struggles that would normally have delayed or canceled vacation plans so that the mandatory trip to Chicago could still be completed. Charles Spencer, a sales agent for Henry Clay Frick, planned to take his wife, Mary, and two oldest children to the exposition in the spring while leaving their two younger children in Pittsburgh with his mother-in-law and the children's nanny. When their nanny quit a month before their planned departure, the entire trip was put in jeopardy. As recalled by daughter Ethel, her mother was in a state of despair at the prospect of missing the fair, so Charles immediately placed an ad in the local papers seeking a new nanny. Taking advantage of the fact that many were struggling in the financial Panic of 1893, he quickly hired a woman "into domestic service [though] socially she belonged several pegs above it."[12] With order restored by June, the four Spencers made their trip to see the fair.[13]

In late June, Moorhead Holland, the eight-year-old son of Western University of Pennsylvania chancellor William J. Holland, severely burned his face while attempting to light a firecracker, putting his family's trip to see the Columbian Exposition's July 4th celebration in peril. The chancellor, who coincidentally did not want to miss what fair organizers promised to be a spectacular firework display in Chicago, sought medical attention for his son and, with his recovery still uncertain, boarded the entire family on a westbound train on the evening of July 1.[14] On July 3, the elder Holland assured Moorhead's grandparents that doctors were confident the boy's burns would not permanently disfigure his face, thereby justifying his decision to follow through with their visit to the fair.[15] Not even bodily harm was an excuse to miss the once-in-a-lifetime opportunity.

Of course, without the railroads mass westward travel to visit the fair would not have been possible. Local newspapers featured advertisements by companies like the Pennsylvania, Pittsburgh & Lake Erie, Baltimore & Ohio, and other railroads promoting discounted rates for tickets to Chicago. While Pittsburgh travelers in June 1892 could secure round-trip tickets to Chicago for as little as $7, by May 1893 companies offered round-trip tickets for $16. Eventually, after the exposition's slow start, ticket prices fell to $12 for a round trip after July 4. This rate held steady during the most popular travel period from late August through early October. To attract last-minute visitors and return trips to get one last look at the great attraction, companies implemented tiered or decreased ticket pricing during the last two weeks of the fair. Journeying to Chicago with access to a sleeper car in late October cost anywhere from $11 to $18, while traveling the same route in coach cost $10.50. In mid-October, the Pennsylvania Railroad even began to offer half-price tickets for children under twelve years old.

In addition to standard round-trip tickets, railroads and other companies organized special excursions that included transportation, as well as lodging, meals, and even side trips to other destinations. In early July the Baltimore & Ohio Railroad offered a seven-day trip to Chicago including round-trip train tickets, admission to the fairgrounds, lunches, and lodging for $95 per person. A two-week July expedition organized by Pittsburgh agents Knap and Weaver included train tickets and lodging with one day in Detroit, two days in Mackinac Island, and six days in Chicago with admission to the world's fair. In mid-August, the World's Columbian Exposition Transportation Company offered a six-day visit to Chicago for $25. A month later that same price purchased twelve first-class meals and six days' lodging at Chicago's Great Eastern Hotel, in addition to round-trip tickets on the Pittsburgh, Fort Wayne & Chicago Railroad. [16]

Some Western Pennsylvania businesses planned shutdowns or organized trips to Chicago so their employees could visit the fair. Westinghouse Electric and Air Brake facilities closed for ten days beginning on the afternoon of July 1. Hundreds of employees took advantage of the $12 excursion ticket price on the Fort Wayne line and Westinghouse paid the $2 difference in cost to the railroad company. [17] The Pittsburgh & Lake Erie Railroad provided vacations and free transportation for its employees who wanted to visit the Columbian Exposition in August. [18]

While Pittsburgh was the start of the journey to the fair for Western Pennsylvanians, it also served as a stop along the way for travelers from the East Coast and abroad. When Chicago was named the site of the exposition, Pittsburghers immediately supported the decision because they saw an opportunity to host businessmen and entrepreneurs from all over the world during their trip to or from the White City. If the city's reputation did not initially draw them in to tour the steel mills or Westinghouse's laboratories, certainly their review of Pittsburgh's treasures on display at the Columbian Exposition would pique their interest for a visit on their way home.

Area companies were anxious to host visitors with legitimate interest in their operations and products, and the Pittsburgh Chamber of Commerce was eager to provide those travelers, even sending agents to Europe to identify and woo potential sightseers.[19] The Edgar Thomson Works, the locomotive works of H. K. Porter, and Allegheny County Light Company all welcomed guests from European countries including Germany, France, and England, as well as more far-flung countries such as Korea.[20] Many foreign visitors were interested in steel production and other local industries. For example, engineers from the Krupp Gun Works in Essen, Germany, spent weeks with their host, Carnegie Steel's Charles Schwab, reviewing the rolling of armor plating at the Homestead Steel Works.[21] The fact that his steel companies drew so many tourists during the summer of 1893 seems to indicate that Andrew Carnegie was at least partially justified in his dismissal of exhibiting in Chicago.

Other visitors were simply looking to break up their tedious trek after their voyage across the Atlantic. English steamship line superintendent T. A. Goodwin confessed, "I am heartily glad that there is such an interesting city as Pittsburg on the route to relieve the monotony of the journey." Among those stopping in Pittsburgh included a group of Scottish artisans, a Brazilian fruit and spice exporter, English professors, a German tanner, a Japanese mirror manufacturer, and numerous others making their way to and from Chicago.[22] Government delegates from several countries also passed through Western Pennsylvania, including Count Zarwitski of Russia, whose false teeth fell out of his mouth and a train window as he sat agape while taking in the sites of Connellsville.[23] Truly, the region was a sight to behold.

While city boosters prepared for the world's fair, another approach to tourism in Pittsburgh began to formulate. Instead of focusing on industry as a primary attraction, there was a movement to promote the region's natural beauty and urban advancements as a means of attracting potential tourists. This tactic was implemented by the Pittsburgh Chamber of Commerce in the pamphlet it produced for distribution at the Columbian Exposition, which boasted of several sightseeing tours throughout the area. For its part, the Pennsylvania Railroad further promoted Pittsburgh in its 1893 guidebook as a city of beauty and progress, stating, "In point of fact, however, Pittsburg is a manufacturing city of no mean importance, and not only that, but a handsome city as well. Its natural beauties have been enhanced by public and private improvements. No more healthy city can be found in America, and in some of the essentials of comfort it has no rival. Natural gas is abundant, and is supplied at low rates for heating and cooking in private houses, as well as for manufacturing. Charitable, educational, and reformatory institutions abound, and its public edifices are numerous and imposing."[24] Thanks to these glowing, sometimes exaggerated, descriptions of Pittsburgh, the city became a destination for business and sightseeing travelers alike.

Thousands of Western Pennsylvania families made the pilgrimage to Chicago to explore the World's Columbian Exposition despite the onset of hardships brought on by the beginning of the financial Panic of 1893. Upon their arrival in the Windy City, tourists made their way to their lodgings to drop off their luggage and settle in before heading to the fairgrounds. Those who could afford to do so stayed at the opulent Palmer House in downtown Chicago, not far from the Art Institute building that hosted many of the World's Congress Auxiliary conferences. Others took advantage of the dozens of hotels built by opportunistic entrepreneurs throughout Chicago's South Side in anticipation of the fair. While some hotels were within walking distance of an entrance to the exposition, many visitors relied on the city's streetcars and railway systems to deliver them to Jackson Park. In a letter, Margaret Mitchell of Pittsburgh described a typical journey from the Great Eastern Hotel, located just past the western end of the Midway Plaisance. "We are about nine miles from town and two blocks from the entrance to Plaisance but as the Plaisance is a mile long we are quite a little distance to the main entrance but we can walk a block then take a Cottage [Avenue] car ride several blocks then walk another block and enter at the 61st Street entrance."[25] Meanwhile, more affluent Pittsburghers such as Adelaide Frick, the wife of Henry Clay Frick, were able to purchase carriage rides from their hotel to the fair gates and, once within the fairgrounds, chair rides throughout the White City and Midway.[26]

Once inside, Pittsburghers were in awe of what they saw. In the White City, the architecture and landscape immediately struck the visitors. Mitchell eagerly notified her father, Judge Christopher Magee, "The Horticultural and the Transportation buildings are beautiful and Agricultural Hall is very beautiful and most interesting the old farmers seem to cling to it with great pride. The grounds are beautiful."[27] It is not hard to imagine her delight, while visiting those buildings, in finding exhibits with familiar Western Pennsylvania names like Heinz and Westinghouse. Two days later, she wrote to her mother about displays of fine china, Tiffany and Company's exhibit, and "things from all over the world." For Mitchell, the fair in Chicago was not only a chance to peruse goods; it offered a glimpse into the world outside of her Pittsburgh home. Experiencing so many fineries all in one place, she gushed to her mother, "The things are magnificent and it is almost as good as going to Europe or perhaps as traveling around the world. . . . It is all such a splendid way of seeing this world."[28]

If Mitchell thought the exhibits of the White City offered a view of the world, the living anthropological displays of the Midway provided an immersive experience. She explained to her father, who would make his own visit to the fair at the end of June, "The Plaisance is a great place it is like a little world in itself. One meets Turks, Egyptians, South Sea Islanders, Austrian bar maids, Java boys, Donkey boys from Cairo, Normandy peasants, Dahomey people, the Sumoli, pretty Irish girls are all in native dress. . . . The Plaisance is a little bit in the great foreign world and gives me a pretty good idea of how those people live."[29] In writing to her young daughter, Mitchell focused her description on aspects that would appeal to a small child, noting the "lovely dolls from France, beautiful wigs from Germany, great trained lions and wild animals from Hamburg, tall camels from Egypt and lovely little donkeys from Cairo. I can buy one for $40.00. Just big enough for you to ride on."[30] For all of the worldly displays on the Midway, though, Mitchell also noted a connection to home, remarking, "The biggest thing in the Fair is the Ferris Wheel made by a Pittsburgher."[31]

While visitors could easily become overwhelmed while surrounded by such wondrous and exotic sights, some fairgoers were able to grasp the educational value of the exposition. After reviewing the exhibits, Western Penitentiary chaplain John L. Milligan observed that "the education that the exposition affords to young people is unmeasurable, and for a young man who some day hopes to travel around the world he can learn as much and perhaps more by visiting Chicago." Noting the stories circulating about high prices in Chicago, Milligan also sought to reassure Pittsburghers that "the question of expense is not so great as the papers say it is, and any young man of limited means can go and stay a week without having to spend a fortune, as is now believed. I would not have missed the ten days I spent there for ten times the sum it cost me."[32] This was music to the ears of Pittsburgh's growing middle class, which was eager to acquire a more refined taste while also on a budget. Even well-traveled members of Pittsburgh's elite recognized the benefits of the fair. After one of his visits to Chicago, H. J. Heinz wrote in his diary that "the Fair is a wonderland and a great educator and pronounced the greatest the world has ever seen and not likely to see soon again."[33]

One potential group of fair visitors, however, were not as eager to make the trip to Chicago. African Americans had been excluded at every turn from participating in the planning and exhibitions of the Columbian Exposition. As a result, many in the Black community recognized that they were not represented in their country's displays and, therefore, not part of the aspirational vision of the United States presented in the fairgrounds. As described in the African Methodist Episcopal (AME) newspaper the *Christian Recorder*, which was founded in Pittsburgh and published in Philadelphia, the African American community instead saw the pavilion erected by the country of Haiti as a surrogate display and point of pride for African Americans in response to their omission.[34] Prominent African American activist Frederick Douglass was invited to oversee the Haitian building and he decided to take the opportunity to advocate for the advancements and inclusion of the Black American community at the fair.

In addition to using the Haiti pavilion as a headquarters for African Americans at the fair, Douglass and fellow activist Ida B. Wells sought to publish a pamphlet for distribution at the exposition outlining why there were few exhibits of African American achievements in Chicago. Former Pittsburgh citizen and then Ohio shoe manufacturer Frederick J. Loudin suggested that the publication should also include information about lynchings and other brutalities against African Americans to draw attention to issues facing Black people. Douglass and Loudin made the initial donation to print the pamphlet and Chicago's African American community provided the rest.[35] Titled *The Reason Why the Colored American Is Not in the World's Columbian Exposition*, the handout included essays by Wells, Douglass, I. Garland Penn, and Ferdinand Barnett that addressed the exclusion of African Americans from the fair, atrocities committed against the Black community since emancipation, and advancements made by African Americans. One former Pittsburgher, Henry Ossawa Tanner, the son of AME bishop Benjamin Tucker Tanner, was put forth as an example of progress in African American art.[36] While there may have been few physical displays at the Columbian Exposition, *The Reason Why* served as a written exhibit of African American advancements.

Another person who was hesitant about the fair was Andrew Carnegie. After laying the groundwork for his successful companies Carnegie spent much of his time abroad and the summer of 1893 was no exception. While many flocked to Chicago from all over the world, Carnegie traveled through Europe and then New England before finally making his way to the Windy City on September 21 to take in the Columbian Exposition. Shortly after his visit to Chicago, Carnegie received a letter from John R. Dunlap, editor of the *Engineering*

Magazine, asking him to write an article about the economic value of the fair for its special retrospective edition. For his contribution, Dunlap offered Carnegie a fifty-dollar honorarium. Reflecting on his visit in the January 1894 issue, Carnegie waxed poetic about the great exhibits of art found at the fair, particularly the architecture, sculpture, and American paintings. He also cited the Parliament of Religions as being the most novel and noteworthy of the World's Congress Auxiliary conferences, stating that it "may be credited with having set in motion many forces tending to the harmonizing, and ultimately to the unifying, of the principal forms of religious belief."[37]

While he conceded that world travelers might jeer at the attractions of the Midway Plaisance, Carnegie also acknowledged that the various cultural displays were a suitable facsimile for many Americans who desired to travel the world but lacked the means. Thinking more locally, he also noticed similarities between the exposition and state fairs. Just as annual fairs brought together people from all over a given state and instilled in them a sense of place and pride, so too did the world's fair succeed in bringing together people from all over the country. Carnegie posited, "Every citizen became not only prouder than ever of his country, of whose position and greatness the exhibition was the outward and visible symbol, but he became acquainted for the first time, perhaps, with his fellow countrymen of other States."[38] Taking many of these attributes to heart, Carnegie began to consider how he might incorporate the same exposure to art and world cultures at his new library being constructed in Pittsburgh's Oakland neighborhood.

The allure of Chicago as a suitable replacement for a European vacation, at least during the summer and fall of 1893, was not easily earned as the city fought the stigma of being uncultured, crime ridden, and dirty. As author J. Philip Gruen explains, Chicago's "size, crowds, noise, smells, grime, and smoke proved overwhelming for many visitors, who often found themselves teetering on the precipice of Hell."[39] However, tourists from Pittsburgh, a city once famously described as hell with the lid off, likely identified with these surroundings and did not find the city as appalling as other fairgoers did. Upon her arrival, Mitchell succinctly described her first impressions in a letter to her mother. "Chicago is a dirty city. From drainage and disagreeable odors, but" she noted optimistically, "the weather is perfect."[40] Two days later, after experiencing more of Chicago and the fair, her impression changed. Mitchell commented to her father, "I am agreeably surprised in regard to Chicago. Everyone is kind and attentive and not grafting as I had fancied."[41]

While Chicago and the exposition may not have been as treacherous as many had feared—a worry that may have been supported by the exposition's plea that each city of over twenty-five thousand people send at least two of its own policemen to assist the Columbian Guard—there were dangers associated with so many people converging in Jackson Park.[42] One precarious situation was the combination of thousands of eager vacationers and overcrowded public transportation. In the waning months of the fair, two Pittsburgh-area men were pulled under streetcars near the fairgrounds, resulting in one losing a leg and the other damaging his spine and suffering internal injuries.[43] Crime was also a concern for many travelers visiting the fair, but Chicago criminals and the influx of unemployed men seeking work at the fairgrounds were not the only offenders. On September 23 Columbian Guards arrested Westinghouse foreman E. Cavanaugh for assaulting a woman from New Brunswick, Maine, and stealing her leather bag containing three hundred dollars in cash and diamonds. The attack occurred in the shadows of an archway on the western wing of the Fine Arts Building. Cavanaugh escaped into a nearby room where Westinghouse electricians were working, but he was quickly discovered by guards and identified by the victim.[44]

While the focus was on the dangers of Chicago, crime struck Western Pennsylvanian fairgoers even at home. Lewis Lynch was jailed for breaking into the Baldwin residence of deputy sheriff J. B. McDonough while he was in Chicago visiting the fair. A friend who came to check on the house in McDonough's absence found it illuminated and he gathered a posse of armed neighbors to investigate and capture the intruder. After a hearing for burglary, for which there was no evidence, Lynch was released, and he subsequently returned to take up residence in the McDonough home. This time there was no attempt to remove him from the house until McDonough returned from Chicago. Once back at home, he found several items and cash were missing, and that Lynch had consumed all the food and coal in the house. When Lynch was discovered in a neighboring barn, he had several of the missing items on his person and, this time with sufficient evidence of burglary, he was once again jailed.[45] It seems the world's fair offered an opportunity for crime both in Chicago and at home in Western Pennsylvania.

From the earliest days of planning the fair, many in the Pittsburgh area and throughout the country were concerned whether the Columbian Exposition would be open to the public on the Christian Sabbath. The world's fair emerged at a time when Western Pennsylvanian Protestants sought to curb the influence of immigrants and Catholics, the rise of which was evident in the region's participation in exhibits and congresses, by calling for strict adherence to existing Sabbath laws in order to preserve their neighborhoods' established character. In the late 1880s, this included the creation of organizations to coordinate their efforts and even the hiring of lawyers to prosecute offenders.[46] Others, however, saw the exposition as a major step in breaking with established Sunday laws and promoting equity among all people with access to leisure and self-improvement. The two positions were set to collide throughout the early 1890s.

On one side were sabbatarians, primarily Methodists and Presbyterians, who wished for the Sunday closure of the fair so that everyone could observe a traditional solemn holy day. These people were concerned that an increase in recreational activity on Sundays would have an adverse effect on the number of people attending religious services. They were also worried that popular amusements would encourage an atmosphere that infringed upon the solemnity required by those who chose to observe the Christian Sabbath.[47] In their view, such a large-scale disregard of religious services in favor of a centralized gathering for amusement would disturb those who sought a quiet day of rest and reflection. In October 1890 the Pittsburgh conference of the Methodist Episcopal Church and a meeting of the United Presbyterian Synod in Greensburg both requested that the "managers of the Columbian exposition in Chicago to close its doors on Sunday."[48]

The Western Pennsylvania Sabbath Association held its annual meeting the following month and the first topic they discussed was whether the exposition should be open on Sundays. In the eyes of the association, to keep the fair open on the Sabbath would be the first major step toward a total collapse of Sunday observances and blue laws. The group felt that commissioners were intentionally not addressing the issue so that exhibitors would not hesitate to spend money on a display that would only be available six days a week. To get ahead of the issue and force a decision immediately, they proposed distributing a circular to exhibitors encouraging them to refuse participation in the fair until it was agreed to close the fairgrounds on Sundays, a tactic that had proved successful during the 1876 Centennial Exhibition in Philadelphia. The association proposed several resolutions lobbying the fair's executive committee, citing the Sunday laws of Illinois and the exhibitors' states, the right to a day of rest for the exposition's employees, and the trouble that increased traffic would cause pious Chicagoans should the grounds be open on Sunday. The conventioneers had stewed over violations of Pennsylvania's blue laws for some time, citing newsboys, hired cars, and even the railroads as ubiquitous offenders. By enforcing these laws on a global stage at the Columbian Exposition, they hoped to encourage more strin-gent enforcement of the law at home in Allegheny County.[49]

The issue festered in some circles throughout the region over the next several years as the fair's opening drew closer. During a January 1, 1893, sermon at the Central Reformed Presbyterian Church in Allegheny, Reverend J. W. Sproull railed against the idea of opening the upcoming world's fair on Sundays. He preached, "There is a determination to destroy the character of the Sabbath and make it a mere day of work and worldly pleasure," but also quickly pointed out that "the friends of the Sabbath lately gained a signal moral victory when they induced congress to condition the appropriation to the Columbian exposition so that the gates should remain closed on the Sabbath." He went on, "The question as to whether the day shall be continued as a Sabbath day or shall hereafter be a holiday depends largely on the answer of congress. If they repeal their former action it will be a national indorsement [sic] of the continental Sunday. If that is introduced it will change the morals of the nation."[50] For those who wanted the fair closed on Sundays, it would be bad enough for the American people to ignore the Sabbath, but to do so in order to partake in commercial amusements, at the expense of forcing others to work so the fair's commissioners could make money, was especially disturbing.[51] To Reverend Sproull and others like him, the fate of the Sabbath and the values of the entire country relied on the strict enforcement of Congress's stipulation that it would provide its $5 million contribution to the fair only if the directors closed the gates on Sundays.

On the other side of the debate were those who spoke in favor of the fair remaining open on Sundays so that those who worked six days each week could also enjoy the exhibits on their day off. This group advocated for and was influ-enced by the masses of immigrant workers who had brought to America their own ideas and traditions of how to observe the Sabbath. Many of these groups incorporated games, drinking, and other festivities into their observances because as members of the working class they only had one day for recreation. For them, the exclusion of amusements on Sunday meant they would no longer be able to enjoy the lighthearted moments of an otherwise hard and tiresome life.[52] Proponents of keeping the exposition open, including at least some groups within the American Federation of Labor and the Knights of Labor, which were quite active in Western Pennsylvania, felt that cutting off workers' access to the fair was counter to the very values sabbatarians claimed they wanted to preserve. This group included not only workers but progressive religious lead-ers and members of the upper class who felt that closing the fair on Sundays was an act of hypocrisy. They believed that excluding the working class in this manner was the antithesis of the republican values of the exposition and the very Christian ideals the sabbatarians hoped to maintain. To offer an opportunity for everyone to visit the fair would mean that laborers could benefit from the cultural enlightenment they would surely experience in Chicago, thus making them more productive and desirable members of American society.[53] These people perceived the enforced observance of the Sunday Sabbath as a deliberate attack by the upper and middle classes to assert dominance over the working class by restricting a means of advancing their status.

After the first two weeks of Sunday closures at the fair, a May 17 editorial in the *Press* presented a thoughtful, Pittsburgh-centric argument for why the exposition should remain open on Sundays. The article begins with the assertion that the primary function of world's fairs was not to make a profit but rather to educate, and so if more people would benefit from the fair being open seven days a week then that is what should be done. The article then claims that Congress had no authority to impose such a regulation on the fair, explaining, "The United States government has no more right to interfere with it than it has to come into Pennsylvania to enforce the blue laws of 1794. This being the case, the local directors of the fair should be legally safe in disregarding the conditions imposed by congress, even without paying back the money." Offering a local comparison to the situation of laborers in Chicago, the author noted, "In Pittsburg there would be 50,000 working people who could not attend conveniently on any day save Sunday. They work hard every day all the week and are too exhausted to go to places of entertainment in the evening. But on Sunday they need recreation, and, in the summer, they find it by going to Schenley or Highland [Park] in thousands, to the Phipps conservatory and to the Carnegie library." The article closes by reminding readers that the opening of these Pittsburgh recreational facilities on Sundays was also met with resistance, but that initial outcry was quick to subside. "When it was decided to open the Phipps' conservatory on Sunday it gave a shock to some of the Sabbatarians of the two cities, but they have recovered now, and no apparent harm has resulted from the opening of the parks, greenhouses and library on the day on which they can best be enjoyed by those who need them most." The editorial concludes by prophesizing that the controversy surrounding the world's fair would end in a similar fashion.[54]

On Sunday, May 28, the commissioners of the World's Columbian Exposition opened the gates to the public, but the fair these visitors encountered was not the same experience fairgoers had the other six days of the week. Exhibitors opposed to the Sunday opening did not staff their exhibits, and several state buildings, including Pennsylvania's, were not opened. At a June 5 meeting of its board of trustees, the Western University of Pennsylvania chose to cover its exhibit in observance of the Christian Sabbath.[55] Methodists threatened to withdraw their exhibits in protest, but when it was pointed out that they were contractually obligated to remain on the fairgrounds, they covered their exhibits every Sunday as well.[56] Reflecting on the legacy of the exposition after it had closed, an editorial in the *Commercial Gazette* pointed to the Sunday opening as a "moral blemish" in which the directors "ignored a solemn contract and violated a law of congress intended to protect the civil institution of the Sabbath," all in the name of greed.[57]

Meanwhile, members of the federal government were displeased that the commissioners went against their wishes and took immediate legal action. Attorney general Richard Olney filed an injunction to force the exposition's closure for its remaining Sundays; however, a federal appeals court denied the government's plea in June. After years of debate leading up to the summer of 1893, the fair officially won the right to open its gates every day for the duration of the exposition. The question then became whether people would use their one day of rest to visit the attractions.

After a few weeks of good attendance, the number of people visiting on Sundays began to decline. By mid-July, reporters wondered if all the debate over the Sunday question had been worth it. A correspondent from the *Press* "said that the people of Chicago are too busy beating carpets, hanging out washing and doing other things of a business nature to go to the fair on Sundays. They have not the time. They are not at church, nor spending the day in some serious way advocated by ministers and other pious and well-meaning people." Since the primary argument for opening the fair was that workers would not have an opportunity to see it otherwise, the Pittsburgh reporter speculated, "Now that the people of Chicago have shown that they do not care enough for the fair to attend in paying numbers there is perhaps no use in keeping it open."[58] Later in July, the *Press* noted that those who did visit the fair on Sundays frequented the Midway Plaisance, where most of the attractions were open for business and more akin to the type of entertainment the working class usually visited on their day off, and not in the educational exhibits of the White City. In that reporter's opinion, "unless the world's fair all over can be made as lively as the Midway in its own peculiar style, there would be no profit, educational or pecuniary, in opening the gates on Sunday."[59]

The commissioners realized too late that they had misjudged the allure the Columbian Exposition would have on the working class, and after a month of low Sunday attendance they decided to close the fair for the remaining Sundays.[60] Unfortunately for them, however, the same court decision that allowed the exposition to be open on Sundays also required them to do so, even if it was against their wishes. Instead of trying to make the best of the situation by providing some incentive to visit the exposition on Sundays, administrators simply opened the gates to the half-functional fair with no special programming and limited concessions. Visitors could still observe the exposition on a Sunday, but they could not truly experience its essence and sense of wonder.[61] In addition to the closure of several exhibits, the onset of the financial panic made many potential working-class visitors hesitant to spend their hard-earned money on admission to the exposition. The Sunday opening of the fair was a financial failure for the exposition's directors, but the fair itself played a key role in changing the way the country viewed Sunday recreation moving forward.

While Pittsburghers disagreed on the Sunday question, other aspects of the fair were more widely accepted. Throughout the entire process of planning the state exhibits for the Columbian Exposition, a sentiment developed that Western Pennsylvania was being ignored, or at least underrepresented. This perceived bias against Pittsburgh, or more appropriately in favor of Philadelphia, placed a chip on the collective shoulder of Western Pennsylvanians as they planned to visit the fair and take in the exhibits. An agitated *Press* reporter complained that during a visit to Chicago he could not find any representation of Pittsburgh in the Pennsylvania State Building. His complaint that items from Western Pennsylvania were lacking when compared to those from the eastern side of the state was true enough, but he later retracted his objection when he realized that organizers sorted regional newspapers alphabetically by county name and so those from Pittsburgh were filed under "Allegheny."[62]

Although the Pennsylvania Board of World's Fair Managers may have overlooked Pittsburgh-related contributions for state committee displays, there was no doubt that Western Pennsylvania made significant contributions to the exposition, most notably by providing electricity and the Ferris wheel. Writers for area newspapers also felt that local intelligence was an important addition to the World's Congress Auxiliary. In reporting on the various area women who had traveled to Chicago to participate in the congresses, the *Press* noted, "Pittsburg on the whole has been given very little show at the great exposition, yet has the smoky city been called upon several times to contribute of its feminine intellect for the various congresses that have been held auxiliary to the fair."[63]

This opinion hits on one of the most important contributions of the Columbian Exposition to Western Pennsylvania—highlighting that Pittsburgh was not just an industrial workhorse but also an emerging center of intellectual and social advancement.

The idea that Western Pennsylvania was being neglected at the fair rose all the way to the office of Pittsburgh mayor Bernard J. McKenna, and by late summer he had seen enough. On August 17, Mayor McKenna expressed his displeasure, proclaiming, "Pennsylvania has a building, but the Pittsburger who visits it is sure to think of Philadelphia and no other city. The Quaker city is monopolizing all the attention given to Pennsylvania, and it is time for Pittsburg to push to the front."[64] Looking ahead to early September, the mayor saw his chance to put the region in the spotlight.

As a means of promoting increased attendance at the exposition, fair officials had designated special themed days throughout the summer. The scheme proved to be a success, with Chicago Day drawing more visitors than any other day of the entire exposition, but it was also not without controversy. Planners designated August 25 as Colored People's Day at the fair, but the decision of whether to participate divided the African American community and, when combined with white Americans' intentional avoidance of the fairgrounds on that day, the celebration was poorly attended. Several states also had their own designated date and organizers scheduled September 7 as Pennsylvania Day. State leaders encouraged citizens from all over the commonwealth to travel to Chicago and join in the festivities at the Pennsylvania Building, but not everyone felt represented. Mayor McKenna expressed his belief that "the state day will be celebrated on September 7, but none of the citizens of Pittsburg and Allegheny will take prominent parts, as Philadelphians are slated to furnish the entertainment."[65]

Rather than attempt to insert the region into the Pennsylvania Day ceremonies at the last minute, Mayor McKenna proposed a novel solution. "I think we should arrange for a western Pennsylvania day at the world's fair and hold it on Saturday, September 9, just two days later than Pennsylvania day. I think we can show that Pittsburg had as much to do with those buildings as any city in the country, and perhaps more. I think something can be done to demonstrate to the people of the world that Pittsburgh is more than a way station on the Pennsylvania railroad." Perhaps anticipating some resistance from state officials, McKenna also suggested that "if the state building could not be obtained, the celebration could be held on the Midway Plaisance, near the Ferris wheel, which was designed by a Pittsburger."[66]

THE TWIN CITY DAY IN CHICAGO.

Miss Chicago Will Welcome Her Eastern Sisters With the Most Profuse Hospitality to the Fair.

Fig. 13. This cartoon shows a woman representing the city of Chicago welcoming another woman, Pittsburgh, and her daughter, Allegheny City, to the Columbian Exposition fairgrounds in anticipation of the proposed Twin City Day. *Pittsburgh Press*, August 27, 1893.

The mayor's idea captured the imagination of Pittsburgh's select and common councils and, when approached for their support, their counterparts in Allegheny. Mayor McKenna formed a committee composed of councilmembers from both cities that worked to secure support and plan programming for what the press termed Twin City Day. He also sent a letter with his proposal to Pennsylvania Board of World's Fair Managers executive commissioner A. B. Farquhar, who agreed on August 25 to provide the State Building for the Twin City Day activities.[67] Mayor McKenna was sure that people would make the trip to participate in the celebration, confidently proclaiming, "The only trouble threatened now is that the building will not be large enough to accommodate the people from Allegheny county. However, if the celebration is the success it promises to be now, we will find a larger building, or hold an outdoor meeting." Programming would be difficult to arrange with only a few weeks to prepare, but groups like the Second Brigade band and Pittsburgh's Welsh choir volunteered to perform at no charge.[68]

With all the support and planning quickly falling into place, the last major factor necessary to ensure a successful event was facilitating the transportation of the people of Western Pennsylvania to the fair. The best means of aiding such a mass movement of citizens was the negotiation of low passenger rates for all the railroad companies that ran between Pittsburgh and Chicago. The Twin City Day committee met with sales agents from several lines, including the Pennsylvania and Baltimore & Ohio, and shared its belief that a reasonable round-trip rate would be eight to ten dollars. The railroad agents countered with proposed rates of ten dollars for coach tickets and thirteen for sleeper car access. They explained that they were reluctant to go any lower because those fares might encourage people to skip Pennsylvania Day and wait to visit the fair during Twin City Day, when the rates were cheaper. While their terms did not appear to be too far off from what the agents proposed, Pittsburgh committee member Kirk Q. Bigham opined, "Hundreds who cannot afford to spend a week in Chicago would go on Friday and return on Monday or Tuesday at an $8 fare, while they would rather remain at home than pay $10."[69] They had reached an impasse, and Western Pennsylvania's day at the exposition was in jeopardy.

Local newspapers reporting on the meeting cast the railroad men in an unfavorable light, depicting them as representatives of greedy corporations unwilling to negotiate. If Twin City Day did not come to fruition, the *Pittsburgh Post* proclaimed, "the residents of the two cities must thank the railroads for putting an end to their plan for booming their homes and enjoying themselves simultaneously." Mayor McKenna explained that the rate would not have been so objectionable if they anticipated that only men would attend, but with such an attraction as the Columbian Exposition they expected that the man's "wife wanted to go also, and she is the one who objects to taking $20 out of the family fund for bare transportation."[70]

The committee once again met with the railroad agents to negotiate passenger rates and after no progress had been made, the committee went into executive session. When the group reconvened they presented a resolution that stated: "It is the sense of this committee that unless a rate of $8 for day coaches and $12 with Pullman privileges can be obtained from the railroads that the project of celebrating Twin City day at Chicago be abandoned."[71] A copy of this resolution was given to each railroad representative in attendance to take back to his office for consideration. The day after the meeting, September I, Mayor McKenna and director of public works Edward Manning Bigelow met with railroad executives in a last-ditch effort to reach a deal and save the event. Bigelow had felt from the beginning that the committee should have started its negotiations with the railroad executives who had benefited from their relationship with the city councils—that is, the Republican political machine—and would have been more likely to agree to the lower rates. Those executives could then have advocated for the discounted tickets with their own agents.[72] Together, the actions of committee members from the two cities hint at the close business relationship railroads had with municipal governments in the I890s.

The next day's description of the pair's efforts was discouraging. The *Post* reported, "The mayor stated yesterday that the railroads showed no inclination to aid in the movement to have a Pittsburgh day, and in fact did not want one. One of the railroad men asked how many would possibly go on a lower rate and the mayor stated that they expected at least I0,000. The railroad man said: 'The roads could not handle them and we don't want them.'" Reflecting the idea that Pittsburgh was always being slighted, the article lamented, "The railroad managers and their usual policy of discrimination against this city have been again manifested in their refusal to make any reasonable concessions, and the mayor has declared the whole matter at an end." Responses to the failed Twin City Day proposal were mixed. Some citizens encouraged the mayor to strictly enforce city ordinances pertaining to railroads as a means of retaliation, while others tried to take a more optimistic approach. One councilman suggested that, should the proposal have succeeded, Western Pennsylvanians would have spent an estimated $200,000 to $300,000 during their travels, thus taking that amount away from the local economy.[73] Since the plan failed, that money would now remain in the area.

On September 5, Governor Robert E. Pattison passed through Pittsburgh on his way to Chicago for Pennsylvania Day with relatively little fanfare. Pittsburgh papers reported the September 7 Pennsylvania Day celebration at the exposition as a success, but there was no representation from the western side of the state during the program, just as Mayor McKenna had feared. In the wake of the aborted Twin City Day event, many area residents had to find local alternatives that could bring a bit of the fair to Pittsburgh for those who could not otherwise afford the trip to Chicago. Harry Davis's Eden Musée featured a miniature reproduction of the Columbian Exposition fairgrounds that included "all the buildings, the fountains, the villages, the Ferris wheel, the [Midway Plaisance] and, in fact, every sight of interest exactly as it is shown in

Chicago."[74] Acts that performed at the exposition, such as the German infantry band led by Edward Ruscheweyh, also stopped to play at Pittsburgh theaters on their way back to Europe.[75]

Another autumn attraction that upheld the intent of Twin City Day was the annual Western Pennsylvania Exposition. Beginning in 1889, the Western Pennsylvania Exposition Society presented forty days of exhibits, concerts, and amusements at its new building at the Point; however, with a global counterpart happening in Chicago at the same time as the regularly scheduled exposition, many did not expect the society to follow through with an event in 1893. Instead of canceling, though, they used the opportunity to experiment, deciding "not only to hold the exposition as usual but to secure greater attractions than ever before and at a heavier cost than that ever risked in Pittsburg amusement management."[76] Even when the financial panic struck that spring, organizers continued to plan their event. Anticipating that the recession would be a brief inconvenience, the *National Labor Tribune* commended the society's work, proclaiming, "This is the right thing to do; stringency will not last, as is evident from present indications, and the way to hustle it into the past is to do just as the Exposition management is doing."[77]

To justify the increased spending, the society echoed many of the same opportunities cited to entice Western Pennsylvanians to care about their involvement in the Columbian Exposition. Using the world's fair as the primary catalyst, the *Press* explained,

> The argument is that more people from other countries will visit the United
> States this year than usual, and that many of them will stop in Pittsburg long
> enough to look at what we have to show them in the way of immense industries
> and a live commercial community. Independently of this, it is believed that
> those Pittsburgers and residents of surrounding towns who go to Chicago will
> only have their appetites whetted for more exhibitions of a similar character,
> and that particularly they will desire to see what can be shown them in the
> way of exhibits of their own products.[78]

Furthermore, a local exposition would do for Pittsburgh what the Columbian Exposition had done for Chicago. The increased attention would highlight the fact that "Pittsburgh presents to-day in the wonderful history of our nation, a city first in industrial energy, in inventive genius, in love of learning, our array of statistics showing an advancement nowhere else equaled; and the establishment of its Exposition is a significant summing up of all the history of our city's past, and a splendid augury for its future."[79]

OUR COMPLIMENTS TO CHICAGO.

The Windy City May Have the Biggest Show This Year, but Pittsburg is Still Modestly in the Swim.

Fig. 14. This cartoon of an enormous globe-headed man representing the Columbian Exposition bowing to a woman holding the Western Pennsylvania Exposition building indicates that Pittsburghers' interest in the world's fair was about to give way to the local attraction. *Pittsburgh Press*, September 10, 1893.

As planning for the Western Pennsylvania Exposition continued, the society distributed promotional materials to surrounding towns. County fairs were drawing their usual numbers and so they believed that "the people of Allegheny, Washington and Butler counties who will attend the agricultural exhibits of fast trotting [Columbian Exposition] probably prefer to spend their money at home, or rather have a good time on an economical basis."[80] The society also handed out these materials within the fairgrounds of the world's fair. Books about the coming attraction boasted, "No organization of its kind in the country, outside of the World's Fair in Chicago, will compare with the Pittsburg Exposition of the season of 1893, or with the magnitude, variety and value of its attractions."[81] Western Pennsylvania Exposition manager J. H. Johnston also attempted to persuade people to come to his attraction at the Point by drawing on the public's knowledge of the Columbian Exposition, saying, "I can assure all visitors that the exhibits this season will surpass those to be seen at any exposition in the country, and will scarcely be excelled even at the world's fair. The latter, of course, is much larger in extent, but in proportion the Pittsburg exposition will compare favorably with that of Chicago."[82]

The Western Pennsylvania Exposition opened on September 6 to great fanfare. About ten thousand to twelve thousand people attended the festivities, which included a performance by Matilda Sissieretta Joyner Jones, an African American opera singer known as Black Patti, who had recently performed at the Columbian Exposition. Comparisons to the fair in Chicago came easy; there were exhibits of local industries and products, concerts, and the area newspapers maintained a ledger in which attendees could register and have their names published in the next day's edition. In addition to similarities, there were also criticisms and claims about how Pittsburgh's exposition actually eclipsed the world's fair. The *Press* reported that opening-night visitors "were satisfied to let Chicago have her lagoon as Pittsburg has three big rivers right at her doorsteps. They were not envious of the gondoliers or other tropical plumaged birds when the Nellie Hudson started out this afternoon to give short trips over rivers which do not smell as rank to heaven as those of Chicago."[83] Even Johnston joined the critics, remarking, "While we have not spent $23,000,000 on our exposition as they did in Chicago, we have been assured by many persons who have attended the world's fair that our own show, in the matter of exhibits, in many cases surpass those made in Chicago." When companies exhibited at both expositions, Johnston noted, "their displays at the Pittsburg exposition are immensely superior in novelty, value and attractiveness."[84]

By the time the Western Pennsylvania Exposition closed on October 21, it had proven that the gambles of the society had been worth the risk. Attendance was steady throughout the entire event and the exposition even made a small profit, but, despite earlier boastful predictions, many could not explain why. Johnston publicly wondered how his attraction could have been so successful, "taking into consideration the depression in commercial circles which exists at present throughout the country, together with the unparalleled attendance during the past few weeks at the [Columbian Exposition]."[85] Perhaps the world's fair did in fact influence Pittsburghers to attend their local, more accessible version of the fair; however, they would not have visited the Western Pennsylvania Exposition if there were nothing of note to see. The society's willingness to embrace the challenge to compete for attendees and make its exposition comparable to that in Chicago proved to be beneficial and would have a lasting effect on the event moving forward.

As Pittsburgh's exposition began to wind down in mid-October, Western Pennsylvanians began once again to look westward to Chicago as the end of the Columbian Exposition rapidly approached. On October 16 a *Press* editorial predicted that the closing day would provide a "demonstration that will outdo anything ever seen in this country in the way of a popular celebration."[86] The ceremonies were to rival those of the fair's dedication and opening days. Instead, an unforeseen tragedy turned the final day of the 1893 World's Fair into a solemn affair.

On the evening of October 28, Patrick Eugene Prendergast shot Chicago mayor Carter Harrison three times as revenge for his delusions of a political appointment going unfulfilled. Harrison's death extinguished the life of the exposition as well. Plans for the October 30 festivities celebrating the success of the fair were instead adapted into a day of mourning and remembrance for the mayor who had brought the world to Chicago. The speeches and cannon fire intended to commemorate the end of the great global gathering turned to a quiet ceremony with a few short remarks and resolutions honoring the fallen mayor. At sunset, officials lowered the American flag and the Columbian Exposition officially closed.[87]

The fair had been omnipresent, and even those who did not travel to Chicago or attend the concerts by performers from the world's fair that visited Pittsburgh still experienced the exposition in their own way. An editorial in the *Press* quipped, "I have thoroughly enjoyed the world's fair without the trouble, expense and fatigue of going there, and with some trifling inaccuracies . . . I could describe the whole show through the kindness of my friends."[88] The summer of 1893 was a cultural phenomenon and it seems few were able to completely avoid the fair. With the gates of the fairgrounds sealed to visitors, the wonders and lessons of the White City, Midway Plaisance, and the World's Congress Auxiliary began to spread throughout the country. In Pittsburgh, the city and its people were ready to benefit from their influence.

6

Bringing the Exposition Home

THE LEGACY of the World's Columbian Exposition began to take shape once the first visitors stepped onto the Chicago fairgrounds. Stories of the wondrous White City, with its neoclassical architecture and the marvels held within its buildings, began to spread throughout the country, enticing millions to make the journey and experience the phenomenon for themselves. Exhibitors and others who had participated in making the fair a success hoped their involvement would lead to personal prosperity as a result of advertising their products and inventions at the exposition. Meanwhile, Daniel Burnham and Frederick Law Olmsted, the White City's chief architect and landscape architect, respectively, could only begin to dream of how their vision of a planned city would influence the American urban landscape for generations to come. Other, unintended consequences of the fair were no less significant, as ideas springing from the meetings of the World's Congress Auxiliary and visitors' general exposure to the city of Chicago set the wheels of social change in motion. Together, these influences formed a bridge from Victorian to modern America, and perhaps nowhere else in the country embodied this transformation as completely as Pittsburgh, Pennsylvania.

Because Western Pennsylvania was already the epicenter of the coal and steel industries, these local companies were able to survive the financial Panic of 1893 and thus did not witness a profound commercial impact resulting from their lack of involvement at the world's fair. Instead, two burgeoning companies in different industries, Westinghouse Electric and Manufacturing Company and H. J. Heinz Company, had influential experiences at the fair that shaped the future of each for years to come. In the case of Westinghouse, the contract to provide electricity for the exposition may have saved the company altogether. As the panic claimed businesses all over the United States, fair officials prioritized cash payments to George Westinghouse above all others as a thank-you for saving the exposition $500,000.[1] Additionally, all twelve dynamos from the exposition lighting plant, as well as three additional dynamos of the same size, were sold for a total of $750,000 by the end of the year.[2] Together, this money was sent to Pittsburgh to pay the Westinghouse workmen, who, as it turned out, were already working on the company's next big endeavor.

For years, entrepreneurs had struggled to find a way to harness the power generated by Niagara Falls. In 1889, after several previous attempts to generate hydroelectricity had failed, a group of New York capitalists invested $2.63 million to form the Cataract Construction Company with the ultimate goal of selecting and implementing the best means to not only harness but also distribute that power.[3] Where previous enterprises had collapsed under the necessity to turn a quick profit in order to remain operational, Cataract had robust financial backing. And unlike earlier companies, this organization formed at the threshold of the war of the currents and a period of great advances in the field of electrical engineering. One of its first tasks was to survey the state of power generation and transmission, soliciting the opinions of several consultants, including Thomas Edison and George Westinghouse. The survey showed that the industry was in a state of constant flux. Luckily, the company could afford to wait and let new ideas be tested and demonstrated before selecting the best fit for its project at Niagara Falls.[4]

In 1892, Cataract was finally prepared to accept bids for the Niagara power plant. Even though Westinghouse was scrambling to complete his newly awarded contract to electrify the Columbian Exposition, he agreed to also submit plans for this project. While working on the bid, Westinghouse invited Cataract representatives to Pittsburgh in January 1893 to test newly designed rotary converters, which turned alternating current to direct current electricity, for its project. By March 1893 he had submitted his proposal for the Niagara plant, which included an alternating current two-phase system. General

Electric, perhaps wiser from its defeat for the world's fair contract and Nikola Tesla's previous demonstrations proving that alternating current could success-fully power motors for implementation at a power plant, abandoned its previous dedication to DC and proposed a three-phase AC system.[5]

Westinghouse once again seized upon the opportunity that presented itself; if he could successfully demonstrate the principles of his Niagara proposal at the Columbian Exposition, surely he would be awarded the contract. The univer-sal system Westinghouse implemented in Chicago confirmed that a centralized two-phase generator, through a system of transformers and rotary converters, could provide alternating and direct current electricity at various voltages and frequencies for lighting and power needs.[6] In addition to demonstrating a suc-cessful system, Westinghouse also proved that alternating current was now accepted by the public by implementing it on an international stage. Cataract sought a solution for the Niagara project that was not only technologically sound but also one that could match the impressiveness of the falls themselves. World's fairs, like Niagara Falls, were popular spectacles in the late nineteenth century and AC was one of the more notable attractions at the exposition, so the exposition made for an apt comparison.[7]

The Westinghouse system at the fair addressed all the issues facing the Cat-aract project, albeit at a much smaller scale. This display played an integral role in convincing those responsible that AC could be transmitted over long dis-tances, and was therefore the most practical current for the Niagara Falls proj-ect.[8] On May 6, just days after the successful debut of Westinghouse's lighting display at the opening of the world's fair, Cataract announced that they would use alternating current at the Niagara Falls power plant; however, rather than awarding the contract to any of the submitted bids, they hired engineer George Forbes to take the best parts of each proposal to make his own unique design. Forbes had been a part of the committee that reviewed the bids, and Westing-house was furious that his company had been deceived into dedicating hard work and developing new technology for a contract Cataract had no intention of awarding. This type of deception proved to not be an isolated incident.

In addition to the battle over the Niagara contract, Westinghouse and Gen-eral Electric were also entwined in a legal struggle in the Pittsburgh courts. On June 7, 1893, three Westinghouse employees; several top administrators of Gen-eral Electric; and the superintendent of the bureau of electricity in Pittsburgh, Morris W. Mead, were charged with conspiracy and larceny of blueprints from the Westinghouse Electric and Manufacturing Company. These blueprints showed the designs and specifications of some of Westinghouse's most prized new machinery. The trial began on September 4, with former Westinghouse draftsman Herbert F. Ashton testifying that he had been paid $160 a month to provide GE with drawings and information about various Westinghouse contracts. At the center of the allegations were blueprints of two projects—the Columbian Exposition and Niagara Falls systems. Ashton also confessed to providing, at the request of a General Electric superintendent, one of the stopper lamps created by Westinghouse to circumvent GE's patents.[9] After losing the contract to light the world's fair, General Electric was desperate to gain a competitive edge over Westinghouse. Since blueprints provide information about the finished product, they contained detailed specifications to be used by workmen to complete the project, so anyone familiar with the type of system shown in the drawings could glean valuable information from them.[10] These particular blueprints would have provided the data necessary to bring GE up to speed on any Westinghouse advancements.

The defense claimed that Ashton had approached General Electric stating that he could provide evidence that the Westinghouse stopper lamps infringed on GE patents, but that this was a setup to instigate the very conspiracy trial in which they were currently engaged. With a conspiracy suit in the courts, litigation pertaining to the patents was put aside by GE lawyers, allowing the stopper lamps to continue burning brightly with Westinghouse-supplied electricity on the fairgrounds of the Columbian Exposition. To prove its point, the defense sought to discredit Ashton by introducing a parade of character witnesses from around Allegheny County, all testifying that he was not a truthful person. A second round of character witnesses from Connecticut, where GE was headquartered, attested to the upstanding character of the several General Electric officials implicated in the suit.[11] The jury eventually deadlocked, with the allegations against both companies being equally terrible and plausible. Even though both companies were publicly shamed during the trial, General Electric and Westinghouse were still the two largest, most capable electrical companies in the country and neither suffered from the publicity of the suit.

In August, just before the conspiracy trial in Pittsburgh began, Cataract contacted General Electric and Westinghouse for bids to build Forbes's proposed dynamos and transformers. While J. P. Morgan backed both Cataract and General Electric, he chose not to exercise his influence to award the contract to his firm. For investors during the Panic of 1893 the Niagara Falls project was too risky a venture for GE because Westinghouse held all of Tesla's relevant AC patents at the time. As a keen businessman, Morgan also did not want to risk the success of the proposed power plant by awarding the contract to GE, a company that was just entering the realm of alternating current. In the long term, a future acquisition of Westinghouse Electric by GE would have been a sounder investment.[12] George Westinghouse, however, was still enraged that Cataract and Forbes had tricked his company into providing the initial designs for the project, but in October, just days before the close of the Columbian Exposition, he agreed to accept the job in order to provide steady work for his men during the financial panic.[13] He did, however, stipulate he would not work directly with Forbes, who had proven to be an industry rival.

The Niagara contract was for the development of three generators, each five times larger than those built for the Columbian Exposition, but Westinghouse engineers were forced to correct or compromise on several of the specifications provided by Forbes. For example, rotary converters did not work well at the previous standard of 60 hertz, so Westinghouse had established a 33½-hertz standard for his converters. The plant's first primary customer, the Pittsburgh Reduction Company, required vast amounts of direct current electricity to reduce aluminum ore, but Forbes had proposed that his converter operate at 16⅔ hertz, which Westinghouse considered too low to be effective. Eventually, Westinghouse settled on 25 hertz for its Niagara converters, which went on to serve as the standard for transmission at the falls until 2006.[14] The first generator was tested in April 1895 and in autumn hydroelectric power from Niagara Falls was sold and distributed.[15] Westinghouse's gamble had paid off; the Columbian Exposition system was a practical example of his work and had validated alternating current as the best means of transmitting electricity, thus securing him the contract to develop the machines that would harness the power of Niagara Falls. A successful implementation at the falls would garner Westinghouse enough work to keep the company on steady footing for the foreseeable future.

With the opening of the first generator, the Pittsburgh Reduction Company was able to greatly expand on the products it exhibited at the Columbian Exposition as well. While the company was an early adopter of the new power source, the ability to implement mass quantities of hydroelectricity marked the start of a new era that used electric furnaces. As a result of its proximity to Niagara Falls, the area became the focal point of the American aluminum industry.[16]

The Westinghouse system also proved to meet Cataract's criteria that the project reach the same majestic benchmark set by the falls themselves. Encased in a building designed by the architectural firm McKim, Mead and White, which had also designed the Agricultural Building at the Columbian Exposition, the plant set the standard for electrical power generation and distribution technologies for decades. When Andrew Carnegie visited Niagara in 1895 he described the power plant, not the falls, as "sublime."[17] Pittsburgh's status as a locus of technological innovation, particularly in the field of electricity, had been secured thanks to two very public demonstrations of Westinghouse ingenuity—the 1893 World's Fair and the Niagara Falls power system.

The experience of H. J. Heinz at the Columbian Exposition garnered very different, but no less meaningful, results. Since the 1876 Centennial Exposition, Heinz had traveled the world showcasing his products and winning awards. These displays hinted at his penchant for advertising, and the pickle charm coupon scheme at the 1893 World's Fair saved not only his exhibit but all of those on the second floor of the Agricultural Building. As a result, Heinz realized his full potential as a marketer. This became an immediate necessity as the Panic of 1893 wore on and the resulting demand for his products carried the company through the worst of the recession.[18] The Heinz Company grew during the depression of the 1890s because it dominated high-end condiments and ventured into low-end staples like canned baked beans, soups, and dill pickles, while also cutting costs through the automation of canning. As a result of this strategy and the fair, the Heinz Company had its best sales year up to that time in 1893. The following year profits shrank only slightly before surpassing the 1893 sales numbers in 1895 and exploding to nearly $2.5 million in 1896 ($82.5 million in 2022).[19]

In addition to the pickle charm, the Chicago fairgrounds also planted the seed for another great Heinz advertising venture, which came to fruition in 1898. After witnessing millions of people traveling to the Midwest to view exhibits of art and artifacts, as well as sample products, Heinz noticed that similar crowds flocked to Atlantic City to spend their leisure time at the New Jersey beaches. He realized he could erect an attraction where people already were, rather than building one from the ground up in the hopes that visitors would find him, and so Heinz purchased the Iron Pier for sixty thousand dollars as the site for his next great exhibit. Extending nine hundred feet into the Atlantic Ocean, the Heinz Ocean Pier, as it came to be called, was an expanded and permanent version of his Columbian Exposition display. Inside the building were hundreds of artifacts, artworks, and curios, some of which had been on exhibit at the 1893 World's Fair. Additionally, lectures and musical concerts were frequent features. Also on display were hundreds of awards Heinz had won at various fairs and expositions—and, of course, arrangements and samples of Heinz products. Admission to the attraction, and the ubiquitous pickle charm, were free to visitors.[20] The Ocean Pier remained a popular attraction in Atlantic City until a September 1944 hurricane destroyed the building.

Fig. 15. Open from 1898 to 1944, the Heinz Ocean Pier in Atlantic City reflected the
architectural style of the White City. Inside, Heinz displayed art, curios, and
awards, much like his many fair exhibits. H. J. Heinz Company Photographs, MSP
57, Detre Library and Archives, Senator John Heinz History Center.

Heinz's advertising acumen manifested in several other initiatives stemming
from the exposition. For example, inspired by the exhibit of the Pope Manufacturing Company, which had previously made its name in bicycles before branching out into vehicles, he purchased an electric-powered delivery wagon in 1899.
Since so few were in operation at the time, Heinz wanted the wagon more for its

novelty than for actual delivery purposes, but it also foreshadowed the importance of motor vehicles to product delivery in the coming decades.[21] Similarly,
by the turn of the century, Heinz billboards and other advertisements were a
common sight throughout the country and any short railroad trip would result
in an encounter with at least one Heinz sign.[22] As part of his signage initiative,
in 1900 Heinz debuted a large electric sign in New York City's Flatiron District
advertising some of its famous fifty-seven varieties. Perhaps influenced by the
large electrical displays at the fair, the Heinz advertisement used 1,200 lightbulbs to outline the sign's words and an image of the iconic Heinz pickle.

With the 1906 publication of Upton Sinclair's *The Jungle*, sanitation and
health concerns surrounding food processing became a national issue. Because
he kept a meticulously clean factory, Heinz welcomed visitors into his buildings
to witness for themselves how his products were prepared and packaged. Much
like the clear glass bottles used to store his products, tours of the factory turned
every aspect of food processing into a transparent exhibit advertising the clean-
liness and purity of Heinz products.[23] Extending this further, Heinz used his
connections to the Western Pennsylvania Exposition to coordinate tours for visitors, thus using his factory as an enormous permanent display. No doubt his
vast exposition experience and fondness for advertising made him a valuable
resource for Western Pennsylvania Exposition planning and promotion in the
early twentieth century. Heinz's interest and success in promoting exhibitions
also led to his role as the second vice-president of Pittsburgh's sesquicentennial
celebration in 1908 and as a delegate to San Francisco's 1915 Panama-Pacific
Exposition.[24]

Where Heinz's exposition experience led to a more robust administrative role in
local exhibitions, the contribution of another Pittsburgher, George Washington
Gale Ferris Jr., revolutionized entertainment around the globe. In addition to
the nearly 1.5 million tickets sold for a ride at the fair, the very idea and image
of the great wheel and its creator also proved to be a marketable commodity.
The Pittsburgh engineer made thousands of dollars selling authorized souvenirs
about or depicting himself and the wheel, including photographs, medals, book-
lets, and a multitude of other trinkets and tchotchkes.[25] For the summer of 1893,
Ferris had become an international celebrity.

After its successful run during the exposition, Ferris intended to operate the
wheel for the remainder of 1893; however, the fair authorities closed the Midway to visitors in mid-November. Having been under the impression that they

had leased the Jackson Park site until the end of the year, the Ferris Wheel Company sued the exposition for lost revenue.[26] During the ultimately unsuccessful suit the wheel stood dormant in the bracing winds and snow of a Chicago winter. Beginning on April 29, 1894, the wheel was dismantled, and Ferris sought a new home for his invention. Interest from sites in New York City, Atlantic City, London, and other locales came and went without much progress. Meanwhile, by June 23, the wheel had been completely packed onto train cars and stored in a siding of the Illinois Central Railroad near the old fairgrounds on 61st Street in Chicago's Woodlawn neighborhood. The wheel spent the next winter in hiding until Ferris arranged for it to be rebuilt as the main attraction for a site on North Clark Street near Chicago's Lincoln Park.[27]

The new location did not last long. From the outset, residents opposed the placement of the wheel. By the time it was operational, the lingering financial depression, fading novelty of the wheel, and the lack of a concentrated crowd of visitors all led to limited financial success. By 1896 the company went bankrupt.[28] Struggling to preserve both his company and his wheel, the overworked Ferris became ill and was admitted to Pittsburgh's Mercy Hospital in November 1896. He died on November 22, likely of typhoid fever. Ferris having separated from his wife prior to his death, his ashes remained unclaimed at a Pittsburgh crematorium for over a year before his brother finally paid the funeral expenses.[29]

In 1903, the Chicago House Wrecking Company, the same firm that was hired to dismantle structures on the Columbian Exposition grounds, purchased Ferris's wheel. They disassembled the attraction during the winter and shipped the pieces to St. Louis, where it was rebuilt as a feature of the 1904 Louisiana Purchase Exposition.[30] After another successful world's fair run, the Chicago House Wrecking Company returned to St. Louis to salvage the site. On May 11, 1906, two hundred pounds of dynamite was used to implode the original Ferris wheel, reducing the steel structure to a pile of debris more than thirty feet high.[31] Pieces of the attraction were sold and distributed around the country to be repurposed, and at least one part was reported to have returned to Western Pennsylvania. William Nagel, operating vice-president of the United Engineering and Foundry Company, claimed that one of the Ferris wheel's engines was eventually sold to Crucible Steel in 1927 to drive its Park Works thirty-five-inch blooming mill in Pittsburgh.[32]

Although other world's fairs had been held in the nineteenth century, the Columbian Exposition was the first to have an area specifically for amusement. The Ferris wheel was at the heart of the Midway Plaisance and so it, like the

Eiffel Tower before it, became the enduring symbol of the fair and its revolutionary shift in priorities. It is not surprising, then, that smaller replicas of
the wheel began to appear throughout the country. Traditionally, county and
state fairs displayed locally and nationally produced commercial goods, but they
also served as a center for recreation that often included amusements typically
only available in cities. After the exposition, popular entertainment and rides
like the Ferris wheel were incorporated into the festivities. So every local fair
would not need to invest in building its own wheel, portable Ferris wheels were
designed to be assembled and disassembled at locations across the nation. The
Columbian Exposition proved that an amusement-centric attraction was a viable business and served as a forerunner to the coming century's mass-consumer
culture. Ferris wheels became an omnipresent symbol of the shifting tastes
of popular culture and were often a featured attraction at traveling carnivals
that provided rural Americans with access to the mechanized rides available in
urban amusement parks.[33]

The directors of the Western Pennsylvania Exposition were also keenly
aware of the impact the Midway had on the world's fair. In comparing the local
exposition to Chicago's, the *Pittsburgh Press* remarked, "It was perhaps doubt-
ful whether the [exposition] society would ever make a great money success of
the exposition until it made a more prominent feature of the pure and simple
amusement of the public. An argument in support of this proposition is found in
the report of the immense earnings of the Midway Pleasance [*sic*]." It went on to
note, "While the visitors to the world's fair examined and admired the exhibits
of the [Columbian Exposition] proper . . . they would feel that they had not seen
the fair at all had they neglected to take a ride in the Ferris wheel."[34]

The *Press* also suggested, "If the Pittsburg Exposition society were to engage
attractions of this kind they could get them cheaply on account of the advertising they would enjoy from the Pittsburg exposition, while the exposition would
reap the benefit of their presence in the increased amusement that would be
afforded to visitors and the consequently larger attendance."[35] This strategy
was accepted by the exposition society, and rides including a merry-go-round
were built at the Point near its buildings. Beginning in 1895 there were two
side-by-side switchback railways at the exposition, later renamed the Gravity
Railway. This railway remained until 1900 and was replaced by a figure-eight
rollercoaster that operated at the exposition from 1901 to 1916.

The wheel also had a broader societal impact. The increasing amount of
leisure time available to the middle class gradually resulted in a shift in popular sentiment toward a favorable view of a recreational Sabbath, and so the

Fig. 16. The buildings of the Western Pennsylvania Exposition were located on the
Pittsburgh side of the Allegheny River. Eventually organizers would add a roller-
coaster next to the main building close to the city's Point. John Gates Photograph
Collection, AIS.1991.22, Archives and Special Collections, University of Pittsburgh
Library System.

Columbian Exposition opened during a period of changing attitudes regarding
Sunday amusements. Initially it was believed that by opening the exposition on
Sunday, the fair would have a chance to enlighten and educate those who would
not otherwise have access, in addition to those who were privileged enough to
attend on any day they chose. The fair attempted to physically separate the educational exhibits of the White City from the undignified, entertainment driven
Midway Plaisance; however, throngs of visitors from every class visited the less-
reputable attractions of the Midway, confirming that all types of people valued
experiential amusements. At the epicenter of those experiences, ushering in the
era of commercialized leisure, was Ferris's great wheel.

The success of the Ferris wheel in Chicago tapped into a suppressed desire to
have fun for fun's sake. For many Americans, this type of experience could occur
only on Sunday, when they were not required to work. The increasing interest in commercial leisure activities, which often emphasized experiences that
brought participants to the brink of their base emotions, threatened both traditional Sunday worship and the values embodied in the Christian Sabbath. This
placed the world's fair at a crossroads in which it both celebrated Victorian
values and aided in their erosion by promoting popular entertainment culture.[36]
The earlier adoption of the bicycle by families as a popular recreational activity

provided them with a sense of independence to determine their own Sunday leisure plans; therefore, as Karl E. Johnston claims, "the bicycle wheel and the Ferris Wheel brought to a climax in the 1890s the amusement revolution that got its start in the 1840s, not only by changing the way people spent their new-found leisure time, but also by affirming the pursuit of pleasure independent of moral or religious ends."[37]

By demonstrating that not every aspect of a person's Sunday activities needed to be dedicated solely to religious pursuits, the Ferris wheel and other forms of commercial recreation bridged the gap between Victorian and modern culture and played a role in developing the leisurely weekend. This cultural shift contributed to the popularity of trolley parks, which quickly evolved into permanent manifestations of fair midways. These amusement parks provided early twentieth-century visitors with experiences that connected them to technological advancements of the day. Given the early twentieth-century fascination with extremes, whether it was size, speed, or technology, attractions that offered riders an experience in going fast or reaching great heights—like the Ferris wheel and rollercoasters—became the quality by which amusement parks and carnivals were evaluated.[38]

In southwestern Pennsylvania, the premier trolley park was Kennywood, which first opened in 1899 with athletic fields, a dance hall, bowling alley, and a carousel. During its first few years of operation, Kennywood added a Ferris wheel, figure-eight rollercoaster, and a cafeteria. In 1903 the park was leased to the Pittsburgh Steeplechase and Amusement Company, which completed the transition of Kennywood from a traditional trolley park to one that more closely mimicked the attractions and atmosphere of exposition midways. Frederick Ingersoll, who had managed several of the rides at Kennywood before it was taken over by Pittsburgh Steeplechase, took note of the park's success once it became a full-blown exposition park, and he looked for an opportunity closer to the city of Pittsburgh to replicate its accomplishments.[39]

Ferris did not set out to change cultural norms with his great wheel, but several influences and initiatives stemming from the Columbian Exposition were made with the aim to alter society. In addition to the fairgrounds serving as an exhibit of scientific and commercial advancement, it was also a marketplace. Souvenirs and purchases at the fair were another way in which members of Pittsburgh's growing middle class could assert their position within the local social hierarchy. Capitalizing on the concentration of wealth descending on

Chicago during 1893, exhibitors and consumers alike were well aware of the significance material goods had on delineating social status. With an expanding middle class eager to mark its place in society, companies at the Chicago fair offered a variety of goods appealing to their needs.[40] The rapid development of middle- and upper-class suburbs in Pittsburgh's East End provided hundreds of new homes that required furnishing with the most impressive items from all over the world, many of which were on display and for sale at the exposition. For example, during their visits to the fair, Judge Christopher Magee and his wife, Elizabeth, purchased a porcelain vase from Chicago's Pitkin and Brooks, a teapot from the Central Association of Japan, Royal Saxon Porcelain Factory tableware imported by New York's Gilman Collamore and Company, and coffee spoons from jeweler Peter Hertz of Copenhagen.[41] The fact that many of these goods were handcrafted items distinguished them from the mechanically produced goods that were becoming ubiquitous in the everyday lives of most Americans, and by association, distinguished their owners as well.

In addition to fair influences that reinforced their social status, the middle class also incorporated lessons that allowed them to shape the urban environment by assisting immigrants and the working class. While visiting Chicago, civic-minded visitors may have encountered Jane Addams or her social settlement project, Hull House. Founded by Addams in 1889, Hull House was one of America's first attempts at creating a settlement house. Based on Toynbee Hall in London, which was begun in 1884 by graduates and teachers from Cambridge and Oxford, settlement houses aimed to provide a place in which members of poor and immigrant communities could thrive. Reflecting the ideas of social Darwinism, which had gained widespread interest by the 1880s, these houses were situated in slum areas and operated by resident workers who planned community activities. These residents would provide an environment that offered guided leisure activities for the working class, introducing them to middle-class values and culture through interaction with reformers.[42] By improving the neighborhood living conditions and offering middle-class ideals of education and leisure, the settlement house sought to better the people residing therein.

While there were certainly philanthropic activities aimed at these communities prior to 1893, Pittsburgh did not have a proper settlement house project until after the close of the Columbian Exposition. At the fair, Addams had participated in several of the world's congresses and was the driving force in organizing the Congress on Social Settlements, which took place from July 19 to 21. In addition to talks concerning the general settlement movement in relation to municipal reform, the arts, labor, and charitable institutions, the achievements and physical space of Hull House were also on display.[43] To Pittsburghers observing the influx of immigrants into their city's older residential areas near the Central Business District, the accomplishments of Addams's Hull House in Chicago seemed to be exactly what the residents of those blighted neighbor, hoods needed.

Two such men, Reverend George Hodges, rector of Shadyside's Calvary Epis, copal Church, and H. D. W. English, a Calvary parishioner and member of the Pittsburgh Chamber of Commerce, founded the first settlement house in Pitts, burgh. In a letter published in *The Meaning of Social Settlement*, Reverend Hodges credited Robert A. Woods's book *English Social Movements* with piqu, ing his interest in the settlement movement; however, given the timing of his idea and the economic status of Calvary's parishioners, it is likely many had vis, ited Chicago to see the Columbian Exposition and several had been acquainted with Addams, or at the very least been made aware of her work at Hull House.[44] The Kingsley Association formed at a meeting on September 21, 1893, and on Christmas Day the Kingsley House, located at 1707 Penn Avenue in Pittsburgh's Strip District, first opened its doors with programming for the neighborhood children.[45] Kate Everest, of the University of Wisconsin, was hired to lead the initiatives at the house, and Amanda Johnson, from Hull House, was placed in charge of the department of work.[46] Serving Irish, Polish, Jewish, and German immigrants as well as American-born families, Kingsley House provided the community with concerts and lectures, including Breeding Speer's 1894 talk on the world's fair, to begin the process of betterment.[47]

By the early twentieth century, the efforts of the Kingsley Association were two-pronged. The Kingsley House continued to concentrate on instill, ing middle-class American ideals in the community children; however, it also took the initiative to confront issues like housing and sanitation, which, if left unaddressed, could interfere with the success of its efforts.[48] Much of this work, both within and outside the house, was conducted by women who were sud, denly thrust into leadership roles concerning civic activism. After becoming acquainted with the living conditions most working-class immigrants endured, women refocused some of the energy they had exerted in aiding families toward revitalizing the city itself, treating it as another entity that required saving.[49] Along with other organizations like the Civic Club of Allegheny County, the Kingsley Association became a driving force of Progressive Era reform in indus, trial Pittsburgh.

While the impetus for the formation of the Kingsley Association is complex, another Pittsburgh settlement house can trace its origin directly to the activities of the Columbian Exposition. Pauline Hanauer Rosenberg, of Allegheny, was Western Pennsylvania's only representative at the Jewish Women's Congress in September 1893. In addition to attending the lectures and meetings, she also delivered an address on how the discovery of America by Europeans affected the Jewish people. On the last day of the congress, a business meeting was called to create a permanent organization for Jewish women based on the success of the congress. Rosenberg proposed that the new group should be called the Columbian Union in honor of the exposition; however, this name was voted down in favor of the National Council of Jewish Women (NCJW).[50] The new organization would be led by a national president and each represented state would elect a vice-president. Rosenberg was selected to serve as the first vice-president for Pennsylvania.[51]

When she returned home, Rosenberg took to organizing a Pittsburgh-area section of the NCJW. On May 2, 1894, she convened a group of local Jewish women to discuss the new organization and the crowd was receptive to her cause. While it was the fourth NCJW section to be founded, it was the only one to adopt Rosenberg's preferred name, the Columbian Council, as a nod to the world's fair where the group formed.[52] They elected Rosenberg as section president and Cassie Weil vice-president. Pittsburgh's Jewish community had always conducted charitable work in response to a specific need; however, the Columbian Council was different. Rather than addressing needs or deficiencies through an ad hoc approach, this group sought to teach immigrants and members of the lower class general skills that would allow them to improve their own lives. In many cases, this training was meant to Americanize immigrants by teaching them English and imparting knowledge that would help them succeed in established society.[53] At the council's first meeting, Rabbi Lippmann Mayer presented a means of accomplishing these lessons by proposing that they form a religious school.

The school opened in January 1896 and on March 20, the council changed the name to the Columbian School. Weil was a great supporter of the school and, likely due to her friendship with Addams and knowledge of her work at Hull House, she brought many settlement movement techniques and activities to Pittsburgh.[54] The school, located at 32 Townshend Street in the Hill District, had many of the same attributes as the Kingsley House, providing classes, lectures, and clubs for the local community. In contrast to Kingsley's multiethnic, religiously diverse neighborhood, though, Columbian School programs were targeted specifically to the expanding Jewish community. As a result, the school was the first attempt to connect the established middle-class central European

Jews with the new, poorer immigrant eastern European Jews, thus helping to establish a more unified Jewish community as Pittsburgh entered the twentieth century.[55]

The school grew quickly under Weil's leadership while Rosenberg focused on her service to the national organization, ultimately becoming president of the NCJW in 1905. In 1899 the Columbian School and Settlement introduced free year-round night classes for adults, which eventually led to similar publicly sponsored courses. As a testament to the school's success, former students would often return to lead some of its clubs and programs. Because of this achievement, the Columbian School outgrew its facilities and so its supporters sought out funding for a new building from a member of one of the Pittsburgh Jewish community's most successful families—Henry Kaufmann. Seeking aid, Weil's husband, A. Leo Weil, and Rodef Shalom rabbi J. Leonard Levy approached Kaufmann about a donation. Henry and his wife, Theresa Kaufmann, decided to give $150,000 to build and endow a new building in honor of their daughter, who died in July 1907. As a result of their contribution the Irene Kaufmann Settlement was formed.[56]

The addition of financial stability to the efforts of the Columbian School and Settlement also led to a change in its leadership. In June 1909, just months after the Kaufmanns announced their gift, Cassie Weil resigned her position as the first president of the school. As historian Ida Cohen Selavan noted, "During all the years when financial support was uncertain and the women had balanced their budget with cake sales and 'begging,' her leadership had been unchallenged. With the arrival of large sums of money and the promise of more, the Board seemed to feel the need for male leadership of the Settlement. Mr. Nathaniel Spear was elected, the first in an unbroken chain of male presidents."[57] The new building was constructed at 1835 Centre Avenue in the Hill District, where it remained until 1964 when it was sold to Hill House.[58]

The Kingsley and Columbian Houses influenced other Pittsburgh-area settlements and together these institutions sought to introduce middle-class ideals to lower-class, often immigrant, communities. As the region reached its peak in immigrant population, their efforts to Americanize these new workers and their children likely provided a common ground and eased tensions among various ethnic communities, but often at the expense of certain aspects of their Old World heritage and almost never crossing the racial divide. Initiatives like the ones organized by settlement houses were further supported by the findings of the Pittsburgh Survey. In 1907 and 1908, a group of researchers sponsored by the Russell Sage Foundation descended on Pittsburgh and the nearby mill town of Homestead to document living and working conditions, the workforce, and the impact of industry on the urban environment. The narrative and statistics compiled for the comprehensive study were punctuated by photographs of workers and their families by Lewis Hine.[59] The published findings chronicled the lives and tribulations of an industrial working class that was ubiquitous in cities across the United States and moved the region into an era of environmental and housing reform that sought to make Pittsburgh a more livable city and continues to affect the region over a century later.

In the wake of the success of the Woman's Building at the Columbian Exposition, well-to-do women in Pittsburgh also sought to continue the cultural and philanthropic activities promoted at the fair. In May 1894 the Twentieth Century Club was founded by Julia Morgan Harding to support the intellectual activities of local women. The club hosted artists and lectures on science, literature, current events, and other topics, entertaining such noted guests as Addams and Booker T. Washington, both speakers at the 1893 World's Fair, and Woodrow Wilson before his career as a politician. Additionally, the Twentieth Century Club supported the work of the Civic Club of Allegheny County and the development of playgrounds in the city. Like the work of the Board of Lady Managers in Chicago, the success of the club in Pittsburgh spawned other women's clubs in the area, continuing the fair's legacy of women's advancement.[60] Taken together, it became clear the women of Western Pennsylvania had benefited greatly from the experience of the 1893 World's Fair.

If the Columbian Exposition and Chicago had a subtle, albeit significant, influence over Pittsburgh's social movements, the fair had a much more apparent effect on the city's built environment. In cities throughout the country, one of the most visible results of the exposition was the evolution of popular tastes toward the neoclassical architecture of Burnham's White City. There has been much interpretation of the use of classical architecture, in which it is particularly noted that the exposition buildings reflected the rise of the United States as a successor to the Roman Empire, but there are also several practical reasons for the selection of this building type. For one, similar architecture was used at the 1889 Paris Universal Exhibition, which had become the benchmark for the 1893 fair. The style was also familiar to the exposition architects, many of whom had studied at the École des Beaux-Arts in Paris. Because the stylistic principles were well known, it was easy to transmit well-understood directions from the architects' offices outside of Chicago to Burnham in the fairgrounds.[61]

Furthermore, the use of this building type for exhibitions was logical because it was "spacious, easier to build, and more effectively illuminated through their vaulted skylights."[62] With an eye toward meeting an impossible opening day deadline and with many important infrastructure decisions still in flux, classical architecture was the only choice that could meet the demands of the fair.

The use of the Beaux Arts style for the buildings may not have been remarkable in and of itself, but the cohesion of the Court of Honor buildings, with a standard cornice line and uniform use of white paint (with the exception of the Transportation Building's polychrome Golden Door), resulted in a temporary city that was greater than the sum of its parts. Hinting at his skill as a city planner, Burnham believed the White City's legacy would be as an example in planning and order, and not in promoting a resurgence in classical styles.[63] The plan was a great success, immediately appealing to the millions of fairgoers; however, because classical architecture was used as a means of demonstrating this order, that style was etched into their minds as the embodiment of everything the Columbian Exposition represented. As a result, Beaux Arts–inspired architecture became the style of choice for grand American buildings like banks and government institutions, but it also crept into private homes and clubhouses.[64]

While the White City gave an illusion of permanence, all the buildings were temporary and faced with a type of plaster called staff, not the white marble they were meant to represent. The challenge of incorporating the Beaux Arts style in buildings throughout the country, then, was the affordability of building materials for such extravagant lasting projects.[65] This transition from buildings faced in faux marble to those of actual stone embodied the country's transformation from the Gilded Age, in which society's most impressive elements were not all they appeared to be, to the Progressive Era, where both capitalism and social reform thrived to form a more ideal urban environment. Western Pennsylvania, with its prosperous iron and steel industry and commercial importance, had become a region of wealthy industrialists and financial institutions eager to build. The political machine of Christopher Lyman Magee and William Flinn, which was connected to many of these companies, actively encouraged building projects in Pittsburgh to garner political support and provide revenue for their interests, ensuring that the area would receive several contributions reflecting the latest architectural trends at the conclusion of the fair.

One example of this strategy connected a name associated with Pittsburgh's contributions to the fair with the name most synonymous with the Columbian Exposition. In 1898, Henry Clay Frick hired Daniel Burnham to design the simple Beaux Arts–styled Union Trust Company building on Fourth Avenue in the Golden Triangle. With four tall columns holding a large pediment, the building was a scaled-down version of the Bank of Pittsburgh, which had been designed two years earlier by another Columbian Exposition architect, George B. Post. These downtown buildings, obviously inspired by ancient Greek temples, reflected the godlike status of finance to turn-of-the-century Pittsburgh. In Allegheny, the new post office designed by William Aiken in the years immediately after the fair included an arched entrance, a large dome, and other elements reminiscent of the Chicago fair's Administration Building by Richard Morris Hunt.

In addition to the influence of the exposition's buildings, Chicago as a city was at the forefront of another architectural trend that would soon sweep the nation. Despite its swampy, unstable location, the Windy City had pioneered the erection of tall office buildings and by 1893 several were on display for visitors to the fair. Apart from Pittsburgh's first tall building, the Carnegie Building, which opened the same year as the exposition, many Western Pennsylvanians had not witnessed such towering structures in person; however, visits to the World's Fair meant traveling to downtown Chicago railroad stations or hotels. After the exposition, several skyscrapers began to rise above the Golden Triangle, likely due to a mixture of Pittsburghers' exposure to similar structures in Chicago and the necessity to expand the capacity of a growing white-collar workforce within the limited geography of the Central Business District. Eventually, the promotion of downtown's tall buildings to tourists visiting Pittsburgh shifted interest in local industries away from the dirty mills and factories where the products were made and toward the more refined elements of the business, much like the trend of visitors seeking out parks and other attractions away from working-class neighborhoods.[66]

Early designs for skyscrapers were varied, but by the early 1890s architects had looked to the classical style, perhaps inspired by the buildings of the White City, to reconceptualize their projects. By treating the tall building like a well-known classical architectural element, the Greek column, they could create three distinct areas of a skyscraper, each with its own design and purpose. As explained by Pittsburgh architectural historian Walter Kidney, "The base would ordinarily be shops, banking rooms, restaurants, spaces that the public would visit in large numbers and that were often two levels. . . . The shaft would contain most of the office spaces. . . . The capital would be a decorated terminal feature, speaking for the building as a whole, announcing it on the skyline, and would include the last few office stories, any service spaces at the top, and a climactic cornice."[67] This building layout is typical of the Pittsburgh

Fig. 17. This 1912 view shows downtown Pittsburgh's expansion upward with skyscrapers such as the Oliver Building, Arrott Building, and People's Savings Bank, among others. Pittsburgh City Photographer Collection, AIS.1971.05, Archives and Special Collections, University of Pittsburgh Library System.

skyscrapers built after the fair, as were the light-colored exteriors made famous at the exposition. White and cream-colored terra cotta, which could be molded into standard or ornamental pieces, were popular in the early twentieth century, even though Pittsburgh's infamous air pollution would quickly discolor the pristine facades.[68]

Some of the best examples of early skyscrapers in Pittsburgh were designed by Daniel Burnham. Between 1898 and 1912, Burnham erected more than fifteen buildings in Western Pennsylvania, with coke and steel tycoon Henry Clay Frick as his most frequent benefactor. As previously mentioned, Frick, who had visited the Columbian Exposition on several occasions and was familiar with his work, hired Burnham for the architect's first Pittsburgh commission in 1898 to design the Union Trust Building. Burnham returned in 1902 to build several skyscrapers, including the Frick Building, its annex in 1905, and his last Frick project, East Liberty's Highland Building, in 1910.[69] While Frick was a demanding client, Burnham could appreciate his artistic eye. Taking advantage of his interest in the arts, Burnham convinced Frick to contribute $100,000 to the American Academy of Fine Arts in Rome, which was founded by a group of architects and artists associated with the Columbian Exposition so they could study art in the surroundings of classical masterpieces.[70] In addition to his Frick projects, Burnham also designed several skyscrapers for another steel baron,

Henry Oliver, a building for the Western Pennsylvania Exposition Society in 1901, and Union Station in 1902 for Pennsylvania Railroad president Alexander Cassatt, brother of artist Mary Cassatt.

Other notable architects of this era also built skyscrapers downtown, many of which have stood for over a century. Post's fifteen-story Park Building, erected in 1896, incorporated elements of the Beaux Arts style, including several Atlas-like figures called telamones that lift the cornice above the rest of the tower. Pittsburgh architect Frederick Osterling contributed several skyscrapers to the city, such as the 1902 Arrott Building, which included columns and an intricate cornice with snarling faces. Benno Janssen, another architect who was most active in Pittsburgh, designed the Buhl Building in 1913. This skyscraper featured white terra cotta tiles elaborately decorated in blue Renaissance patterns.[71] These buildings and others, influenced by classical styles and Chicago's rising skyline, shaped the character of the Central Business District as residential life began to fade away from the Golden Triangle entirely.

In addition to the buildings of the exposition and Chicago influencing those of Pittsburgh, the landscaping of the fairgrounds also played a crucial role in developing the urban environment in Western Pennsylvania. Frederick Law Olmsted, already an accomplished landscape architect, complemented the grand Beaux Arts exhibit halls with meticulously arranged plants, walkways, and a central lagoon. Stressing the necessity of intermingling urban and rural areas to create an ideal city, the White City served as the first widely accessible and publicized example of the principles that would become the City Beautiful movement. Inspired by their experiences at the fair, the middle class in Pittsburgh and many other cities engaged in a variety of social reform initiatives, including the settlement movement, local art committees, environmental activism, and others. Along with the already established chambers of commerce, temperance organizations, and others, they served as a collective force that ushered in the Progressive Era's mission to defeat corruption.[72] Through the City Beautiful movement, these citizens believed they could positively affect the overall moral behavior of the city with the creation of parks, the development of idyllic neighborhoods, the introduction of public art, and other municipal improvements.[73]

One such person in a position of power was Edward Manning Bigelow. In 1888, Pittsburgh's councils named Bigelow as the first head of the city's department of public works. Bigelow, a thirty-eight-year-old civil engineer who had previously worked for Pittsburgh as a surveyor, was a cousin of local political boss Christopher Lyman Magee and was immediately put in a position where he could use his connections to shape the city in a manner of his choosing.[74] An early example of his influence can be found in the East End's Highland Park, which began to implement the Beaux Arts craze shortly following the exposition. The park opened to the public the same year as the Chicago World's Fair and quickly incorporated elements of the fairgrounds. In 1895, Italian sculptor Giuseppe Moretti was hired to design a magnificent entrance to the park. By 1900 this commission resulted in two columned pillars, each hoisting a statue above Highland Avenue. Later, Moretti included shorter, but no less detailed, statues of Castor and Pollux, each with a horse, on either side of the Stanton Avenue entrance.[75] In general, Highland Park, with its grand entrances, fountain, and carefully manicured green spaces, embodied City Beautiful ideals, as well as those of the middle class who were actively developing the surrounding suburban community.

In the wake of the Pittsburgh Survey's critical observations of poor living and working conditions, civic leaders hired Olmsted's son, Frederick Law Olmsted Jr., to evaluate Pittsburgh and suggest potential beautification initiatives and improved municipal efficiency. Envisioning the Golden Triangle as a civic center, or Pittsburgh's version of the White City, the junior Olmsted's 1910 report, *Pittsburgh, Main Thoroughfares and the Down Town District: Improvements Necessary to Meet the City's Present and Future Needs*, laid out plans for improving traffic into town. Developments in transportation, including the expansion and near-complete electrification of the city's traction lines thanks to Westinghouse's successful exhibition at the Columbian Exposition, had facilitated the exodus of white-collar workers out of the Central Business District. Olmsted's plan sought to ease their commute back into downtown for work and leisure activities. Many of his proposals came to fruition, including the connection of downtown to suburbs east and south of the Central Business District with wide streets and tunnels. The Liberty Tunnels, Liberty Bridge, and the Boulevard of the Allies are all direct results of the Olmsted report. His recommendations also led to the development of more publicly accessible waterfronts along the Monongahela and Allegheny Rivers and the regular collection and maintenance of data that could be used in future planning efforts.[76]

While several of Olmsted's recommendations did come to pass, his assumption that downtown would be the home of Pittsburgh's civic center did not. Instead, an unassuming tract of farmland separating downtown from the East End suburbs was on the cusp of embodying many of the legacies of the 1893 World's Fair. It would be the area known as Oakland that benefited most from the Columbian Exposition.

7

Oakland

Pittsburgh's White City

THE FIRST DECADE of the twentieth century witnessed several cities' efforts to permanently capture the spirit of the White City's Court of Honor in the form of new centralized building complexes and urban planning projects. The earliest plans in Washington, DC, Cleveland, and Chicago were all led by Daniel Burnham and had a direct influence on how the City Beautiful movement would be defined and implemented in the years ahead. Burnham stressed that the Columbian Exposition demonstrated the benefits of cohesive rather than piecemeal planning on the overall effectiveness of a project and developed a systematic means of creating those designs.[1] Planning committees spent months studying their locations and developing a meticulous proposal of monumental and landscape architecture before submitting a formal report to their commissioning municipality for approval and adoption. However, when Pittsburgh commissioned Frederick Law Olmsted Jr. to complete his plan for the city in 1910 several factors were working against its full implementation. His proposal for a downtown civic center was set aside because commercial interests around the Allegheny County Courthouse simply would not give way to a new local government building and park complex. This pushed the focus of any centralized project into the developing neighborhood of Oakland, which was already growing into the city's cultural center. Existing projects and political maneuvering prevented Olmsted from providing a detailed vision for Oakland emanating from the entrance to Schenley Park, ultimately leading to the discarding of his plan for the neighborhood.[2] Instead, what developed was a continuation of the very piecemeal arrangement Burnham decried as the antithesis of the White City model; however, the visions of several key planners and architects allowed Oakland to develop around several smaller-scale plans that still effectively incorporated City Beautiful concepts.[3]

The neighborhood of Oakland had already become a refuge for the upper class when it was annexed by the city of Pittsburgh in 1869. Three miles east of downtown, the sparsely populated hillside overlooking the Monongahela River offered a cleaner and quieter environment for their families to live and play when compared to the densely packed residences, busy warehouses, and filthy factories of the Golden Triangle. One of the reasons Oakland managed to remain so pristine late into the nineteenth century was that the landowner, Mary Croghan Schenley, had not sought to develop the area. Schenley had inherited hundreds of acres acquired by her grandfather, James O'Hara, dating back to before the Revolutionary War; however, she eloped to England when she was nearly fifteen years old and did not actively develop her properties during her absence from Western Pennsylvania. Eventually, in 1889, Schenley gave four hundred acres of her Oakland land to the city, creating Schenley Park. Unbeknown to her at the time of her donation, the park would serve as the linchpin of Oakland's incorporation of the City Beautiful movement.[4]

The key player in securing the donation of land for Schenley Park was the city's new director of public works, Edward Manning Bigelow. Believing, as many members in the middle and upper class did in the 1890s, that environment influenced the behavior of urban people, Bigelow sought to use the park as a means of pacifying Pittsburgh's working class, which had been restless ever since the 1877 railroad riots.[5] However, given Schenley Park's proximity to the developing East End suburbs rather than industrial neighborhoods, most of the intended beneficiaries of the park could not afford to travel there regularly. Moreover, even if working-class families could make their way to the park, Bigelow's choice of recreation activities, attractions, and overall ambiance appealed more to the interests and tastes of the upper class than to those he meant the park to benefit.[6]

From its beginning, Schenley Park was tied to the Columbian Exposition.

Industrialist Henry Phipps Jr., who had previously erected a botanical conservatory in Allegheny, offered $100,000 to build its successor in the park under Bigelow's direction.[7] Phipps completed the Schenley Park Conservatory just as the 1893 World's Fair was coming to a close, and Bigelow took advantage of the opportunity to travel to Chicago and acquire some of the more impressive botanical exhibits. Several Pittsburghers donated money to fill the conservatory, and their contributions aided in the purchase of the South Wales collection of tree ferns for $5,000. Other donations included the Drexel Collection of various plants worth over $3,000, from Senator William Flinn; $1,000 worth of plants by a Mrs. Carr; and portions of the exhibits by J. M. Armstrong, Captain Jacob J. Vandergrift, and others.[8] Given his effort to secure these rare plants for the new building, it was clear that the success of Phipps Conservatory was an important first step in Bigelow's overarching goal of creating a nurturing environment for those who sought self-improvement.[9]

In addition to the natural qualities of Schenley Park, both native and imported, there were also attempts to incorporate architecture onto the grounds. In October 1893, Bigelow was approached by Pennsylvania Board of World's Fair Managers member Patrick Foley about acquiring the exposition's State Building for the park. He entertained the notion of moving the copy of Independence Hall to Pittsburgh, but ultimately declined to bid on the building. Nine bids were eventually placed for the rights to the building, ranging from $850 to nothing at all, and the structure was eventually razed. One attraction built near the park entrance was the Schenley Park Casino, which opened in 1895. The casino, which very much resembled an exposition-type building, offered a brief glimpse at the technological marvel of an indoor skating rink, the first artificial ice rink in North America. The casino also served as a theater. The impact of the casino on the greater development of Oakland was cut short, however, when a fire destroyed the building, along with a nearby carousel and bridge, just nineteen months after it opened.[10]

Another aspect of the City Beautiful movement that found its way into Schenley Park was public art. Italian sculptor Giuseppe Moretti had several works installed in the park. In 1895 the city unveiled his statue of Bigelow at the main entry point to Schenley Park just in front of Phipps Conservatory. Later, in 1897, four bronze panther sculptures by Moretti were placed at the corners of the Panther Hollow Bridge, just south of the conservatory. These sculptures combined the appeal of nature and public art to ornament an otherwise utilitarian aspect of the park. Examples of animal sculptures on bridges were found

Fig. 18. The main entrance to Schenley Park served as the keystone of the early
   development of Oakland, with the Carnegie Library (left) and Phipps Conservatory
   (right, background) greeting visitors on either side of the Schenley Bridge. Pittsburgh City Photographer Collection, AIS.1975.01, Archives and Special Collections,
   University of Pittsburgh Library System.

throughout the White City, which made fauna an acceptable subject for serious
artists. This feature reinforced the notion that Schenley Park was a destination
to encounter both the wilderness and culture.[11]

In 1898, Bigelow instructed Schenley Park superintendent William Fal-
coner to commission John C. Olmsted, another son of Frederick Law Olmsted,
to design and erect a grand entrance to the park near Forbes Avenue. The proposed neoclassical structure was to separate the urban world from the park,
but as the idea of expanding City Beautiful ideals throughout Oakland began
to take hold at the turn of the century, planners abandoned the idea. Moretti
and several other artists and architects also designed proposed park entries in
the Beaux Arts style, often implementing the colonnades and peristyles of the
White City's Court of Honor. Like Olmsted's design before them, the idea was
ultimately abandoned in favor of the Schenley Memorial Fountain, which was
dedicated in 1918.[12] Even without the grand entry, Schenley Park embodied the

principles of the City Beautiful movement, and just beyond the park arose ves-
tiges of the architectural and intellectual legacy of the Columbian Exposition.

———————

Shortly after the establishment of Schenley Park, Andrew Carnegie saw an
opportunity. The once untouchable land owned by the overseas heiress was
suddenly up for grabs to anyone who could make a convincing argument that
they could responsibly steward her property for the good of Pittsburgh's citizens. Previously, in 1881, Carnegie had offered to donate $250,000 to build a
free library in Pittsburgh, but the city had no authority to tax citizens in order
to raise money for the $15,000 annual maintenance provision and so the pro-
posal was declined. In 1887 the state assembly changed the law, but even with
the roadblock resolved, Pittsburgh officials placed Carnegie's plan on the back
burner. At the suggestion of his friend William J. Holland, he eventually offered
the city $1 million on February 6, 1890, for an even more ambitious plan. This
gift not only was intended to build a library but also provided for an art gallery
and meeting space in the main library, as well as branch locations throughout
the city.[13] As a site for his ambitious plan, Carnegie selected the entrance to
Schenley Park.

For the next three years, headlines outlining the progress of both the Carnegie Library and the Columbian Exposition shared the pages of Pittsburgh's
newspapers and, in a way, the success of the world's fair justified Carnegie's
proposal. To some, the White City served as evidence that an unsophisticated
industrial city could achieve the status of a cultural mecca in a short period of
time. If a temporary city could accomplish this in Chicago, why couldn't a permanent institute in Pittsburgh do the same? In 1891, Carnegie announced a competition to select the building design for the library and the firm of Longfellow,
Alden and Harlow emerged victorious from over one hundred entries. Digging
for the foundation began in 1892 and construction on the building began in July
1893. Continuing through the worst of the ongoing financial panic, construction of the building finished in 1895.[14]

Upon its completion, the Carnegie Institute, as it came to be called, embodied several key milestones for Pittsburgh. The institute was the first cultural
institution planned and located outside of the Central Business District, moving
closer to the developing suburbs in the East End. The building, inspired by the
Medici Palace in Florence, was also the largest example of Beaux Arts architecture in the city and, along with the development and design of Schenley Park,
acted as the impetus for future civic center development in Oakland. It also

served as a grand announcement of Pittsburgh's enlightenment.[15] While Western Pennsylvania had some of the earliest higher education institutions west of
the Allegheny Mountains, their benefits were only available for a select few;
the Carnegie Institute, like the Columbian Exposition, was developed for the
betterment and education of all citizens.

Although Carnegie's vision for public libraries had been previously realized
in several Allegheny County locations and in Scotland, the Carnegie Institute
consisted of not only a library but also a music hall, museum, and art gallery.
The museum quickly evolved into one of natural history, exhibiting animals,
plants, and minerals from the region, as well as ancient and medieval works of
art. Perhaps most famously, the museum also included paleontological exhibits,
particularly dinosaurs. In 1901, the institute acquired a nearly complete skeleton of a *Diplodocus* and Carnegie had casts of the bones produced and shipped
to institutions around the globe. There was also a collection of industrial exhibits, featuring samples of the raw materials used in steel, glass, and other local
industries.[16] Taken together, these displays replicated many of the types of
exhibits found at the Chicago fair and, consolidated under one roof, aimed to
provide in a few hours what thousands of Pittsburghers spent weeks experiencing during the summer of 1893.

In 1907, Carnegie funded an addition to the original institute building to
expand the museum to accommodate a proposed new exhibit—the Hall of
Architecture. In true Beaux Arts fashion, the latest structure incorporated
classical influences. Inspired by the Seven Wonders of the Ancient World, the
architects of Alden and Harlow designed the Hall of Architecture to resemble
the Mausoleum of Halicarnassus, with a pyramidal roof and vast open exhibit
hall.[17] Similarly, they designed the accompanying Hall of Sculpture with the
same dimensions as the ancient Greek Parthenon.[18] Carnegie was stirred to
create a collection of casts after viewing the cast exhibit at the Columbian
Exposition; however, his plan deviated from the displays traditionally found in
museums. While the institute did display sculptural casts like other American
museums, it was the featured grand architectural casts that set it apart from the
rest. Because these reproductions were more difficult to create, and thus more
expensive, Carnegie's Hall of Architecture was a statement of not only Pittsburgh's affluence but also its commitment to culture.[19] At a time when many
American architects and their benefactors strove to reproduce classical architecture in the wake of the 1893 World's Fair, Carnegie went right to the source
and unabashedly commissioned copies of the original buildings they sought to
replicate and placed them in his museum for public consumption.

As part of the institute's addition, Carnegie commissioned local artist John White Alexander to paint a mural for the walls surrounding a grand staircase. After the Columbian Exposition, murals had become integral components of new public buildings such as courthouses, government buildings, libraries, and museums, just as they were in the White City. Pittsburgh's new Palace of Culture was to be no different. Alexander's Carnegie Institute mural, *The Crowning of Labor*, was not only one of the largest and most expensive examples of these projects but also one that embodied the best qualities of mural painting and City Beautiful movement concepts of social betterment. Fifteen panels on the first floor depict laborers working tirelessly in filthy factories and mills, forming the foundation upon which the subject of the artwork on the second floor rests. These panels show classically dressed winged women representing the products of Pittsburgh's efforts. This portion of the mural, called "The Apotheosis of Pittsburgh," shows the women crowning a knight who represents the city and looks suspiciously like Carnegie himself. The next floor's murals depict the people of Pittsburgh gazing up to the last level, which was to illustrate the various activities of the institute; however, Alexander died before the final panels were completed. The story told in the mural reinforces the lives and beliefs of City Beautiful benefactors like Carnegie, specifically that the product of the toiling workers elevated the city, or more accurately a small set of wealthy industrialists, to prominence so they could provide arts and education for the improvement of all citizens. Furthermore, with the institute at the top, the mural bolsters the idea that cultural philanthropy is the noblest contribution a millionaire could make to his community, echoing the message Carnegie put forward in his "Gospel of Wealth," while also reinforcing to viewers that all citizens should strive to benefit from those institutions created for their own good.[20]

In addition to the classical architecture and sculpture found in its halls, as well as Alexander's mural, the Carnegie Institute also included an art gallery for the display of paintings and other original works. During the closing weeks of the Columbian Exposition, friends like L. G. Laureau, a juror for several of the fair's art competitions, contacted Carnegie about the possibility of purchasing artwork from the displays for future exhibit "at some museum."[21] Perhaps using these requests as inspiration, Carnegie sought to utilize the art gallery, much like the Palace of Fine Arts at the exposition, to garner local interest and cultivate a taste for American modern art. To ensure a steady stream of new works Carnegie approved the creation of a "chronological collection" in 1896 comprising annual acquisitions of works by American artists.[22]

A fine arts committee of the Carnegie Institute's board of trustees provided direction for the art gallery. Members of the committee included Henry Clay Frick, William N. Frew, David Thompson Watson, and John Caldwell, all avid local art collectors. Another member, Edward Manning Bigelow, was, as the city's director of public works, as invested as Carnegie in the cultivation of Pittsburgh's culture. Joseph Ryan Woodwell and Alfred Bryan Wall were the only two artists on the fine arts committee when it first formed.[23] Both artists had also exhibited works at the Chicago World's Fair. The committee selected another Pittsburgh artist, John Wesley Beatty, to address the lofty goals of the art museum as its first director. Beatty's experience as an advisory committee member at the Columbian Exposition, as well as connections to established American artists who trained in Europe, made him exceptionally qualified to lead not only the initiative of developing the chronological collection but also the most innovative contribution of the museum—the Carnegie International Exhibition.[24]

As early as 1894, local artists had expressed their desire for the institute to use part of Carnegie's endowment to provide prize money to attract top talent to a Pittsburgh exhibition. Carnegie was up to the task and he expressed his own desire to create an annual exhibition based on the art exhibits popular in Paris and at world's fairs, which would also provide a selection of works from which the museum could acquire art for its permanent collection.[25] Much like his plaster cast exhibit, Carnegie put his own grander spin on traditional American museum conventions. Whereas most American exhibitions focused on art from the United States, Carnegie's exhibit was international in scope, bringing a popular feature of the world's fairs home to Western Pennsylvania and introducing Pittsburgh to the best American and European artists.

In addition to the likely genesis of the international exhibition idea being the Columbian Exposition, early participants and works in the Carnegie International were also present at the fair. Impressionist painter William Merritt Chase was both a juror at the exposition and a judge at early Carnegie International exhibitions. Mary Cassatt, whose controversial mural appeared in the Woman's Building at the Columbian Exposition, was still prominent in Europe and served as an advisor to several early Internationals. Furthermore, her 1891 painting *Young Women Picking Fruit* was purchased for the museum's permanent collection through the Patron's Art Fund in 1899.[26] While bringing pieces into the Carnegie Institute's own holdings, the International also contributed to the region's private collections. For example, Andrew Mellon purchased Frank Millet's *Anthony Van Corlaer, the Trumpeter of Amsterdam*, in 1896 after it was exhibited at the Chicago fair and the 1895 Carnegie International. Together, the Columbian Exposition and the Carnegie International inspired local interest in viewing and collecting art from all over the globe at the close of the Gilded Age.[27]

While Carnegie and Bigelow opened the door for the City Beautiful–inspired development of Oakland, two men burst through to mold the area with their imaginations—Franklin Nicola and Henry Hornbostel. Originally from Cleveland, Nicola came to Pittsburgh to work with a lumber company before branching out into real estate. In 1898 Nicola made his first mark in Oakland with the opening of the Hotel Schenley on land purchased from Mary Schenley. The landscaping around the hotel was contracted to the Olmsted firm, which was in the midst of developing a proposal for the entrance to Schenley Park. It is likely that Olmsted intended for the two projects to meet each other near the present corner of Forbes Avenue and Bigelow Boulevard; however, the entrance plan never came to fruition.[28]

Soon after the hotel's opening, Nicola began to acquire and sell parcels of land throughout the neighborhood. In 1901 he sold the block north of the Carnegie Institute to its benefactor's former colleague and newfound enemy, Henry Clay Frick. This lot eventually became the home of the University of Pittsburgh's towering Cathedral of Learning. Soon after, in 1905, Nicola's Schenley Land Company purchased the rest of Mary Schenley's land in the neighborhood and set in motion a plan to make Oakland the type of civic center romanticized in the City Beautiful movement. After purchasing over one hundred acres of the Schenley dairy farm, Nicola partitioned the land into three distinct zones that would house residential, public, and semipublic spaces. For Nicola, Oakland would be a model suburban community that included homes as well as civic and cultural institutions wrapped in the Beaux Arts architecture popularized by the 1893 World's Fair.[29]

Nicola intended for Oakland to be a planned city based on the model of the White City, but unlike its Columbian Exposition inspiration, where visitors learned and played, people would live there, too. The residential component became Schenley Farms, a planned community for upper- and middle-class families consisting of homes built by some of the most prominent architects in the region. The most conspicuous features of Nicola's plan, however, were enormous monuments and buildings all in the Beaux Arts style. The most ambitious contributor to this plan was architect Henry Hornbostel. He had visited the

Columbian Exposition just prior to leaving for Paris to study at the École des Beaux-Arts in 1893 to receive the traditional architectural instruction of the day.[30] Benefiting not only from the same education that informed the architects of the White City but also from witnessing their cohesive implementation of those lessons in Chicago, Hornbostel entered the arena of Pittsburgh architecture seeking a chance to build his own urban environment in that same style. With the growing number of opportunities in Oakland, Hornbostel seized his moment.

Hornbostel found his first Oakland commission with Andrew Carnegie and his newly formed Carnegie Technical Schools. The school purchased a site on a plateau overlooking Junction Hollow, to the east of the Carnegie Institute, and a competition to design the campus was held in 1904. The contest was timely for Hornbostel because, in the wake of the exposition where the education of the masses was a primary goal, urban campuses offered a perfect opportunity for city planning, and thus City Beautiful ideals, in miniature.[31] Schools already reflected the Victorian obsession concerning order, with fields of study organized into departments, students sorted into classes, and faculty, as the superior class, positioned above it all. The implementation of City Beautiful principles, then, further embodied these divisions. As places of higher learning, classical architecture was a natural fit for campuses harkening back to times of great intellectual advancement. Furthermore, colleges became increasingly more reliant on the donations of alumni or wealthy members of the community, and so monumental architecture became a preferred method of ensuring that donors' contributions would be properly acknowledged.

Using his affinity for elements from the White City, Hornbostel won the contest, even defeating world's fair architect George B. Post. His design incorporated several buildings influenced by classical or Renaissance styles all surrounding a central open space, much like the grouping of buildings found in the White City's Court of Honor. By providing a central mall, Hornbostel encouraged visitors to take in the entire campus from that vantage point and consequently imposed the sense of a more cohesive plan for the buildings.[32] This became more evident during the annual Carnegie Tech Exhibition, which served as an open house to educate and entertain both the community and prospective students. Much like the fair, a planned entry point directed visitors onto campus, controlling their viewing experience to achieve maximum effect.[33]

In addition to the campus design, several buildings echoed elements of the world's fairs that were increasingly popular at the turn of the century. Both the White City and the Carnegie Tech campus used the name Machinery Hall, with

Fig. 19. Henry Hornbostel's plan for the new campus of the Western University of
Pennsylvania, soon to be called the University of Pittsburgh, climbed the Oakland
hillside and resembled the Acropolis of ancient Athens. University of Pittsburgh
Historic Photographs, Archives and Special Collections, University of Pittsburgh
Library System.

the latter containing the school's power plant and engineering shops instead of
exhibits. However, there were exhibition spaces in other buildings. The School
of Applied Design contained all the artistic disciplines and featured a grand
exhibition hall in its entry. Given the variety of works that might be on display
at a given time, visitors would recall such exposition features as the Palace of
Fine Arts or the cultural exhibits at the national buildings and pavilions.[34]

Soon after Carnegie Tech's formation in Oakland, another university
already in existence sought to relocate to the neighborhood. With a small campus in Allegheny, the Western University of Pennsylvania (WUP) began to find
itself farther from the families who provided the majority of its student population, many of whom had relocated to the rapidly developing East End. Since the
1890s, the university had also formed partnerships with several professional
schools, leaving WUP in need of a larger campus should they ever wish to bring
all its affiliates to one location. The university acquired over forty acres of land
in Oakland and in 1908 issued its own campus design competition, which Hornbostel also ultimately won. Whereas the Carnegie Tech site was entirely lev-
eled, the WUP site, purchased from Nicola for $537,000, required Hornbostel
to distribute thirty buildings along winding hillside roads and paths.[35] With
Beaux Arts–inspired columned, temple-like buildings on the hilltop, the Hornbostel design came to be known as the Acropolis Plan, after the ancient Greek
site in Athens.

The Columbian Exposition had a clear influence on its new campus, but
Western University had been reflecting on the fair since it closed its gates in

October 1893. The university received donations of several items that had been on display at the fair, including samples of minerals, petroleum, sugar, and glass from all over the world.[36] Because interest in electrical engineering had sky-rocketed after George Westinghouse's impressive display in Chicago, he asked Chancellor Holland to hire Dr. Reginald Fessenden to teach a new generation at Western University. Fessenden's patents concerning the use of iron-based filaments in bulbs had aided in Westinghouse's ability to win the exposition contract, and it seems he was eager to return the favor and bring Fessenden into the fold. When the school's budget would not allow them to provide a salary that would attract the Purdue University professor, Westinghouse hired Fessenden as a consultant to supplement his income and lure him to Pittsburgh. As part of the WUP faculty, Fessenden secured some of the electrical equipment from the fair for his new laboratory, which gave the school one of the most modern electrical engineering labs in the country.[37] In 1900 Fessenden left Pittsburgh to work for the United States Weather Bureau and later he became a pioneer in the development of radio transmissions.

As for Western University's exhibit of photographs and student work from the exposition, it was put on permanent display in the school's main building in Allegheny. Having been located near the exhibit of the University of Pennsylvania in Chicago, the WUP exhibitors also realized an emerging problem with the school's name. Many visitors mistook the university as being an affiliate of Philadelphia's University of Pennsylvania. So, while in the midst of building its new campus, the board of trustees created the Committee on the Change of Name of the University to explore the possibility of renaming the school. By 1908 WUP had affiliated with several other institutions, including the Western Pennsylvania Medical College, Pittsburgh College of Pharmacy, and Pittsburgh Dental School, so the trustees decided to rebrand the university once all the schools were located on a single campus. Furthermore, the city of Pittsburgh was undergoing a great expansion with the annexation of Allegheny City in 1907 and a groundswell of civic pride during the city's sesquicentennial celebration the following year. With all of this taken into consideration, the committee recommended that the school be renamed the University of Pittsburgh.[38]

Ultimately, the Acropolis Plan proved too ambitious for the newly renamed university. Architecture archivist and author Martin Aurand has pointed out that Hornbostel intended his design to share an axis with his earlier Carnegie Tech campus. This focus on the Carnegie Tech axis provided for his striking symmetrical competition drawing of the Acropolis Plan; however, in reality, the point of view shown in these sketches could rarely be achieved by visitors to

Fig. 20. By the early 1910s Oakland could boast several Beaux Arts buildings, including the Twentieth Century Club, Pittsburgh Athletic Association, Carnegie Institute, the campuses of the University of Pittsburgh and Carnegie Technical Schools, Soldiers and Sailors Memorial, Hotel Schenley, and Logan Armory, as well as Forbes Field. University of Pittsburgh Historic Photographs, Archives and Special Collections, University of Pittsburgh Library System.

the university and, therefore, became less attractive to administrators as the first buildings were erected on the hillside. Ultimately only four buildings from Hornbostel's original plan were constructed before waning financial resources and the outbreak of World War I ended the project, with only Thaw Hall remaining today.[39]

In addition to the two university campuses, Hornbostel made two other significant Beaux Arts–inspired contributions to the area. The first was the 1907 Rodef Shalom Temple, which is technically in Shadyside, a neighborhood adjoining Oakland. Rodef Shalom was the first Jewish congregation in Western Pennsylvania and had operated a synagogue in downtown Pittsburgh since 1861. With the addition of Rabbi J. Leonard Levy the size of the congregation grew rapidly and during the same period many of the congregants moved to the East End. This move effectively distinguished the established Reform German-Jewish community from the immigrant Orthodox eastern European Jews. The classical influence of Hornbostel's synagogue mirrored the beliefs of Reform Judaism in that both adapt historical tradition for a modern society.[40] The other building is the Allegheny County Soldiers' and Sailors' Memorial Hall, at the foot of the Acropolis Plan. Hornbostel won the 1907 design contest with a giant monument with features taken from the Mausoleum of Halicarnassus, which had also influenced the Carnegie Institute's Hall of Architecture that was being built nearby at the same time.[41] Hornbostel reoriented the building, originally designed to face what is now Bigelow Boulevard, toward Fifth, which added a long forecourt and placed the focus of the surrounding blocks in the same direction.

Hornbostel's attempts to link his projects into one cohesive plan may not have been realized, but it is clear that he saw Oakland as his own personal fairground. All of his Oakland projects were monumental in scale, meeting one of the requirements for any world's fair. Hornbostel also took a page from the planners of the White City by using a singular color palette and group of building materials. When taken in together, then, the buildings form one project that is greater than the sum of its individual parts, just like the Court of Honor in Chicago.

Another architect who produced several Beaux Arts buildings for Oakland was Benno Janssen. Also a product of the École des Beaux-Arts in Paris, Janssen built on Hornbostel's vision for Oakland by designing Alumni Hall (now Eberly Hall) for the University of Pittsburgh in 1921, which almost seamlessly inserted itself into the design of the abandoned Acropolis Plan. Janssen's most notable contributions to Oakland, however, are his clubhouses. His 1911 Renaissance-inspired Pittsburgh Athletic Association and the 1914 ancient Greek-style Masonic Temple exemplify the relocation of Pittsburgh social life from downtown to Oakland. Later, Janssen would add the Twentieth Century Club and Young Men's Hebrew Association to his list of clubhouses, as well as the enormous neoclassical Mellon Institute.[42] Since the monumental buildings of Oakland were designed by a small handful of architects instead of the work of one lone designer, the neighborhood benefited from the same characteristics of the White City, particularly a sense of uniformity without monotony.

In addition to the educational and social aspects of Oakland, it also became a center of leisure. Schenley Park emerged as a popular destination for picnics, footraces, and other athletic events, particularly during summer holidays like the Fourth of July. Among prominent East Enders who owned horses, trail riding and races were popular park activities. As golf became prevalent among the Pittsburgh elite, Frick built a golf course in the park for his own private and business use before the city claimed it as a public course in 1910. Once automobiles began to appear in the area, a racing oval was also installed in Schenley Park.[43] While Bigelow claimed that the park was intended to help provide a better environment for working-class men to thrive and achieve self-betterment, the amenities provided in the park clearly indicate that, in reality, the desired visitors came from the middle and upper classes.

Besides the emphasis on recreation in Schenley Park, entrepreneurs built and operated other nearby facilities specifically for more popular amusement. Soon after the Columbian Exposition, an attraction called the Musatorium was built across from the Carnegie Institute construction site. The Musatorium included some of the most popular activities of the day, including a billiard parlor, bicycle shop, and a rollercoaster; however, the building burned down only two months after the nearby Schenley Park Casino did. A few blocks away, a trolley barn was renovated in 1896 to hold the world's largest indoor ice rink, which became Pittsburgh's hockey arena for the first half of the twentieth century. Known as Duquesne Gardens, the facility also hosted basketball games, boxing matches, concerts, and other large gatherings until it was demolished in 1956.[44]

In 1909 the Pittsburgh Baseball Club opened Forbes Field across from the Carnegie Institute near the entrance to Schenley Park. Barney Dreyfus, owner of the Pittsburgh Pirates franchise, chose to move his team away from its small existing accommodations in Allegheny to the growing Oakland neighborhood, as had the Western University of Pennsylvania. This provided the team's fan base with a stadium in closer proximity to their East End homes and away from the heavily polluted Allegheny River that flooded the field throughout the sea-son. The stadium was one of the first to be constructed of steel and concrete, and also included the arched windows and terra cotta facade often used in Beaux Arts architecture. In addition to Pirates baseball, Forbes Field also served as a home for the University of Pittsburgh collegiate and, eventually, Pittsburgh Steelers professional football teams, as well as a site for boxing matches, Negro League baseball games, concerts, political rallies, and more.[45] In 1925 the University of Pittsburgh opened another athletics venue in Oakland—Pitt Sta-dium. This arena, which resembled the Roman Colosseum, replaced Forbes Field for football games and hosted university track and field meets and basket-ball games.

In addition to athletic contests, visitors to Oakland could also participate in the types of amusement that were most popular on the Midway Plaisance, albeit only briefly. Frederick Ingersoll had previously entered the world of entertain-ment by working with his father in the coin-operated game business. After being inspired by the rise in the number of trolley parks that began to attract more visitors with rides, Ingersoll secured the rights to construct figure-eight coasters in 1898 and incorporated Ingersoll Construction Company in 1901 to build them.[46] After achieving rapid success as a rollercoaster designer, Ingersoll began working with the owners of Coney Island's Luna Park to select a site for a similar attraction in Allegheny. Coney Island had become a hotbed for amusement parks beginning in 1895 and Luna Park was formed in 1903 when several parks were consolidated. The success of Luna Park set off a race to build other exposition parks nearby while Luna's owners sought to expand their company to other cities.[47] After several months of partnership in seeking a site, the two parties were unable to reach an agreement and so Ingersoll sought to establish a park on his own. After failing to secure property near Recreation Park in Allegheny and the estate of George Singer in Point Breeze, Ingersoll set his sights on a piece of land in North Oakland.[48]

On the eastern side of Herron Hill sat the estate of Annie Aspinwall. In December 1904, Ingersoll purchased the property for $115,000 ($3.5 million in 2022) as the site for his new venture. Ingersoll hired the contractors Booth and Flinn, a beneficiary of the Magee-Flinn political machine, for $80,000 to begin work on the attraction. Ingersoll sought to open the park for the 1905 season and implemented several of the tactics used at the Columbian Exposition to meet his deadline. Much like the rushed early construction of the Ferris wheel in Chicago, workers used dynamite to loosen the frozen ground to begin leveling the site. The Ingersoll attraction also required the installation of new water mains and electrical wires. Like the Columbian Exposition, the buildings of Pittsburgh's Luna Park were similarly constructed of wooden frames covered in staff and painted to look like marble or stone. Also, just like the 1893 World's Fair, the park opened before all its attractions were completed.[49]

Once Luna Park opened on June 5, 1905, though, it became an immediate hit. An enormous white-and-gold entrance was covered in electric lights and many of the other buildings were similarly outlined, totaling over sixty thousand lights. Inside, visitors could play carnival games on a midway called The Pike, go bowling, observe fish at a large aquarium, and eat at one of the restaurants or concession stands. They could also ride on a scenic railway or the Shoot the Chutes, in which boats carried riders down a steep hill into a pool at the center of the park. Ingersoll renovated the Aspinwall home into an Infant Incubator attraction in which nurses cared for premature babies in full view of park guests, an idea that had premiered at the 1896 Berlin Exposition.[50] While Westinghouse motors powered the trolleys delivering visitors to the park, once inside the grounds guests could view such Thomas Edison innovations as Kinetoscopes and motion pictures.[51] As at the Columbian Exposition, foreign cultures were

Fig. 21. With several buildings encircling the pool of the Shoot the Chutes ride, Oakland's Luna Park incorporated elements of the Columbian Exposition's Court of Honor and Midway Plaisance. Detroit Publishing Company, "Luna Park, Pittsburg, Pa.," 1905, Prints and Photographs Division, Library of Congress.

also on display. The Japanese Pavilion was built by carpenters from Yokohama and featured Japanese food, games, music, flora, and more. There was also a market that sold Japanese goods to eager Pittsburghers.[52]

At the end of its inaugural season, Luna Park had hosted eight hundred thousand visitors, but while the park was a success due to its accessibility to the East End, it was also popular because attendance was exclusive.[53] Many members of the working class were unable to afford the trolley ride to the park, let alone the nickel admission and additional fees to enjoy the attractions and rides, thus making Luna a middle-class refuge from the hoi polloi. Furthermore, from its hillside location, the park sat awash in electric light and frivolity while overlooking the slum of Skunk Hollow situated in the valley below. Researchers for the Pittsburgh Survey even noted that the park seemed to mockingly hover above one of the most destitute neighborhoods in the city.[54] But this type of disparity was not new, particularly for an urban attraction that seemed to

spring from the ground overnight. This same dichotomy had presented itself at
the Columbian Exposition when visitors contrasted the fair's White City to the
Black City of its surrounding industries and their workers.

While Ingersoll made several additions to the park each season to make it
more desirable, Luna Park was open for a very short period of time. One major
factor in its ultimate demise was a decision early on to ban alcohol from the
grounds and close the park on Sundays. Kennywood had previously received
backlash for being open on the Sabbath, as well as hosting rides that encouraged riders to be close together, so the managers of Luna opted to avoid that
conflict.[55] This proved to be a fatal misjudgment when other recreational
spaces like Highland Park, Schenley Park, and the Carnegie Institute were all
crowded with visitors on Sundays.[56] In addition to this error in management,
the park was also the scene of a tragic accident during the 1907 season when a
lion escaped from its cage and fatally mauled Anna Hucke, a sixty-three-year old
German immigrant who lived in the Uptown neighborhood.[57] Luna was sold at
a sheriff's sale in 1908 and the 1909 opening of Forbes Field, which provided a
better location for the types of acts typically hosted at the park, ensured that
it would be its last season of operation. By then the success of amusement parks
depended on locations that could accommodate expansion and reinvention; the
era of the urban exposition park was waning. The site of Luna Park ultimately
gave way to automobile garages and showrooms, the next big influence on transportation and recreation. From 1905 to 1909, however, Luna Park served as
Oakland's Midway Plaisance.

Outside of Chicago, the World's Columbian Exposition left its most lasting legacy in Pittsburgh's Oakland neighborhood. In comparing the 1893 World's Fair
to the developing area, the architecture journal the *Builder* remarked in 1912
that "few will dispute, after seeing it, that one of the finest Civic Centers possessed by any city in the country, or the world, for that matter, is to be found in
Pittsburgh. At no time since the Columbian Exposition at Chicago in 1893 has
there been brought together such an imposing grouping of architectural art. The
Columbian Exposition was temporary; Pittsburgh's is permanent."[58] The successful development of the Oakland civic center in the image of the fair, which
featured a loose coordination of private and public efforts, was perhaps the first
successful attempt at cohesive urban planning in the region. This later served as
an example for the planning efforts of downtown Pittsburgh that proved to be
critical in the city's redevelopment during the mid-twentieth century.[59] To be

sure, just as the Columbian Exposition fully executed the ideals of urban planning, albeit only temporarily, with monumental architecture, meticulous land-
scapes, and a balance of educational and entertainment attractions, the Oakland
civic center, at its peak, was the epitome of these same principles, making it
Pittsburgh's very own White City.

Epilogue

BY THE TIME Chicago hosted another world's fair in 1933, the world was a wildly different place than it had been in 1893. Many of the products that had debuted at the Columbian Exposition were now commonplace; technologies and inventions that were barely ideas presented at the 1893 fair, like automobiles and motion pictures, had developed into lucrative industries and were already being taken for granted. Not only was flight shown to be possible, it had also proved to be a necessary component of modern warfare, as demonstrated in the Great War just fifteen years earlier. Alternating current, once maligned by the great Thomas Edison until he was proven wrong by George Westinghouse's lighting of the 1893 exposition's fairground, was the current of choice for electric companies throughout the nation. When the Century of Progress Exposition opened its gates in 1933, it was undeniable that its predecessor forty years earlier had left its mark on the world.

There were similarities between the fairs of 1893 and 1933, notably that each operated and succeeded during a widespread financial depression; however, while the Columbian Exposition, and all American world's fairs up to that time, relied on federal money supplemented by private subscriptions to pay for its construction, the 1933 fair was funded privately and did not require tax-payer money.[1] The later exposition also proved to be such a valuable boost to the economy that President Franklin D. Roosevelt, after his own visit to the fair, requested that it resume in 1934. Once the exposition's directors received per-mission from the mayor of Chicago and the governor and legislature of Illinois to reopen, President Roosevelt encouraged the creation of legislation that would allocate money to ensure the government's continued participation in the fair for another season.[2]

Like the Columbian Exposition, the 1933 fairgrounds were also placed on the shore of Lake Michigan, but this time closer to the heart of Chicago, on 424 acres in Grant Park and the Museum Campus north of the 1893 fair's Jackson Park location. This was the same spot that commissioners in 1890 had hoped to use as part of their dual-site plan. While the Ferris wheel did not make an appearance at the Century of Progress, the two 625-foot-tall steel towers sup-porting the Sky Ride took its place as the fair's premier attraction. Nonetheless, visitors from Western Pennsylvania still found familiar names in the exhibits of the 1933 World's Fair—H. J. Heinz Company; Westinghouse Electric and Manufacturing Company and Air Brake Company; Pittsburgh Equitable Meter Company; Union Switch and Signal; and the Aluminum Company of America (formerly the Pittsburgh Reduction Company) all exhibited in Chicago.[3] New-comers like the Irene Kaufmann Settlement and Gulf Refining Company also had displays at the 1933 exposition.

Architecture played a significant role in defining the Century of Progress Exposition and the Columbian Exposition, but in very different ways. In 1893 the use of Beaux Arts architecture was aimed to tie the United States to the established legacies of ancient empires, thereby creating legitimacy for the expanding American empire of the day. In contrast, the Century of Progress's use of modern styles attempted to connect specific corporations to America's future with little explicit history or heritage. The plan for the 1933 fair and its buildings failed to grasp the country's architects as its predecessor had for a number of reasons, including a national decline in the number of building projects, the utilitarian design of the exhibit halls, and an outpouring of neg-ative press led by Frank Lloyd Wright in response to his exclusion from the fair's building committee.[4] Whereas the Columbian Exposition had a cohesive plan and style, the Century of Progress buildings were more varied and thus less powerful; however, the use of color and new gaseous tube lighting resulting from the *collaboration* of Westinghouse and General Electric scientists was, overall, the bigger legacy than the plan or architectural styles.[5] Furthermore, new building techniques and products that were used in the Century of Progress pavilions, such as plywood and gypsum board, had a greater impact than the building designs.[6] While these practical contributions are still in use today, twentieth-century American cities had little opportunity or appetite to implement the modern styles of the Century of Progress buildings wholesale.

Much like the rest of the world, Pittsburgh had also changed a great deal by the 1933 opening of the Century of Progress Exposition. Many of the region's business titans associated with or influenced by the Columbian Exposition—Heinz, Westinghouse, Carnegie, Frick—had all since passed, but their legacies and that of the fair remained. The Westinghouse and Heinz names lived on with their companies, while Carnegie's mills and Frick's mines formed the centerpiece of the 1901 creation of the United States Steel Corporation orchestrated by Carnegie Steel executive Charles Schwab and New York financier J. P. Morgan. In the Golden Triangle, skyscrapers streaked the skyline as a testament to the city's financial and commercial success. The building boom in the early twentieth century and the First World War ushered in a new era of steel production and facility expansion in Western Pennsylvania, bringing along with it a wave of eastern European immigrant laborers. Whereas in 1890 Pittsburgh was the thirteenth-largest city in the United States with just over 250,000 people—344,000 including the population of Allegheny City, which was annexed by Pittsburgh in 1907—by 1930 the city was the tenth largest in the nation with nearly 670,000 residents.[7]

The influence of the 1893 World's Fair on the city's architecture had waned by 1933, partly due to the Great Depression and partly because of changing tastes. Architects of modern skyscrapers preferred to include sleek Art Deco motifs instead of the classical Greek, Roman, and Renaissance ornamentation of the White City. Benno Janssen's mid-1930s Mellon Institute served as the climax of Beaux Arts architecture in Oakland and the last gasp of the exposition's influence on the now crowded canvas of the once pristine neighborhood. The building's size and aesthetic would have been right at home in the 1893 fairgrounds; however, its sixty-two solid limestone columns rising over thirty-six feet into the air were the epitome of permanency, funded by and testifying to the incomparable wealth and influence of Pittsburgh's Mellon family.[8]

While Janssen's monumental columns sprang up along Fifth Avenue, the city's gleaming Beaux Arts civic center was giving way to the University of Pittsburgh, which had abandoned its Acropolis Plan in favor of its own skyscraper that used a style more familiar to American college campuses. Charles Klauder's neogothic Cathedral of Learning, which had been under construction since 1926, quickly became the centerpiece of the university and Oakland when it was dedicated in 1937. Inside the tower, nationality classrooms, which committees designed and decorated in traditional Old World styles representing various nationalities present in the Pittsburgh community, harkened back to the model villages and streets that lined the Midway Plaisance. In fact, several rooms benefited from gifts of furniture and artifacts that were displayed in national pavilions at the 1939 World's Fair in New York. Meanwhile, outside the Cathedral of Learning, the halo of surrounding Beaux Arts–influenced buildings remained a testament to the neighborhood's influential impetus.

One of those buildings, the Carnegie Institute, also continued to serve as a reminder of the fair's influence on Pittsburgh as a cultural center. Each of the Institute's Carnegie Internationals brought examples of contemporary art to the city to supplement its growing permanent collection of paintings and other works, but the impact on art acquisitions in the region did not end there. Henry Clay Frick became synonymous with art collecting by the turn of the century and his extensive collection of paintings formed the foundation of a museum in New York City, which opened in 1935. Another Pittsburgher, former treasury secretary Andrew W. Mellon, donated his art collection and an endowment to establish the National Gallery of Art in Washington, DC. Housed in a building inspired by the ancient Roman Pantheon, the gallery ensured that the world would remember Pittsburgh as a place of culture and not just a smoky city.

Much as Pittsburghers had hoped when Chicago was selected as the site of the Columbian Exposition, the fair served as an advertisement for the burgeoning industries of the region by drawing visitors into the city's factories and mills; however, the exhibits and speeches featured by Western Pennsylvanians at the 1893 World's Fair and its World's Congress Auxiliary also provided examples of Pittsburgh's ingenuity and intellectuality. Perhaps unpredictably, though, the exposition also proved to be a source of inspiration for the thousands of Pittsburghers who journeyed to the fairgrounds. While some of the resulting developments may have been inevitable, it is not a coincidence that the years immediately after the fair witnessed a rise of social and cultural organizations, as well as the realization of City Beautiful ideals throughout the city. In 1889 a promoter for Chicago's Columbian Exposition campaign proclaimed that "Pittsburg has been like a mother to us" in the wake of that city's great fire; in 1893, Chicago and its world's fair became Pittsburgh's muse, influencing its social, intellectual, and cultural development well into the twentieth century, shaping the city into its modern form.

Appendix

Western Pennsylvania Exhibits
at the Columbian Exposition

DEPARTMENT	CONTRIBUTOR	LOCATION	EXHIBIT	AWARDS
A. Agriculture	Allegheny County Home	Woodville	Wheat	
	Corry Creamery Company	Corry	Butter	Group 7. Dairy and Dairy Products
	A. P. Dale	Oil City	Rye	
	Erie Preserving Company	Erie	Canned vegetables	Group 6. Preserved Meats and Food Preparations
	James Glass	South Burgettstown	Ewe and ram	
	A. Guckenheimer and Brothers*	Pittsburgh	Rye whiskey	Group II. Whiskeys, Cider, Liqueurs and Alcohol
	H. J. Heinz Company*	Pittsburgh	Pickles, apple butter, horse-radish, malt vinegar, etc.	Group 6. Preserved Meats and Food Preparations Group 8. Tea, Coffee, Spices, Hops, and Aromatic and Vegetable Substances Group II. Whiskeys, Cider, Liqueurs and Alcohol
	James L. Iams	Swartz	Ewe	
	Joseph Jenkin	Mercer	Corn and oats	Group I. Cereals, Grasses and Forage Plants
	Mr. Kerstella	Oil City	Rye	Group I. Cereals, Grasses and Forage Plants

Large Distilling Company*	Pittsburgh	Whiskey	Group 11. Whiskeys, Cider, Liqueurs and Alcohol
John C. McClintock	Meadville	Creamery butter	Group 7. Dairy and Dairy Products
J. R. McNary	Burgettstown	Wheat	Group 1. Cereals, Grasses and Forage Plants
Charles Robinson	Mercer	Corn	
Schuetz, Renziehausen and Company*	Pittsburgh	Rye whiskey	
Lee R. Scott	South Burgettstown	Ewe and ram	Group 9. Wool in the Fleece
United States Baking Company*	Pittsburgh	Crackers and biscuits	

B. Horticulture

Allegheny Park	Allegheny	Plants	
Allegheny City Park*	Allegheny	Ferns, etc.	Group 22. Floriculture
Charles Clark	Pittsburgh	Plants	
J. W. Elliot*	Pittsburgh	Plants, blooming shrubs, sketches	Group 22. Floriculture
Berthold Frosch*	Pittsburgh	Plan of parks	
Captain Jacob J. Vandergrift	Pittsburgh	Plants	

DEPARTMENT	CONTRIBUTOR	LOCATION	EXHIBIT	AWARDS
E. Mines	Allegheny Valley Railway Company	Pittsburgh	Quartzose sandstone from Bell	
	Amy and Company	Greenville	Blue stone	
	Association of American Tin Plate Manufacturers*	Pittsburgh	Tin plate	Group 52. Metallurgy of Tin, Tin-Plate, etc.
	Beaver Falls Art Tile Company	Beaver Falls	Specimens showing the process; embossed tiles glazed to show various effects to a single color	Group 46. Graphite and Its Products; Clay and Other Fictile Materials; Asbestos
	Berwind White Coal Mining Company	Horatio	Bituminous coal vein sections from near Horatio, Aneta, and Houtzdale	Group 43. Mineral Combustibles—Coal, Coke, Petroleum, Natural Gas, etc.
	Brady's Run Fire Clay Company	West Bridgewater	Fire clay	
	Samuel S. Brown*	Pittsburgh	Safety incandescent lamp for mines; coal mining machines; lift for mines and vessels	
	Carborundum Company	Monongahela	Carborundum	Group 45. Grinding, Abrading and Polishing Substances

Carnegie Steel Company	Pittsburgh	Scotia iron ore, bombshell ore, lump ore, small-sized jigged ore	Group 49. Metallurgy of Iron and Steel, with Products
Thomas Carson	Layton's Station	Sandstone from Youghiogheny River	
Clearfield Fire Brick Company	Clearfield	Fire clays	
Consolidated Stone and Mining Company	Pittsburgh	Sandstone from Rock Point	
Crescent Steel Company*	Pittsburgh	Open hearth and crucible steel	
Davis and Harris	Rock Point	Beaver Valley sandstone	
Dixon Woods Company	Pittsburgh	Fire clay for furnace block	
Eclipse Lubricating Oil Works	Franklin	Burning oils and waxes; crude, refined, and lubricating petroleum products	
John Feeney	Walker's Mills	Blue stone	
H. C. Frick Coke Company	Scottdale	Bituminous coal vein section for Connellsville Coke; coke and coal; model of coke works	Group 43. Mineral Combustibles —Coal, Coke, Petroleum, Natural Gas, etc. Group 63. Moving, Storing and Delivering Ores, Coals, etc.

DEPARTMENT	CONTRIBUTOR	LOCATION	EXHIBIT	AWARDS
	H. C. Frick Coke Company (continued)			Group 67. History and Literature of Mining and Metallurgy
	W. S. Gresley	Erie	Column of coal	
	F. M. Guffey	Pittsburgh	Oil well boring samples from McDonald oil field, well No.12, Oakdale	
	Fred Guinmed	Allegheny	Beaver Valley sandstone	
	Harbison and Walker	Pittsburgh	Benezet fire clay	Group 46. Graphite and Its Products; Clay and Other Fictile Materials; Asbestos
	Joseph Hartman and Son	Pittsburgh	Dimension sandstone, New Galilee	Group 44. Building Stones, Marbles, Ornamental Stones and Quarry Products
	Keystone Driller Company*	Beaver Falls	Well-drilling machines	Group 61. Boring and Drilling Tools and Machinery, and Apparatus for Breaking out Ore and Coal
	Arthur Kirk and Son*	Pittsburgh	Mining tools and artificial packages of explosives	
	J. P. and E. A. Knox	Allegheny	Beaver County sandstone	

Exhibitor	Location	Exhibit	Group
George A. MacBeth Company	Pittsburgh	Sand, salt, limestone and other materials used in glass making; sample of first optical glass made in America	Group 46. Graphite and Its Products; Clay and Other Fictile Materials; Asbestos
E. M. McConnell	New Castle	Carbonate iron ore; inter conglomerate carbonate iron ore; brown hematite ore	
Monongahela Gas Coal Company	Pittsburgh	Bituminous coal vein section from First Pool Mine, Allegheny County	Group 43. Mineral Combustibles—Coal, Coke, Petroleum, Natural Gas, etc.
Alban Motsch	Erie	Foundation stone, blue slate stone	
National Cement Company	Pittsburgh	Beaver Valley sandstone	
National Iron and Steel Publishing Company	Pittsburgh	*The American Manufacturing & Iron World*	Group 67. History and Literature of Mining and Metallurgy
Oil Well Supply Company	Pittsburgh	Oil well boring samples drilled at the 1890 Western Pennsylvania Exposition; tools and methods of producing oil	Group 42. Minerals, Ores, Native Metals, Gems and Crystals—Geological Specimens; Group 43. Mineral Combustibles—Coal, Coke, Petroleum, Natural Gas, etc.

DEPARTMENT	CONTRIBUTOR	LOCATION	EXHIBIT	AWARDS
	Oil Well Supply Company (continued)			Group 61. Boring and Drilling Tools and Machinery, and Apparatus for Breaking out Ore and Coal Group 62. Pumps, Engines and Apparatus Used in Mining for Pumping, Draining and Hoisting Group 69. Motors and Apparatus for the Generation and Transmission of Power—Hydraulic and Pneumatic Apparatus (Dept. F) Group 71. Machine Tools and Machines for Working Metals (Dept. F)
	Pittsburgh Coal Exchange*	Pittsburgh	Miniature steamboat for coal barges	
	Pittsburgh Consolidated Coal Company	Pittsburgh	Bituminous coal vein section from Jumbo Mine, Washington County	Group 43. Mineral Combustibles—Coal, Coke, Petroleum, Natural Gas, etc.
	Pittsburgh Crushed Steel Company, Ltd.	Pittsburgh	Crushed steel and steel emery samples	Group 45. Grinding, Abrading and Polishing Substances Group 58. Quarrying and Working Stone

Pittsburgh Reduction Company*	Pittsburgh	Aluminum	Group 66. Assaying Apparatus and Fixtures
Pittsburgh Stone Company	Pittsburgh	Sandstone from Layton's Station	
Pittsburgh Testing Laboratory*	Pittsburgh	Analytical chemistry exhibit and specimens	Group 66. Assaying Apparatus and Fixtures
Frank Senger	Erie	Sandstone from LeBoeuf	
Shaner Gas Coal Company	Pittsburgh	Bituminous coal vein section from Shaner Mine, Westmoreland County	
Singer, Minick and Company*	Pittsburgh	Steel	Group 51. Copper and its Alloys, Metallurgy
Joseph Soisson and Sons	Connellsville	Fire clay used in mill and coke oven bricks	
Soisson and Kilpatrick	Connellsville	Flint fire clay	
Star Encaustic Tile Company, Ltd.	Pittsburgh	Specimens to illustrate the process of manufacturing plain and encaustic tiles	Group 46. Graphite and Its Products; Clay and Other Fictile Materials; Asbestos
H. F. Stark	Greensburg	Sandstone from Bull Rock, Bolivar	
Sterling Steel Company*	Pittsburgh	Steel armor-piercing projectiles	Group 49. Metallurgy of Iron and Steel, with Products

DEPARTMENT	CONTRIBUTOR	LOCATION	EXHIBIT	AWARDS
	David H. Taylor	Freeport	Sandstone	
	Tyler Tube Company*	Washington	Charcoal iron blooms and boiler tubes	Group 49. Metallurgy of Iron and Steel, with Products
	Uniontown Firestone Company	Uniontown	Firestone for lining cupolas and Bessemer converters	
	Walker's Mills Quarry Company	Walker's Mills	Sandstone	
	Welch, Gloninger and Maxwell	Pittsburgh	Flint fire clay; soft or interior fire clay used in fire brick and buff building brick; red clay for paving brick	Group 46. Graphite and Its Products; Clay and Other Fictile Materials; Asbestos
	Welch, Gloninger and Company	Pittsburgh	Fire clay used in fire bricks and buff building bricks	
	Westmoreland Fire Brick Company	Pittsburgh	Fire clay for furnace bricks; buff building bricks	
	Wilson Brothers and Company	Ellwood City	Beaver Valley sandstone	
	John A. Wood	Pittsburgh	Map to accompany report of the Commission on the Lake Erie and Ohio River Ship Canal	
	W. Dewees Wood Company*	Pittsburgh	Iron and steel sheets and plates	Group 51. Copper and its Alloys, Metallurgy

F. Machinery			
Woodland Fire Brick Company, Ltd.	Woodland	Fire clays	
Ball Engine Company	Erie	Engines	Group 69. Motors and Apparatus for the Generation and Transmission of Power—Hydraulic and Pneumatic Apparatus
Brown Folding Machine Company*	Erie	Folding machine	Group 74. Machines and Apparatus for Type Setting, Printing, Stamping, Embossing and for Making Books and Paper Working
Downie Pump Company*	New Brighton	Pumps and valves	
Erie City Iron Works*	Erie	High speed automatic cut-off engines	Group 69. Motors and Apparatus for the Generation and Transmission of Power—Hydraulic and Pneumatic Apparatus
Franklin Portable Hoist Company*	Franklin	Crane and hoist	
Charles L. Goehring*	Allegheny	Molding and carving machines	Group 73. Machines for Working Wood

DEPARTMENT	CONTRIBUTOR	LOCATION	EXHIBIT	AWARDS
	W. W. Grier*	Verona	Ingraining machine	Group 73. Machines for Working Wood
	Jarecki Manufacturing Company*	Erie	Screw-threading machines	Group 69. Motors and Apparatus for the Generation and Transmission of Power—Hydraulic and Pneumatic Apparatus
	William E. Leard*	New Brighton	Connecting rods, etc.	
	J. J. Mannion and Company*	Pittsburgh	Silk looms	
	Phoenix Iron Works*	Meadville	Engines	Group 69. Motors and Apparatus for the Generation and Transmission of Power—Hydraulic and Pneumatic Apparatus
	Stearns Manufacturing Company*	Erie	Boilers, engines, and sawmill machinery	Group 69. Motors and Apparatus for the Generation and Transmission of Power—Hydraulic and Pneumatic Apparatus Group 73. Machines for Working Wood

Company	City	Product	Group
N. A. Watson*	Erie	Boiler feeder	Group 69. Motors and Apparatus for the Generation and Transmission of Power—Hydraulic and Pneumatic Apparatus
Wilson, Snyder Manufacturing Company*	Pittsburgh	Pumps	

G. Transportation

Company	City	Product	Group
Duff Manufacturing Company*	Allegheny	Compound lever jacks	
A. French Spring Company*	Pittsburgh	Nut lock and washers; elliptic and spiral springs	Group 80. Railways, Railway Plant and Equipment
Arthur Kirk*	Pittsburgh	Navigation lock	
McConway and Torley Company*	Pittsburgh	Passenger coach platforms and couplers	
Noble Nut Lock and Washer Company*	Pittsburgh	Nuts, locks and washers	
Norris Box Lid Company*	Pittsburgh	Journal box lids	
Pennsylvania Railroad Company*	Altoona	Refrigerator, stock, freight, and passenger cars; suburban station with footbridge	Group 80. Railways, Railway Plant and Equipment

DEPARTMENT	CONTRIBUTOR	LOCATION	EXHIBIT	AWARDS
	Pittsburgh Locomotive and Car Works*	Pittsburgh	Locomotive tenders	Group 80. Railways, Railway Plant and Equipment
	H. K. Porter and Company*	Pittsburgh	Locomotive and steam motors	
	Schoen Manufacturing Company*	Pittsburgh	Railroad ties and special steel articles for ties	Group 80. Railways, Railway Plant and Equipment
	Schoen Pressed Steel Brake Beam Company*	Pittsburgh	Brake beam	
	Frederick Schwitler*	Allegheny	Milk wagon	
	Verona Tool Works*	Pittsburgh	Steel track tools	Group 80. Railways, Railway Plant and Equipment
	Westinghouse Air Brake Company*	Pittsburgh	Air brakes and train signaling apparatus	Group 80. Railways, Railway Plant and Equipment
H. Manufactures	Charlotte Arrowsmith*	Mercer	Silk weaving	Group 100. Silk and Silk Fabrics
	John Bradley Company*	Pittsburgh	Cutaway coat	Group 104. Clothing and Costumes
	Joseph Callery and Company*	Pittsburgh	Harness and shoe leather	
	Mrs. C. E. Cooper*	Oil City	Oak inlaid table	Group 90. Furniture of Interiors, Upholstery and Artistic Decoration

Company	City	Product	Group
Dawes and Myler*	New Brighton	Bathtubs and laundry trays	Group 120. Plumbing and Sanitary Materials
James H. Dias*	Irwin	Horseshoes	
Fayerweather and Ladew*	Clearfield	Belting and sole leather	
William Flaccus and Sons*	Pittsburgh	Leather	Group 111. Leather and Maufactures of Leather
Belinda Fluke*	Kittanning	Embroidered center pieces	Group 106. Laces, Embroideries, Trimmings, Artificial Flowers, Fans, etc.
Griswold Manufacturing Company*	Erie	Hollow ware	Group 116. Refrigerators, Hollow Metal Ware, Tinware, Enameled Ware
A. Groetzinger and Sons*	Allegheny	Sole leather; shoe and leather building	Group 111. Leather and Maufactures of Leather
J. Groetzinger and Company*	Allegheny	Harness leather; shoe and leather building	
George A. MacBeth Company*	Pittsburgh	Optical and lamp glass	Group 94. Glass and Glassware
Mayer Pottery Company, Ltd.*	Beaver Falls	Glazed printed earthenware	Group 91. Ceramics and Mosaics
Conroy Prugh and Company*	Allegheny	Mirrors	Group 94. Glass and Glassware

DEPARTMENT	CONTRIBUTOR	LOCATION	EXHIBIT	AWARDS
	Metric Metal Company*	Erie	Gas and water meters	Group 112. Scales, Weights and Measures
	Standard Manufacturing Company*	Pittsburgh	Bathtubs and plumbers' ironware	Group 120. Plumbing and Sanitary Materials
	J. S. Thomas*	Erie	Refrigerators	
	U.S. Glass Company*	Pittsburgh	Glassware, blown glass, and pressed glass	Group 94. Glass and Glassware
	Werner Itschner and Company*	Mercer	Silk ribbon	Group 100. Silk and Silk Fabrics
	Women's Silk Couture Association Company*	Mercer	Superior reeled silk and flags	Group 100. Silk and Silk Fabrics
J. Electricity	Phoenix Glass Company*	Pittsburgh	Electrolier globes and shades	Group 129. Lighting by Electricity
	Standard Underground Cable Company*	Pittsburgh	Static arresters	
	Westinghouse Electric and Manufacturing Company*	Pittsburgh	Induction coils and converters; transformers, motors, and dynamos; meters and switches; Columbian Exposition power plant	Group 81. Street Car and Other Short Line Systems (Dept. G) Group 122. Apparatus Illustrating the Phenomena and Laws of Electricity and Magnetism Group 123. Apparatus for Electrical Measurements

Group 125. Machines and Appliances for Producing Electrical Currents by Mechanical Power—Dynamical Electricity

Group 126. Transmission and Regulation of the Electrical Current

Group 127. Electric Motors

Group 128. Application of Electric Motors

Group 129. Lighting by Electricity

Group 138-A. Progress and Development in Electrical Science and Construction, As Illustrated by Models and Drawings

Group 140. Paintings in Oil

K. Fine Arts

Edward T. Boggs	Pittsburgh	Architectural design for monument
Thomas Shields Clarke	Pittsburgh	Oil painting: *A Fool's Fool*
Ida Joy Didler	Allegheny	Oil painting: *Portrait*
Martha Goldman	Pittsburgh	Oil painting: *Portrait of Gustav Goldman*
George Hetzel	Pittsburgh	Oil paintings: *Wood Scene* and *Study from Nature*
D. B. Walkley	Pittsburgh	Oil painting: *The Potter*

DEPARTMENT	CONTRIBUTOR	LOCATION	EXHIBIT	AWARDS
	Alfred Bryan Walls	Pittsburgh	Oil painting: *Across the Meadows*	
	Johanna K. Woodwell	Pittsburgh	Oil painting: *Study, Head of a Young Lady*; water-color: *Portrait of Miss L.*	
	Joseph Ryan Woodwell	Pittsburgh	Oil paintings: *White Rocks, Magnolia, Mass.; A Rocky Coast, Magnolia, Mass.; Cobblestone Beach, Magnolia, Mass.; and Rocks at Low Tide, Magnolia, Mass.*	
L. Liberal Arts	Allegheny Public Schools	Allegheny	Student work	Group 149. Primary, Secondary and Superior Education
	Altoona Public Schools	Altoona	Student work	Group 149. Primary, Secondary and Superior Education
	Benedictine Academy*	Allegheny	Student work	Group 149. Primary, Secondary and Superior Education
	John Brashear*	Allegheny	Telescopes	Group 151. Instruments of Precision, Experiment, Research and Photography; Photographs

Carroll Aluminum Manufacturing Company*	Meadville	Aluminum dental surgical instruments	Group 148. Instruments and Apparatus of Medicine, Surgery and Prosthesis
Central Public High School	Pittsburgh	Student work	Group 149. Primary, Secondary and Superior Education
Colby Piano Company	Erie	Pianos	Group 158. Music and Musical Instruments—The Theatre
Corry Public Schools	Corry	Student work	Group 149. Primary, Secondary and Superior Education
George Washington Gale Ferris Jr.*	Pittsburgh	Ferris wheel	Group 152. Civil Engineering, Public Works, Constructive Architecture
Holy Cross School*	Pittsburgh	Student work	Group 149. Primary, Secondary and Superior Education
Holy Family School*	Latrobe	Student work	Group 149. Primary, Secondary and Superior Education
Holy Ghost College*	Pittsburgh	Student work	Group 149. Primary, Secondary and Superior Education

DEPARTMENT	CONTRIBUTOR	LOCATION	EXHIBIT	AWARDS
	Johnstown Public Schools	Johnstown	Student work	Group 149. Primary, Secondary and Superior Education
	McMillan Sash Balance Company*	Pittsburgh	Sash balance and lock	Group 152. Civil Engineering, Public Works, Constructive Architecture
	Meadville Public Schools	Meadville	Sewing	
	Charles H. Miller*	Pittsburgh	Appliances for cleansing water mains	
	Pittsburgh Diocese Colleges and Academies*	Pittsburgh	Class work	
	Pittsburgh Public Schools	Pittsburgh	Student work	Group 149. Primary, Secondary and Superior Education
	Shaw Piano Company	Erie	Pianos	Group 158. Music and Musical Instruments—The Theatre
	Slippery Rock Normal School	Slippery Rock	Student work	
	Soldier's and Sailor's Home	Erie	Photographs	Group 147. Physical Development, Training and Condition—Hygiene
	Saint Agnes School*	Pittsburgh	Student work	Group 149. Primary, Secondary and Superior Education

School	Location	Category	Group
Saint Andrews School*	Allegheny	Student work	Group 149. Primary, Secondary and Superior Education
Saint Augustine School*	Pittsburgh	Student work	Group 149. Primary, Secondary and Superior Education
Saint Benedicts School*	Pittsburgh	Student work	Group 149. Primary, Secondary and Superior Education
Saint Bridget's School*	Pittsburgh	Student work	Group 149. Primary, Secondary and Superior Education
Saint George's School*	Pittsburgh	Student work	Group 149. Primary, Secondary and Superior Education
Saint James School*	Pittsburgh	Student work	Group 149. Primary, Secondary and Superior Education
Saint John Baptist School*	Pittsburgh	Student work	Group 149. Primary, Secondary and Superior Education
Saint John's School*	Pittsburgh	Student work	Group 149. Primary, Secondary and Superior Education
Saint Joseph's Academy*	Greensburg	Student work	Group 149. Primary, Secondary and Superior Education

DEPARTMENT	CONTRIBUTOR	LOCATION	EXHIBIT	AWARDS
	Saint Joseph's School*	Allegheny	Student work	Group 149. Primary, Secondary and Superior Education
	Saint Joseph's School*	Pittsburgh	Student work	Group 149. Primary, Secondary and Superior Education
	Saint Joseph's School*	Sharpsburg	Student work	Group 149. Primary, Secondary and Superior Education
	Saint Kieman's School*	Pittsburgh	Student work	Group 149. Primary, Secondary and Superior Education
	Saint Malachy's School*	Pittsburgh	Student work	Group 149. Primary, Secondary and Superior Education
	Saint Mary of Mercy School*	Pittsburgh	Student work	Group 149. Primary, Secondary and Superior Education
	Saint Mary's Academy*	Pittsburgh	Student work	Group 149. Primary, Secondary and Superior Education
	Saint Mary's Male School*	Allegheny	Student work	Group 149. Primary, Secondary and Superior Education

Saint Mary's School*	Allegheny	Student work	Group 149. Primary, Secondary and Superior Education
Saint Mary's School*	Pittsburgh	Student work	Group 149. Primary, Secondary and Superior Education
Saint Michael Male and Female School*	Pittsburgh	Student work	Group 149. Primary, Secondary and Superior Education
Saint Patrick's School*	Pittsburgh	Student work	Group 149. Primary, Secondary and Superior Education
Saint Paul's Female School*	Pittsburgh	Student work	Group 149. Primary, Secondary and Superior Education
Saint Paul's Male School*	Pittsburgh	Student work	Group 149. Primary, Secondary and Superior Education
Saint Paul's School*	Butler	Student work	Group 149. Primary, Secondary and Superior Education
Saint Peter and Paul's School*	Pittsburgh	Student work	Group 149. Primary, Secondary and Superior Education
Saint Peter's School*	Allegheny	Student work	Group 149. Primary, Secondary and Superior Education

DEPARTMENT	CONTRIBUTOR	LOCATION	EXHIBIT	AWARDS
	Saint Peter's School*	Pittsburgh	Student work	Group 149. Primary, Secondary and Superior Education
	Saint Thomas' School*	Braddock	Student work	Group 149. Primary, Secondary and Superior Education
	Titusville Public Schools	Titusville	Student work	
	Ursuline Convent*	Pittsburgh	Student work	Group 149. Primary, Secondary and Superior Education
	Western Penitentiary	Allegheny	Model of cell house and cell blocks; prison work samples	
	Western University of Pennsylvania	Allegheny	Photographs, publications, instruments, and faculty and student work	Group 149. Primary, Secondary and Superior Education
M. Ethnology	William Spriesterbach*	Pittsburgh	Historical section	
N. Forestry	Armstrong Brothers and Company*	Pittsburgh	Cork	

* = Private exhibit not part of the Pennsylvania State Exhibit

Note: Exhibit list compiled from *Catalogue of the Exhibits of the State of Pennsylvania and of Pennsylvanians at the World's Columbian Exposition.* Award information compiled from "List of awards, as copied for Mrs. Virginia C. Meredith, Chairman, Committee on Awards, Board of Lady Managers, from the official records in the office Hon. John Boyd Thacher, Chairman, Executive Committee on Awards" [1895].

Notes

INTRODUCTION

Epigraph: Margaret Mitchell to Elizabeth Louise Magee, June 11, 1893, box 4, folder 8, Magee Family Papers, Archives and Special Collections, University of Pittsburgh Library System.

1. Patton, "'Sell the Cookstove If Necessary,'" 44. Other notable debuts included Juicy Fruit gum and the United States Postal Service's first commemorative stamps. The fair is also where the Pabst Brewing Company earned its now famous blue ribbon.

2. Doenecke, "Myths, Machines and Markets," 535, 546. Doenecke argues that the use of beautiful and familiar art and architecture helped visitors overcome the shock associated with their encounters with massive machinery. Because the imagery used harkened back to ancient Greece and the Roman Empire, fairgoers also made the connection that for the United States to succeed these great powers they would need to rely on such technologies.

3. Karlowicz, "American Expositions and Architecture," 275. Appelbaum, *Spectacle in the White City*, 15.

4. Schlereth, *Victorian America*, 148. Doenecke, "Myths, Machines and Markets," 545.

5. Schlereth, *Victorian America*, 171. Trachtenberg, *Incorporation of America*, 231. By reinforcing elite culture the exposition, in turn, informed developing middle-class ideals and culture.

6. Rydell, *All the World's a Fair*, 6, 40, 67. Rydell has established himself as the expert on the role of ethnicity and racism in world's fairs. Cotkin, *Reluctant Modernism*, 71.

I: A FAIR HISTORY OF PITTSBURGH

1. Grom, *Physician-Soldiers at the Forks*, 92. Dahlinger, "Pittsburgh Sanitary Fair," 100. Daniel, "Sanitary Fair," 156.

2. Grom, *Physician-Soldiers at the Forks*, 89. Daniel, "Sanitary Fair," 147.

3. Grom, *Physician-Soldiers at the Forks*, 89. Daniel, "Sanitary Fair," 147.

4. Dahlinger, "Pittsburgh Sanitary Fair," 98–99. Dahlinger provides more specific information about the exact location of the fairgrounds and the work that went into preparing the site.

5. Grom, *Physician-Soldiers at the Forks*, 89.

6. Daniel, "Sanitary Fair," 152. Dahlinger, "Pittsburgh Sanitary Fair," 99.

7. Address of the Planning Commission, April 15, 1864, quoted in Grom, *Physician-Soldiers at the Forks*, 90. The Birmingham referenced in the address is the present-day South Side of Pittsburgh. Daniel, "Sanitary Fair," 148–49, also quotes the address and includes the names of the executive committee.

8. Daniel, "Sanitary Fair," 153–54.

9. Grom, *Physician-Soldiers at the Forks*, 95.

10. Daniel, "Sanitary Fair," 156.

11. Dahlinger, "Pittsburgh Sanitary Fair," 100. Daniel, "Sanitary Fair," 156–57. Grom, *Physician-Soldiers at the Forks*, 92. For a list of the full parade procession, see "Military and Civic Procession for the Formal Opening of the Pittsburgh Sanitary Fair," *Daily Commercial*, June 1, 1864, and "Pittsburgh Sanitary Fair," *Pittsburgh Gazette*, June 1, 1864. For descriptions of the opening parade and ceremonies, see "The Great Fair," *Daily Commercial*, June 2, 1864, and "Opening of the Sanitary Fair," *Pittsburgh Gazette*, June 2, 1864.

12. Daniel, "Sanitary Fair," 154–58. Dahlinger, "Pittsburgh Sanitary Fair," 100. Detailed descriptions of the buildings and their decorations can be found in "The Great Fair," *Daily Commercial*, June 2, 1864.

13. Daniel, "Sanitary Fair," 151. "The Great Fair," *Daily Commercial*, June 2, 1864.

14. "Catalogue of the Old Curiosity Shop," *Pittsburgh Gazette*, June 17, 1864. Daniel, "Sanitary Fair," 151, 158–59. Daniel provides a more comprehensive list of the items on display.

15. "Sanitary Fair," *Daily Commercial*, June 7, 1864. For example, evening entertainments in the auditorium for the week of June 6 included several German concerts and religious meetings, among other events.

16. Dahlinger, "Pittsburgh Sanitary Fair," 101.

17. Daniel, "Sanitary Fair," 145. Dahlinger, "Pittsburgh Sanitary Fair," 101. For comparison, Dahlinger provides the per capita donations for St. Louis ($3.44), Philadelphia ($1.83), Cleveland ($1.81), Brooklyn ($1.50), New York ($1.47), and Cincinnati ($1.46). Dahlinger also claims that "it was a rule of the management that no tickets should knowingly be sold to negroes," which seems to contradict the claim in Glasco,

WPA History of the Negro in Pittsburgh (99), that Susan Vashon, an African American woman, raised several thousand dollars for the fair. In "Double Burden: The Black Experience in Pittsburgh," Glasco places Pittsburgh's Black population at between 1,100 and 2,000 people at this time.

18. "The Sanitary Fair," *Gazette*, June 1, 1864. Daniel, "Sanitary Fair," 151, claims that the Pittsburgh fair was also the most organized, which aided its success.

19. Wolmar, *Blood, Iron, and Gold*, 222. In chapter 9, Wolmer discusses the impact the railroad had on several countries throughout the world.

20. Miller, "Pennsylvania's Petroleum Industry," 201. Miller's article provides a cursory overview of the oil industry in Western Pennsylvania.

21. Couvares, *Remaking of Pittsburgh*, 10. These figures are compared to the doubling of employment in coal and glass and the tripling of capital investment and product value of other industries in Allegheny County.

22. Morris, *Tycoons*, 119. For a contemporary description of the 1876 World's Fair, see McCabe, *Illustrated History of the Centennial Exhibition* and Ingram, *Centennial Exposition Described and Illustrated*.

23. Rydell, *All the World's a Fair*, 10–11.

24. Morris, *Tycoons*, 120. For a detailed account of opening day, see Ingram, *Centennial Exposition Described and Illustrated*, 65–88.

25. Norton, *Frank Leslie's Illustrated Historical Register*, 261. Entries for Pittsburgh glass exhibits can be found in Centennial Exhibition Philadelphia, Pa., *International Exhibition, 1876*, part I, 108–9, 114.

26. For leather crafts, see Centennial Exhibition Philadelphia, Pa., *International Exhibition, 1876*, part III, 114, and for harvesting tools part IV, 25–32. McCabe, *Illustrated History of the Centennial Exhibition*, 473. Other companies from Western Pennsylvania included J. C. Bidwell; Speer, Alexander and Sons; Stratton and Cullum; John A. Hafner; and Rankin Manufacturing Company.

27. Centennial Exhibition Philadelphia, Pa., *International Exhibition, 1876*, part III, 45–48.

28. Leupp, *George Westinghouse*, 64–71. Prout, *Life of George Westinghouse*, 21–76. Because George Westinghouse destroyed or otherwise did not maintain his personal correspondence, much of what is known about his life and career comes from biographies written shortly after his death and personal reminiscences of colleagues and employees.

29. *Description of the Westinghouse Air Brake Co.'s Exhibits*. Centennial Exhibition Philadelphia, Pa., *International Exhibition, 1876*, part III, 46.

30. Centennial Exhibition Philadelphia, Pa., *International Exhibition, 1876*, part III, 38, 53.

31. Centennial Exhibition Philadelphia, Pa., *International Exhibition, 1876*, part I, 55–59. Other Western Pennsylvania companies included McKeesport Iron Works; Black Diamond Steel Works; Crescent Steel Works; Soho Iron Mills; Sligo Iron Mills; Cambria Iron and Steel Company; Hussey, Wells and Company; William Clark and Company; Reese, Graff and Woods; Brown and Company; Wayne Iron and Steel Works; Wilson, Walker and Company; Singer, Nimick and Company; Pennsylvania Lead Company; and four of Andrew Carnegie's companies: Edgar Thomson Steel Company, Lucy Furnace, Carnegie Brothers and Company, and Keystone Bridge Company.

32. McCabe, *Illustrated History of the Centennial Exhibition*, 354. Centennial Exhibition Philadelphia, Pa., *International Exhibition, 1876*, part I, 55–56.

33. Ingram, *Centennial Exposition Described and Illustrated*, 193. The Eads Bridge project was a watershed moment for Carnegie's iron and steel ventures. The project was fraught with adversity and the lessons Carnegie learned while building the bridge likely shaped his business practices for decades thereafter. See Morris, *Tycoons*, 93–94; and Nasaw, *Andrew Carnegie*, 134–36.

34. Nasaw, *Andrew Carnegie*, 140–41. Centennial Exhibition Philadelphia, Pa., *International Exhibition*, part IV, 147.

35. Butko, "Heinz," 24. Alberts, *Good Provider*, 28.

36. Skrabec, *H. J. Heinz*, 71. While Skrabec claims that Heinz had a small booth with pickles, mustard, and ketchup at the Centennial Exposition, the fair's official catalog does not list such an exhibit.

37. Ingram, *Centennial Exposition Described and Illustrated*, 576–78. Ingram refers to the schoolchildren excursion as "Pittsburgh's Day" and explains that it was an example of how meticulous planning and organization could lead to a successful trip to the fair.

38. Parke, *Recollections of Seventy Years*, 133–34. "Western Pennsylvania Exposition Society," box 2, folder 4, Britta C. Dwyer Papers, Detre Library and Archives, Senator John Heinz History Center, Pittsburgh.

39. Couvares, *Remaking of Pittsburgh*, 101. Couvares attributes some of the exposition's early success to its manager, William C. Smythe, who had experience as a reporter and a theater manager, making him just the right person to appeal to the masses.

40. Alberts, *Good Provider*, 15. "Pittsburgh Tradesmen's Institute Supplement," *Frank Leslie's Illustrated Historical Register*, December 11, 1875, consists of four pages describing all the exhibits of the inaugural exposition with illustrations. Couvares, *Remaking of Pittsburgh*, 101, notes that there were halls of machinery and horticulture, a local artist exhibit, and several candy and soda vendors.

41. Samber, "Networks of Capital," 62.

42. Muller, "Industrial Suburbs," 66. Muller also notes that the growth of these

ancillary industries along rail lines connecting major manufacturing companies to natural resources, in addition to topographical features in Western Pennsylvania, led to
expansion well outside of Pittsburgh's traditional locus.

43. Samber, "Networks of Capital," 138. Harvey, *Henry Clay Frick*, 39–43. Frick's
persistence resulted in two $10,000 loans to build an additional one hundred beehive
coke ovens.

44. Samber, "Networks of Capital," 50. These numbers are estimates based on contemporary chamber of commerce reports.

45. Tarr, "Infrastructure and City-Building," 228. Tarr notes that the high cost of
transportation forced blue-collar workers to live within walking distance of their jobs,
necessitating increases in population clustered around expanding manufacturing centers. Couvares, *Remaking of Pittsburgh*, 80–81, shows that in 1880 the combined population of Pittsburgh and Allegheny constituted 66 percent of the people in Allegheny
County. By 1900 that number shrank to 58.5 percent, a testament to steel mill expansion outside of city limits, particularly along the Monongahela and Ohio Rivers, as well
as the early development of suburbs.

46. Couvares, *Remaking of Pittsburgh*, 33. The transition to steel and the employment of more unskilled workers, which took power away from the old guard ironwork-
ers, in a way made the steel mill a more democratic workplace because employment and
pay was no longer based on personal relationships, thus benefiting the incoming immigrant population and allowing them to influence worker culture.

47. Schlereth, *Victorian America*, 171. Jucha, "Anatomy of a Streetcar Suburb,"
explores the rise of the Shadyside neighborhood in the East End as an example of this
trend. New houses, built to order, provided the perfect opportunity for middle-class
families to furnish them with the latest appliances, technologies, and frivolities. For an
example of what family life looked like in the developing East End, see Spencer, *Spencers of Amberson Avenue*.

48. Kleinberg, "Technology and Women's Work," 68, 71.

49. Hays, "Development of Pittsburgh," 436. Muller, "Industrial Suburbs," 70, succinctly explains that commuters and the railroads pushed the boundaries of the city and
local venture capitalists benefited from the need to develop infrastructure.

50. Couvares, *Remaking of Pittsburgh*, 64. Bernstein, "Pittsburgh's Benevolent
Tyrant," 36–38. Steffens, *Shame of the Cities*, 155. Steffens's exposé of the Magee-Flinn
machine was first published in *McClure's Magazine* in May 1903 and was republished
as a chapter in his 1904 book along with articles about corruption in Philadelphia, St.
Louis, Minneapolis, Chicago, and New York. The book became one of the earliest examples of muckraking journalism.

51. Steffens, *Shame of the Cities*, 157. Couvares, *Remaking of Pittsburgh*, 64, also

points out that since the upper class benefited from the machine, it in turn became the enemy of the labor movement because it impoverished the working class and threatened unions as its primary source of influence.

52. Bernstein, "Pittsburgh's Benevolent Tyrant," 39. Steffens, *Shame of the Cities*, 177, provides the example that "the building of bridges is one function of the municipality as a servant of the traction company. . . . When the Magee railways went over [the bridges] some of them had to be rebuilt."

53. Davis, "Tycoon Medievalism," 787–88, 792. Carnegie, *Gospel of Wealth*.

54. *Seventh Annual Pittsburgh Exposition, 1883*, 7, 54. Parke, *Recollections of Seventy Years*, 135.

55. Couvares, *Remaking of Pittsburgh*, 101.

56. *Seventh Annual Pittsburgh Exposition, 1883*, 9. Admission for children under twelve years of age was fifteen cents. Couvares, *Remaking of Pittsburgh*, 16, shows that laborers at rolling mills made on average only about $1.25 per day in 1880.

57. Parke, *Recollections of Seventy Years*, 136.

58. *Seventh Annual Pittsburgh Exposition, 1883*, 54–55, contains a detailed description of the buildings and grounds. The Pittsburgh Baseball Club formed in 1882 as a founding member of the American League and was often referred to as the Alleghenys. The Pirates name would not take root until 1891.

59. Crow, "Report of the Chief Engineer," 252–61, contains a detailed list of the losses from the fire, including a brief description of the exhibits, their owners, and their insurance coverage. The list includes familiar names like Heinz, Kaufmann, Boggs & Buhl, Brashear, and Westinghouse, among others. Fleming, *History of Pittsburgh and Environs*, 2:135.

60. *Seventh Annual Pittsburgh Exposition, 1883*, 68. Other expositions that year were scheduled in Boston, Cincinnati, Denver, Louisville, and Milwaukee. There were also about twenty-five state and district fairs in North America.

61. Fleming, *History of Pittsburgh and Environs*, 2:135. Alberts, *Good Provider*, 94. Skrabec, *H. J. Heinz*, 112.

62. Tome, "Western Pennsylvania Exposition, 1889–1916," 21. Alberts, *Good Provider*, 94, and Skrabec, *H. J. Heinz*, 112, also reference the opening celebration concerts.

63. Tome, "Western Pennsylvania Exposition, 1889–1916," 27.

64. Tome, "Western Pennsylvania Exposition, 1889–1916," 28.

2: PLANNING FOR THE EXPOSITION

1. *Universal Exhibition, Paris, 1889*. For a contemporary American review of the fair, see Brownell, "Paris Exposition."

2. *Reports of the United States Commissioners* contains government reports; lists

of American delegates, commissioners and jurors; and exhibitors and awardees from the United States.

3. Brownell, "Paris Exposition," 23.

4. Brownell, "Paris Exposition," 24. The lack of confidence in American artists, architects, and designers was also the exact perception the exposition sought to overcome on a global scale, much like the Centennial Exposition sought to promote the resurgence of American business and industry on a world stage.

5. Brain, "Discipline & Style," 831.

6. Handy, *Official Directory*, 41–42, reports that two people claimed credit for the Columbian Exposition idea—Zaremba and Alexander D. Anderson of Washington, DC. While both men claimed years of work in promoting the concept, Zaremba is acknowledged in official fair publications as the originator of the idea, likely because he lived in Chicago. See "Originator of the World's Columbian Exposition," *World's Columbian Exposition Illustrated*, October 1892, 192–93.

7. "They Want the Fair," *Pittsburg Dispatch*, July 26, 1889. It was reported that a total of sixty prominent New York City residents would be responsible for coordinating with city, state, and national organizers to bring the fair to New York.

8. Andrew Carnegie to J. Lowber Welsh, January 22, 1874, box 9, folder 3, Records of the Carnegie Steel Corporation, Detre Library and Archives, Senator John Heinz History Center, Pittsburgh. Nasaw, *Andrew Carnegie*, 140. Livesay, *Andrew Carnegie*, 113. Carnegie's iron ventures were relatively new in 1874 and so the exposition contracts were important not only for the short-term success of his companies but also for the long-term promotion of iron as a construction material. In comparison, by 1889 Carnegie's steel empire was under a constant state of expansion and swimming in profits.

9. Lederer, "Competition for the World's Columbian Exposition," 387. For an overview of the New York campaign, see Parmet, "Competition for the World's Columbian Exposition."

10. "A Macedonian Call," *Pittsburg Dispatch*, October 19, 1889. For a short biography of William Bennett Cunningham see Campbell, *Biographical History with Portraits*, 556.

11. Committee for the International Exposition of 1892 of the City of New York, *Address to the Senate and House of Representatives*, 25. Among other interesting features of this publication are the lists of committees working to bring the fair to New York for which the members were a veritable who's who of American business and society, including William Rockefeller, J. P. Morgan, Cornelius Vanderbilt, William Waldorf Astor, Jay Gould, P. T. Barnum, Joseph Pulitzer, and Henry Hilton, among others.

12. Committee for the International Exposition of 1892 of the City of New York, *Address to the Senate and House of Representatives*, 5–8.

13. Johnson, *History of the World's Columbian Exposition*, 1:7–13. Bancroft, *Book of the Fair*, 1:39–40. For more information on the Chicago bid's finances and preparations for its congressional presentation, see Lederer, "Competition for the World's Columbian Exposition."

14. "Chicago's Day," *Pittsburgh Post*, February 25, 1890. The front-page article chronicled every ballot, documenting the sentiments of Western Pennsylvanian congressmen.

15. "Pittsburgh Pleased with the Selection of Chicago for the Big World's Fair of '92," *Pittsburg Dispatch*, February 25, 1890. By this time Andrews was a famous engineer known for solving complex design problems.

16. "Chicago Deserves It," *Pittsburgh Press*, February 25, 1890.

17. *Pennsylvania and the World's Columbian Exposition*, 28. For more on the final bill and a complete list of commissioners, see Johnson, *History of the World's Columbian Exposition*, 1:15–20.

18. Downey, *Season of Renewal*, 108.

19. Bancroft, *Book of the Fair*, 1:196–234. *Official Manual of the Board of Lady Managers*, 29–31.

20. *Pittsburgh Post*, July 5, 1890. "Still in a Muddle," *Pittsburgh Post*, August 19, 1890.

21. "Gourley Scores Chicago," *Pittsburgh Press*, September 18, 1890. Gourley's statement was in relation to the two-site idea, which he did not support.

22. "The Fair and the Site," *Pittsburgh Post*, September 26, 1890.

23. Karlowicz, "D. H. Burnham's Role," 251. The debate over the site was also a public struggle for authority between the national commission and the local board of directors.

24. "View of the Columbus Dome According to Revised Plans," *Pittsburgh Post*, November 28, 1890. This article was republished from the *Chicago Tribune* based on information provided in a circular authored by Hallock.

25. Downey, *Season of Renewal*, 29–30. For a complete account of attractions in the Midway, see Flinn, *Official Guide to Midway Plaisance*, and Johnson, *History of the World's Columbian Exposition*, 2:333–40. For the transition of the Midway concept, see Larson, *Devil in the White City*, 159–60.

26. Karlowicz, "D. H. Burnham's Role," 253. The selection of architects from around the nation also ensured approval from the national commission, thus preventing the same delays that had plagued the selection of the fair's site. For an extensive review of Burnham's pursuit of architects for the Columbian Exposition, see Larson, *Devil in the White City*, 77–84.

27. Downey, *Season of Renewal*, 18–21. Burnham et al., *Final Official Report of the Director*, I:2, 33–62. Larson, *Devil in the White City*, 106–7.

28. *Pittsburgh Post*, February 21, 1891. Larson, *Devil in the White City*, 119. Hines, *Burnham of Chicago*, 103, points out, "Burnham felt that the timely and temporary nature of the exposition warranted the directors' decisions to avoid dealing with organized unions and risk, thereby, the possibility of a totally destructive strike." While he conceded to hire union men on an individual basis in 1891, another two years passed before he agreed to pay workers a minimum wage. For an in-depth examination of the fair's workforce, see Silkenat, "Workers in the White City."

29. "Windom Advises Economy," *Pittsburgh Post*, October 22, 1890. Windom calculated that at its existing rates, one-seventh of federal money not allocated for the fair's government building would be spent on salaries.

30. "He Shrank from Boodle," *Pittsburgh Post*, December 16, 1890.

31. Downey, *Season of Renewal*, 64. Bancroft, *Book of the Fair*, 2:432–33. When the fair opened there were buildings for thirty-six of the forty-four states and an additional building representing the territories of Arizona, New Mexico, and Oklahoma.

32. *Pittsburgh Press*, January 6, 1891.

33. Henry Clay Frick to Andrew Carnegie, June 8, 1891, box 8, volume 2, Henry Clay Frick Business Records (hereafter Frick Records), Archives and Special Collections, University of Pittsburgh Library System.

34. Frick to George H. Welshons, June 19, 1891, box 8, volume 2, Frick Records.

35. *Minutes of the Board*, 2.

36. *Minutes of the Board*, 2.

37. *Minutes of the Board*, 4–5. *Pennsylvania and the World's Columbian Exposition*, 6. The remaining board members included John Mundell, L. Clark Davis, Simon Muhr, A. W. Taylor, Edward H. Williams, Robert Purvis, Robert L. Brownfield, and Thomas Bradley, of Philadelphia; Thomas P. Merritt, Berks County; Rodney A. Mercer, Bradford County; John I. Carter, Chester County; E. A. Bigler, Clearfield County; Joel A. Herr, Clinton County; Mrs. Thomas M. Jones and Luther S. Bent, Dauphin County; J. K. P. Hall, Elk County; Benjamin Whitman, Erie County; H. J. McAteer, Huntington County; Joseph C. Walker, Lancaster County; Robert E. Wright, Lehigh County; Lewis Emery Jr., McKean County; R. S. Searle, Susquehanna County; Charles S. Wolfe, Union County; and A. B. Farquhar, York County. Philadelphians John W. Woodside and P. A. B. Widener were members of the committee because of their role on the national commission and Harriet Anne Lucas and Ida. A. Elkins Tyler similarly served due to their membership on the Board of Lady Managers.

38. *Minutes of the Board*, 38.

39. "A Great Floral Display," *Pittsburgh Press*, September 9, 1891. Ten other men were named to the committee, including Robert Craig, of Philadelphia.

40. *Pennsylvania and the World's Columbian Exposition*, 64, lists the committee members. Subcommittee work and calls for material are found in society publications such as the *Bulletin*, March 12, 1892, 8.

41. *Minutes of the Board*, 69–70.

42. Meeting minutes, November 30, 1891, 286, Greater Pittsburgh Chamber of Commerce Records, Detre Library and Archives, Senator John Heinz History Center, Pittsburgh.

43. Meeting minutes, November 30, 1891, 287, Greater Pittsburgh Chamber of Commerce Records.

44. Meeting minutes, December 14, 1891, 290, Greater Pittsburgh Chamber of Commerce Records. Hall, *America's Industrial Centre*, 6–13, lists chamber members and their businesses. Other members included Jonathan H. Ricketson, James B. Scott, Reuben Miller, William McConway, M. Atwood, W. L. Abbott, George H. Anderson, Jonathan F. Dravo, Morrison Foster, Henry Holdship, J. Morton Hall, Albert J. Logan, George A. Macbeth, John Bindley, Arthur B. Wigley, David C. Herbst, Peter Dick, Alexander Murdock, John B. Jackson, and S. L. McHenry.

45. For more on the International American Congress's Pan-American delegation and their stop in Pittsburgh, see "The Gates Open," *Pittsburgh Commercial Gazette*, November 6, 1889; "With Opened Gates," *Pittsburg Dispatch*, November 6, 1889; "Civic Guests," *Pittsburgh Commercial Gazette*, November 7, 1889; and "All America Here," *Pittsburg Dispatch*, November 7, 1889.

46. Mayor Henry Gourley to the Select Council, January 25, 1892, *Municipal Record: Minutes of the Proceedings of the Select Council of the City of Pittsburgh for the Year 1891–2*, 172.

47. "Their First Banquet," *Pittsburgh Press*, May 27, 1892.

48. "The Chamber of Commerce," *Pittsburgh Post*, May 28, 1892, attributes the region's lack of self-promotion to a fear that external enterprises would infiltrate the city and steal away with its resources.

49. *Toasts and Responses at the Banquet Given by the Chamber of Commerce of Pittsburgh, May 27th, 1892, at Duquesne Club*, 17–21, box 12, folder 1, Greater Pittsburgh Chamber of Commerce Records. The toasts and speeches in this booklet provide an overview of Pittsburgh industry in 1892.

3: COMING ATTRACTIONS

1. Jay, "Taller Than Eiffel's Tower," 150–53. Jay provides a detailed illustrated account of the evolution of tower ideas associated with the Columbian Exposition.

2. Jay, "Taller Than Eiffel's Tower," 153. For contemporary accounts and reactions to Eiffel's proposal see "The Eiffel Tower," *Washington Post*, August 28, 1891; "An Eiffel Project for Chicago," *Iron Age*, August 13, 1891; and "World's Fair Progress," *New York Times*, August 22, 1891.

3. "The American Tower," *Iron Age*, December 17, 1891, 1068–71. "The Columbian Tower," *Scientific Machinist*, January 1, 1892, 1, 5. "Eclipse of Eiffel," *Pittsburg Dispatch*, October 17, 1891. For more on Morison, see Griggs, "George S. Morison," 54–57.

4. Meeting summary, October 12, 1891, box 7, folder 3, Henry Clay Frick Business Records, 1892–1987, Archives and Special Collections, University of Pittsburgh Library System (hereafter Frick Records). Present at the meeting were Henry Clay Frick, A. L. Griffin, C. L. Strobel, Lewis T. Brown, Henry M. Curry, W. P. Palmer, and A. H. Childs.

5. A. L. Griffin to C. L. Strobel, October 12, 1891, box 7, folder 3, Frick Records. Griffin instructed that the proposition must meet the following terms: the cost for construction would be $0.0525 cents per pound; the tower could only use sections already made by Carnegie, Phipps; modifications to bend tests and structure; guaranteed payments to specifications; and prompt provision of the tower drawings.

6. Andrew Carnegie to Frick, December 3, 1891, box 482, folder 8, Frick Records. It is unclear whether Carnegie is referring to a site on the Midway Plaisance or a location completely external to the fairgrounds.

7. Philander Knox to Frick, October 19, 1891, box 7, folder 4, Frick Records. Knox had previously represented the South Fork Fishing and Hunting Club in suits filed against it relating to the 1889 Johnstown Flood. He would go on to serve as a United States senator, attorney general, and secretary of state. A copy of the agreement in question can be found in box 7, folder 2, Frick Records.

8. Frick to Griffin, October 19, 1891, box 7, folder 4, Frick Records. It was Frick's impression that the McArthur brothers used Griffin to sign a premature agreement so they could use the Carnegie name to entice people to invest in the tower. Frick was in correspondence with John Fleming of Carnegie Brothers and Company in Chicago at the same time to feel out how reputable the McArthur firm was after learning from Fleming that he determined there was no money in the tower project.

9. Strobel to Frick, October 19, 1891, box 7, folder 4, Frick Records.

10. Griffin to Frick, telegram, October 19, 1891, box 7, folder 4, Frick Records. Strobel also alluded to hiring another firm to erect the tower in his letter of the same date. Griffin to Frick, October 23, 1891, box 7, folder 4, Frick Records. Griffin's resignation was evidently not accepted, as he continued to be a correspondent after his proposed last day of November 1.

11. Griffin to Archibald and Arthur McArthur, October 28, 1891, box 7, folder 4,

Frick Records. By blaming the McArthur brothers for misusing Carnegie's name, Griffin was able to shift the blame Frick laid on him to the McArthurs and save face for making a premature agreement with them.

12. George Morison to Frick, October 31, 1891, box 7, folder 4, Frick Records.

13. Frick to Morison, November 9, 1891, box 7, folder 4, Frick Records.

14. Griffin to Carnegie, December 11, 1891, and Gardner to Carnegie, December 10, 1891, box 482, folder 9, Frick Records. This proposal was the exact fear Frick had expressed to Griffin when the press named Carnegie as supporting the tower to gain further interest.

15. Carnegie to Griffin, December 12, 1891, box 482, folder 9, Frick Records.

16. "The Columbian Tower," *Scientific American*, January 2, 1892, 9.

17. Anderson, *Ferris Wheels*, 46–48. Petroski, "Ferris Wheel on the Occasion," 218. Fincher, "George Ferris Jr.," 110–11. Weingardt, *Circles in the Sky*, 32–46. Weingardt's is the most comprehensive Ferris biography to date.

18. Anderson, *Ferris Wheels*, 50. Weingardt, *Circles in the Sky*, 53–55. *Industries and Wealth of Pittsburgh and Environs*, 86.

19. Daniel Burnham to G. W. G. Ferris, September 25, 1891, Daniel H. Burnham Collection, Art Institute of Chicago. This letter specifies iron inspection for the Transportation, Administration, Woman's, and Electricity Buildings at a rate of seventy cents per ton.

20. Anderson, *Ferris Wheels*, 53. Larson, *Devil in the White City*, 178. Muccigrosso, *Celebrating the New World*, 176, claims that Ferris had pondered the idea of a large pleasure wheel for years before his initial Columbian Exposition design, making the idea of the quickly drafted drawings slightly less impressive.

21. Burnham to Harlow Higinbotham, March 4, 1892, Burnham Collection. In the letter, Burnham seems to defer the decision of pursuing an observation tower to Higinbotham and the ways and means committee.

22. Anderson, *Ferris Wheels*, 55.

23. Larson, *Devil in the White City*, 179.

24. Anderson, *Ferris Wheels*, 46. W. H. Wachter's design called for a 220-foot-tall wheel with swinging baskets that could accommodate eight people each. See "Electricity at the World's Fair," *Western Electrician*, July 30, 1892, 58, and *Chicago Journal of Commerce and Metal Industries*, July 28, 1892, 30.

25. Ferris to Luther V. Rice, December 12, 1892, George Washington Gale Ferris Papers, Chicago Historical Society.

26. Anderson, *Ferris Wheels*, 55–57. Suppliers list, Ferris Papers.

27. Luther V. Rice, "Ferris Wheel," 477. Anderson, *Ferris Wheels*, 58. Petroski, "Ferris Wheel on the Occasion," 219. Larson, *Devil in the White City*, 193.

28. *Scientific American*, July I, 1893, 8.

29. Rice, "Ferris Wheel," 477. Anderson, *Ferris Wheels*, 58.

30. *Scientific American*, July I, 1893, 8. Anderson, *Ferris Wheels*, 58. Rice, "Ferris Wheel," 477.

31. For an overview of Tesla's time with Westinghouse Electric in Pittsburgh, see Jonnes, *Empires of Light*, 179–82.

32. *Warning from the Edison Electric Light Co.* In addition to the danger of alter-nating current, the publication also calls out Westinghouse's business practices and the illegality of his patent use.

33. Jonnes, *Empires of Light*, 208–13. Leupp, *George Westinghouse*, 152–55. The *New York Times* and other newspapers proclaimed that the electric chair would never catch on as an effective and humane means of execution.

34. Prout, *Life of George Westinghouse*, 274–76. Jonnes, *Empires of Light*, 215–19.

35. Leupp, *George Westinghouse*, 157–61. Jonnes, *Empires of Light*, 220–24.

36. Jonnes, *Empires of Light*, 228–29. Cheney, *Tesla*, 72–74. As the story goes, Tesla believed the only way he could share his polyphase system with the world was through Westinghouse's company, leading him to destroy the patent contract and free Westinghouse of his financial liability.

37. Jonnes, *Empires of Light*, 233–34. The war of the currents was fought as much in the courtroom as in the science laboratory, so freedom from lawsuits was no little thing.

38. Jonnes, *Empires of Light*, 242–43.

39. Jonnes, *Empires of Light*, 248, 253. Hines, *Burnham of Chicago*, 107, states that Burnham invited Edison to meet with him to discuss the needs of the exposition in May 1891.

40. Jonnes, *Empires of Light*, 248.

41. Jonnes, *Empires of Light*, 248–49.

42. Jonnes, *Empires of Light*, 249. Leupp, *George Westinghouse*, 163.

43. Jonnes, *Empires of Light*, 249.

44. Lewis, *Early Encounter with Tomorrow*, 32. Edison also donated $5,000 to the New York City Columbian Exposition bid in 1889, though this was likely not widely known at the time.

45. E. H. Heinrich, Reminiscences of George Westinghouse, Jr., 29–30, box 77, folder 15, Records of the Westinghouse Electric Corporation, Detre Library and Archives, Senator John Heinz History Center, Pittsburgh (hereafter Westinghouse Corp. Records). Jonnes, *Empires of Light*, 250.

46. Jonnes, *Empires of Light*, 254–55. Jonnes also claims that Westinghouse and Coffin were enemies, raising the stakes even further.

47. E. E. Keller, Reminiscences of George Westinghouse, Jr., 3–11, box 78, folder 1,

Westinghouse Corp. Records. The machinery is also described in "The Westinghouse World's Fair Exhibit," *Electrical Engineer*, January 25, 1893, 100.

48. Fessenden, *Fessenden*, 62. Leupp, *George Westinghouse*, 164–65. Prout, *Life of George Westinghouse*, 136–37.

49. Leupp, *George Westinghouse*, 166–68. Prout, *Life of George Westinghouse*, 136. Jonnes, *Empires of Light*, 259–61.

50. Keller, Reminiscences of George Westinghouse, Jr., 6–7, box 78, folder 1, Westinghouse Corp. Records.

51. Hogg, "Homestead Strike of 1892," 143–55. For more information on the strike see Krause, *Battle for Homestead, 1880–1892*. For its impact on the relationship between Carnegie and Frick, see Nasaw, *Andrew Carnegie*, and Standiford, *Meet You in Hell*.

52. Elizabeth Louise Magee to Margaret Mitchell, October 21, 1892, box 4, folder 7, Magee Family Papers, Archives and Special Collections, University of Pittsburgh Library System.

53. *Minutes of the Executive Committee*, November 10, 1892, 120. For a description of the ceremony see Johnson, *History of the World's Columbian Exposition*, 1:258–306.

54. "Pittsburg's Day Pageant," *Pittsburgh Press*, last ed., October 21, 1892.

55. "Many Railroaders Saw It," *Pittsburgh Post*, February 9, 1893.

56. *Catalogue of the Exhibit of the Pennsylvania Railroad Company*. "Moving the Big Cannon," *Pittsburgh Post*, March 30, 1893, and "Krupp's Monster Gun," *Pittsburgh Press*, April 10, 1893, describe the Pennsylvania Railroad's efforts to move the artillery across the country.

57. Handy, *Official Directory of the World's Columbian Exposition*, 199. Local newspapers reported various sizes for the gun, often settling on a weight of 124 tons with a length of 47 feet.

58. *Commercial Gazette*, April 6, 1893. Small notes about the Krupp cannon peppered Pittsburgh newspapers from late March until it reached the city in mid-April.

59. "Krupp's Big Cannon Here," *Pittsburgh Post*, April 12, 1893.

60. "Viewing the Big Gun," *Pittsburgh Press*, April 12, 1893. Larson, *Devil in the White City*, 207. Masich, "Rodman's Big Gun," 27–29.

61. "The Historic John Bull," *Pittsburgh Press*, April 13, 1893.

62. "Patriotic Pennsylvanians," *Pittsburgh Press*, April 27, 1893. "Liberty Bell!," *Pittsburgh Post*, April 27, 1893. For planning for the reception of the Liberty Bell and its delegation, see "To Receive Liberty Bell," *Pittsburgh Post*, April 20, 1893; "The Old Liberty Bell," *Pittsburgh Press*, April 26, 1893; and "The Liberty Bell," *Pittsburgh Post*, April 26, 1893.

63. "The Liberty Bell," *Pittsburgh Press*, April 27, 1893.

64. "Advertising and Patriotism," *Pittsburgh Press*, April 27, 1893.

65. David Whitten, "Depression of 1893," EH.Net Encyclopedia, ed. Robert Wha-ples, August 14, 2001, http://eh.net/encyclopedia/the-depression-of-1893/. This article distills the major factors of the Panic of 1893, which are greatly expanded upon in Stee-ples and Whitten, *Democracy in Desperation*. For a summary of the panic as it relates to the gold standard see Brands, *Reckless Decade*, 73.

66. Larson, *Devil in the White City*, 237. Jonnes, *Empires of Light*, 263.

67. Johnson, *History of the World's Columbian Exposition*, I:351. "Electricity at the Opening of the Fair," *Electrical Engineer*, May 10, 1893, 457.

68. Cheney, *Tesla*, 99.

69. Johnson, *History of the World's Columbian Exposition*, I:351.

70. "Lighting the White City," *Electrical Engineer*, April 26, 1893, 404. The capac-ity for the number of bulbs and candlepower vary from report to report in trade jour-nals throughout the construction and premiere of the machinery.

71. Jonnes, *Empires of Light*, 267–68. Leupp, *George Westinghouse*, 169.

72. Jonnes, *Empires of Light*, 268. Leupp, *George Westinghouse*, 169. Prout, *Life of George Westinghouse*, 140.

73. *Pittsburgh Post*, May 1, 1893. The article reported that the fair was a month behind schedule at the time of its opening.

74. "The Opening Day," *Commercial Gazette*, May 1, 1893.

75. "The Opening Day," *Commercial Gazette*, May 1, 1893.

76. *Pittsburgh Post*, May 1, 1893.

4: PITTSBURGH ON DISPLAY

1. Johnson, *History of the World's Columbian Exposition*, I:233. Unless otherwise stated, all mention of exhibits receiving awards comes from "List of awards, as cop-ied for Mrs. Virginia C. Meredith, Chairman, Committee on Awards, Board of Lady Managers, from the official records in the office Hon. John Boyd Thacher, Chairman, Executive Committee on Awards," Chicago History Museum, accessed October 27, 2020, http://chsmedia.org/media/fa/fa/LIB/WCE_AwardsList_Domestic.htm. The list likely dates from late 1893 or 1894.

2. Handy, *Official Directory*, 200, 209–10. Johnson, *History of the World's Colum-bian Exposition*, I:234–38, explains that the Board of Lady Managers was responsible for issuing lithographs of medals and diplomas to individual laborers and principle cre-ators of winning works; however, exhibitors complained that facsimiles would devalue the original awards, so the board renamed them "Diplomas of Honorable Mention."

3. Litwicki, "Influence of Commerce, Technology, and Race," 128. Rydell, *All the World's a Fair*, 40.

4. Cotkin, *Reluctant Modernism*, 52, 70–71. Rydell, *All the World's a Fair*, 67.

5. Bancroft, *Book of the Fair*, 3:434–35. Downey, *Season of Renewal*, 70–78.

6. Burg, *Chicago's White City of 1893*, 238. For a list of all the proposed congress departments and their scope, see *List of World's Congress Departments*. For an overview of the World's Congress Auxiliary, see Higinbotham, *Report of the President*, 325–36; Johnson, *History of the World's Columbian Exposition*, vol. 4; and Bancroft, *Book of the Fair*, 5:921–55. The number of sessions and speakers varies in each account. For a list of published papers and reports of the congresses, see Bonney, "Bibliography of World's Congress Publications," 7–10, and the bibliography of Johnson, *History of the World's Columbian Exposition*, 4:497–508.

7. Burg, *Chicago's White City of 1893*, 284. Higinbotham, *Report of the President*, 333.

8. Information on the Eclipse exhibit is found in *Catalogue of the Exhibits of the State of Pennsylvania*, 77.

9. For a list of Department F, Machinery, exhibits from Pennsylvania, see *Catalogue of the Exhibits of the State of Pennsylvania*, 187–91.

10. For a list of contributors to the Pennsylvania exhibit in Department E, Mines, see *Catalogue of the Exhibits of the State of Pennsylvania*, 46–112, and private exhibits, 183–85.

11. Andrew Carnegie to Henry Clay Frick, May 14, 1890, box 481, folder 8, Henry Clay Frick Business Records, Archives and Special Collections, University of Pittsburgh Library System (hereafter Frick Records). In a postscript Carnegie noted that the subscription should come from Keystone Bridge Company, specifically its Chicago engineer C. L. Strobel.

12. Carnegie to Frick, December 16, 1891, box 482, folder 9, Frick Records. Carnegie wrote this letter in the waning days of the tower project fiasco, further souring Carnegie's impression of the fair.

13. Planning of the Carnegie Steel exhibit can be found in letters from Frick to Carnegie and Frick to Strobel, December 26, 1891, box 8, vol. 2; Frick to Strobel, August 12, 1892; and Frick to John C. Fleming, August 20, 1892, box 11, vol. 1, Frick Records. For a description of the proposed exhibit and Carnegie's impressions, see Carnegie to Frick, September 3, 1892, box 710, folder 9, Frick Records.

14. Frick to Fleming, January 28, 1893, box 11, vol. 1, Frick Records. Frick sent an urgent telegram to Fleming in Chicago and an additional letter on the same date further explaining the decision.

15. Thomas Lynch to Frick, February 1, 1892, box 522, folder 4, Frick Records. Lynch also explained that technical plans of coke ovens would not be of interest to

fairgoers and, for those few with an interest in such plans, it would not be a wise business decision to share them.

16. Frick to Lynch, February 2, 1892, box 522, folder 4, Frick Records. Frick's recommendation to produce an informational pamphlet for people to take home also points to his desire to exhibit for a general audience and not his industry peers.

17. Lynch to Frick, April 12, 1892, box 522, folder 6, Frick Records. "The Great Coke Exhibit at the World's Fair," *Black Diamond*, July 1, 1893, 8–9. Lynch had the model of the Standard Mine built at a one-twenty-fourth scale. Sixty-four tiny ovens contained real flames thanks to a gas connection, demonstrating the coking process. Compressed air moved cars around tracks throughout the model. The same amount of detail that went into recreating the mine model was also stressed in the workers' cottages. For a detailed account of the exhibit, see Vivian, *Hidden History of the Laurel Highlands*.

18. "The Great Coke Exhibit at the World's Fair," *Black Diamond*, July 1, 1893, 8–9. This article and others about the display were found in a scrapbook in box 503, vol. 16, Frick Records.

19. "Frick Coke at the Fair," *Connellsville Courier*, October 13, 1893. "All Roads Lead to the World's Fair," *Chicago Record*, September 6, 1893.

20. "The Great Coke Exhibit at the World's Fair," *Black Diamond*, July 1, 1893, 8–9.

21. S. K. Colby to R. A. Hunt, "RE: Aluminum Exhibit at Columbian Exposition—1893," and J. P. Barrett to the Pittsburgh Reduction Company, March 5, 1894, box 101, folder 7, Aluminum Company of America Records, Detre Library and Archives, Senator John Heinz History Center, Pittsburgh.

22. *Locomotives Exhibited by the Pittsburgh Locomotive Works*, 7. This booklet includes specifications and photographs of many of the locomotives on display at the exposition. "H. K. Porter Locomotive Exhibit at the Columbian Exposition," *Engineering News*, October 19, 1893.

23. *Catalogue of the Exhibit of the Pennsylvania Railroad Company*. This book provides specifications, photographs, and drawings of all the objects on display in Chicago for the Pennsylvania Railroad.

24. "Westinghouse Work at the Fair," *Electrical Engineer*, August 16, 1893, 154. For a list of Pennsylvania exhibits in Department G, Transportation, see *Catalogue of the Exhibits of the State of Pennsylvania*, 192–95.

25. Roberts, "Projected Lake Erie and Ohio River Ship Canal," 15. This paper was similar in content to the *Address of Thomas P. Roberts on The Commercial Outlets of the Great Lakes, with special reference to the proposed Lake Erie and Ohio River Ship Canal*, presented to the Chamber of Commerce of Pittsburgh on March 27, 1893.

26. "Report of the Secretary," 24.

27. Soper, "Railway Safety Appliances in the United States," 169.

28. Downey, "Congress on Labor," 132–37.

29. Osman and Klinger, "'Susquehanna,' Pride of the Fish Commission," 35. For information on the Pennsylvania state exhibit in Department D, Fish, see *Catalogue of the Exhibits of the State of Pennsylvania*, 44–45, and private exhibits, 182.

30. *Catalogue of the Exhibits of the State of Pennsylvania*, 181. For an overview of stockyards in East Liberty, see Rotenstein, "Model for the Nation."

31. For a list of Pennsylvania exhibits in Department H, Manufactures, see *Catalogue of the Exhibits of the State of Pennsylvania*, 196–202.

32. For a list of the Pennsylvania state exhibits in Department A, Agriculture, see *Catalogue of the Exhibits of the State of Pennsylvania*, 29–38, and private exhibits, 175–77.

33. Letter to H. J. Heinz, July 19, 1893, box 5, folder 11, H. J. Heinz Company Records, Detre Library and Archives, Senator John Heinz History Center, Pittsburgh.

34. Alberts, *Good Provider*, 122. Skrabec, *H. J. Heinz*, 125–26. Butko, "Heinz," 22.

35. Letter to H. J. Heinz, July 19, 1893, box 5, folder 11, H. J. Heinz Company Records.

36. Alberts, *Good Provider*, 122. "Narrow Escape at World's Fair," *New York Times*, November 15, 1893.

37. Letter to H. J. Heinz, July 19, 1893, box 5, folder 11, H.J. Heinz Company Records.

38. Alberts, *Good Provider*, 122. Butko, "Heinz," 22.

39. "The First Floral Exhibit," *Pittsburgh Press*, November 30, 1892. "Captured the Prizes," *Pittsburgh Press*, September 19, 1893. For a list of the Pennsylvania state exhibits in Department B, Horticulture, see *Catalogue of the Exhibits of the State of Pennsylvania*, 41–43, and private exhibits, 178–80.

40. "Progress in the Electricity Building," *Electrical Engineer*, June 21, 1893, 601; "Westinghouse Work at the Fair," *Electrical Engineer*, August 16, 1893, 153; and "The Westinghouse Railway Exhibit," *Electrical Engineer*, July 5, 1893, 5. For a list of Pennsylvania exhibits in Department J, Electricity, see *Catalogue of the Exhibits of the State of Pennsylvania*, 205–6.

41. "The Magic City of 1893," *Westinghouse News*, box 70, folder 1, Records of the Westinghouse Electric Corporation, Detre Library and Archives, Senator John Heinz History Center, Pittsburgh (hereafter Westinghouse Corp. Records).

42. Cheney, *Tesla*, 100–101. See 76–83 for a description of Tesla's lectures and presentation style.

43. Scott, "Exhibit of Tesla Polyphase System at the World's Fair," in Osterberg, *Proceedings of the International Electrical Congress*, 417–22. For Stillwell's remarks, see 428–29. For local coverage of the talk, see "Dr. Scott Talks on Tesla," *Pittsburgh Post*, August 25, 1893.

44. "The Tesla Mechanical and Electrical Oscillators," in Osterberg, *Proceedings of the International Electrical Congress*, 475–82.

45. Larson, *Devil in the White City*, 259–61. Anderson, *Ferris Wheels*, 58–60.

46. Luther V. Rice to George W. G. Ferris, June 9, 1893, George Washington Gale Ferris Papers, Chicago Historical Society.

47. Ferris to Rice, June 10, 1893, Ferris Papers.

48. Flinn, *Official Guide to Midway Plaisance*, 23. Other descriptions of the wheel and its cars appeared in "The Ferris Wheel Leaflet for the Press," Ferris Papers; Rice, "Ferris Wheel," 478; and "The Great Wheel at Chicago," *Scientific American*, July 1, 1893, 8.

49. Larson, *Devil in the White City*, 269–71. Anderson, *Ferris Wheels*, 60–62.

50. Smith, *Art, History, Midway Plaisance*.

51. Rice to Ferris, June 12, 1893, Ferris Papers.

52. Anderson, *Ferris Wheels*, 64. Larson, *Devil in the White City*, 279–80. Rice, "Ferris Wheel," 478. Telegrams in the Ferris Papers dating from June 12 to June 17 show the speed at which the cars were added to the wheel.

53. Smith, *Art, History, Midway Plaisance*. Descriptions of the day and night views can also be found in "The Ferris Wheel Leaflet for the Press," Ferris Papers.

54. "The Great Wheel at Chicago," *Scientific American*, July 1, 1893, 8. Larson, *Devil in the White City*, 299–301.

55. "To the Board of Directors of the Ferris Wheel Co.," November 7, 1893, Ferris Papers. For a weekly listing of tickets sold, see Anderson, *Ferris Wheels*, 380.

56. Weingardt, *Circles in the Sky*, 94. Ferris himself made this claim in a pamphlet called *Ferris Wheel Souvenir*, Ferris Papers.

57. Larson, *Devil in the White City*, 280.

58. Langley, "The Internal Work of the Wind," in *Proceedings of the International Congress on Aerial Navigation*, 66–100. Bancroft, *Book of the Fair*, 4:942.

59. Keeler, "Wave-Lengths of the Two Brightest Lines," 733–36.

60. Bancroft, *Book of the Fair*, 4:946.

61. Harlan, *Transactions of the World's Columbian Dental Congress*, 1:xxxi, xxxv, 451, 456. For an overview of the Congress of Medicine and Surgery see Johnson, *History of the World's Columbian Exposition*, 4:81–101.

62. McClelland, "Address of Dr. J. H. McClelland," in Dudley, *Transactions of the World's Congress*, 22.

63. Millie J. Chapman, "Pre-natal Medication," in Dudley, *Transactions of the World's Congress*, 1050–58, and for Willard's comments, Dudley, *Transactions of the World's Congress*, 259–60.

64. "School Work," *Commercial Gazette*, April 11, 1893. For a list of contributors to the Pennsylvania exhibit in Department L, Liberal Arts, see *Catalogue of the Exhibits of the State of Pennsylvania*, 127–43, and private exhibits, 207–12.

65. Minutes of the Meeting of the Board of Trustees of the Western University of Pennsylvania, September 29, 1892, Western University of Pennsylvania, Board of Trustees Minutes, Archives and Special Collections, University of Pittsburgh Library System. Selim H. Peabody to William J. Sawyer, December 31, 1892, box 2, folder 12, Agnes Lynch Starrett Research Files, Archives and Special Collections, University of Pittsburgh Library System.

66. William Holland to Francis R. and Eliza A. Holland, May 5, 1893, box 24, folder 9, Holland Family Papers, Detre Library and Archives, Senator John Heinz History Center, Pittsburgh. Holland was also an avid butterfly collector and organizers of the fair were interested in putting some of his collection on display; however, the risk of damage was too great and he declined the invitation. See William Holland to Dr. S. H. Scudder, October 3, 1892, item 35, UA.0.3.2, Archives and Special Collections, University of Pittsburgh Library System.

67. Holland, *Abstract of the Report of the Chancellor*, 141–42.

68. *Catalogue: Catholic Educational Exhibit*, 97–102. *Catalogue of the Exhibits of the State of Pennsylvania*, 208.

69. Hanson, *World's Congress of Religions*, 1196. For an overview of the Parliament of Religions, see Mercer, *Review of the World's Religious Congresses*; Johnson, *History of the World's Columbian Exposition*, 4:221–37; Bancroft, *Book of the Fair*, 5:948–52; and Burg, *Chicago's White City of 1893*, 263–85. For a local opinion on the congress, see "Parliament of Religions," *Pittsburgh Post*, August 21, 1893.

70. Hanson, *World's Congress of Religions*, 1060–162. "The African Methodist Episcopal Congress," *Christian Recorder*, August 24, 1893. *Programme of the World's Religious Congresses of 1893*, 107.

71. *Programme of the World's Religious Congresses of 1893*, 56. Hanson, *World's Congress of Religions*, 1023. For local coverage of the Catholic Congress, see "The Great Meeting," *Pittsburgh Post*, September 3, 1893, and "Catholics Meet," *Pittsburgh Post*, September 5, 1893.

72. *Programme of the World's Religious Congresses of 1893*, 43. For more on the Jewish Congress, see Hanson, *World's Congress of Religions*, 955–69.

73. Rosenberg, "Influence of the Discovery of America on the Jews," in *Papers of the Jewish Women's Congress*, 66–73. For more information on the Jewish Women's

Congress, see Hanson, *World's Congress of Religions*, 969–84, and Mercer, *Review of the World's Religious Congresses*, 284–85.

74. "Uses of the World's Fair," *Pittsburgh Post*, June 19, 1893. For a summary of the congress, see *Report of the Proceedings*.

75. Stearns, *Temperance in All Nations*, 420–34, contains a list of organizations and their attendees with Pennsylvania organizations on 425. For more on the Temperance Congress, see Burg, *Chicago's White City of 1893*, 249–50, and Johnson, *History of the World's Columbian Exposition*, 4:102–17.

76. Stearns, *Temperance in All Nations*, 407–8. For a brief overview of Murphy's influence and activities, see his obituary "Francis Murphy Dead," *New York Times*, July 1, 1907.

77. Stearns, *Temperance in All Nations*, 345–48.

78. Burg, *Chicago's White City of 1893*, 247. For the speeches and papers presented at the Women's Congress, see Eagle, *Congress of Women*. For an overview of the Women's Congress, see Johnson, *History of the World's Columbian Exposition*, 4:15–80.

79. Cara Reese, "We, the Women," in Eagle, *Congress of Women*, 330.

80. Mary Temple Bayard, "Women in Journalism," in Eagle, *Congress of Women*, 436.

81. Bayard, "Women in Journalism," 437.

82. Bertha H. Palmer, "Closing Address," in Eagle, *The Congress of Women Held in the Woman's Building, World's Columbian Exposition*, 824.

83. For information about the banking congress, see *World's Congress of Bankers and Financiers*.

84. Charles H. Howard to Carnegie, February 27, 1892, Andrew Carnegie Papers, Manuscript Division, Library of Congress, Washington, DC. For more on Carnegie's thoughts and activities toward world peace, see Nasaw, *Andrew Carnegie*.

85. W. T. Stead to Carnegie, May 17, 1892, Carnegie Papers. Carnegie published his idea of a Federation of the Race in "A Look Ahead," 685–710.

86. Benjamin Trueblood to Carnegie, July 15, 1893, Carnegie Papers.

87. *Official Report of the Fifth Universal Peace Congress*, 44.

88. For a list of contributors to the Pennsylvania exhibit in Department K, Fine Arts, see *Catalogue of the Exhibits of the State of Pennsylvania*, 115–25. For images of some of the works, see Brownfield, *Pennsylvania Art Contributions*.

89. Chamber of Commerce of Pittsburgh, *Guide to All Points of Interest*.

90. For a list of Pennsylvania contributions to the Woman's Building, see *Catalogue of the Exhibits of the State of Pennsylvania*, 155–62.

91. Mathews, *Mary Cassatt*, 7–15, 75. Cassatt was born in Allegheny in 1844 and her family moved to Lancaster, Pennsylvania, in 1848. Her family lived in Europe in the

early 1850s, making visits to the 1851 Crystal Palace Exhibition in London and 1855 Paris Exposition, Mary's likely first encounters with world's fairs.

92. Mathews, *Mary Cassatt*, 202. Mathews notes that Elizabeth Gardner was Hallowell's first choice of muralist, as she was a more traditional painter, but Gardner declined.

93. Mathews, *Mary Cassatt*, 204. Corn, *Women Building History*, 90, 95. Hutton, "Picking Fruit," 334. Hutton also explores how Cassatt's mural simultaneously fits and breaks the mold of traditional impressionist paintings.

94. Corn, *Women Building History*, 92. Mathews, *Mary Cassatt*, 205.

95. Mathews, *Mary Cassatt*, 205. Corn, *Women Building History*, 175.

96. Corn, *Women Building History*, 174. Mathews, *Mary Cassatt*, 211–12.

97. Corn, *Women Building History*, 99, 122, 133.

98. Mathews, *Mary Cassatt*, 207. Corn, *Women Building History*, 134.

99. Mathews, *Mary Cassatt*, 207. Corn, *Women Building History*, 134. Hutton, "Picking Fruit," particularly focuses on the allegory of the Garden of Eden and its use in the center panel.

100. Corn, *Women Building History*, 146.

101. Corn, *Women Building History*, 11, 172–73. Hutton, "Picking Fruit," attempts to explain the reasons behind the various criticisms directed at the mural and Cassatt.

102. Corn, *Women Building History*, 178. Mathews, *Mary Cassatt*, 252, posits that Cassatt did not contribute to the 1900 World's Fair because of her experience with criticism at the Chicago Fair.

103. Corn, *Women Building History*, 179, claims that Palmer last had the mural in her possession in 1911.

5: "A PEEP INTO PARADISE"

1. Couvares, *Remaking of Pittsburgh*, 83. Couvares explains that when the city accepted steel as its primary influence as evidenced by these changes, Pittsburgh shed its sense of community and essentially became a large company town.

2. Couvares, *Remaking of Pittsburgh*, 11. The shift from wages based on tonnage produced to hours worked is another example of steel mill owners' ability to control and predict expenditures and, consequently, profits.

3. Schlereth, *Victorian America*, 60. Carnegie's system of middle managers allowed him to play them off each other to encourage peak performance through competition. He also positioned himself in an advisory role so that peers and colleagues could not criticize him for his own shortcomings in any one position. See Bridge, *Inside History of the Carnegie Steel Company*, 113–14, and Morris, *Tycoons*, 133, 136.

4. Michael P. Weber and Peter N. Stearns, introduction to Spencer, *Spencers of*

Amberson Avenue, xv. Jucha, "Anatomy of a Streetcar Suburb," 105. Schlereth, *Victorian America*, 29.

5. Jucha, "Anatomy of a Streetcar Suburb," 104–5. Couvares, *Remaking of Pittsburgh*, 82. Schlereth, *Victorian America*, 18.

6. Ingham, "Steel City Aristocrats," 278. Couvares, *Remaking of Pittsburgh*, 33. Litwicki, "Influence of Commerce, Technology, and Race," 189.

7. "At the Theatres," *Pittsburgh Press*, June 4, 1893. The article also noted, "It seems that everybody has felt like going to the theater this season and in some instances indifferent plays have been greeted by good sized audiences." It is possible that the mounting excitement for the Columbian Exposition enticed people to get out and experience cultural events, even if they could not make the trip to Chicago. Peebles, "History of the Pittsburgh Stage," 10, identifies the 1890s as a period of growing awareness that resulted in increased theater attendance.

8. Couvares, *Remaking of Pittsburgh*, 101. See also Tome, "Western Pennsylvania Exposition," and "Western Pennsylvania Exposition Society," box 2, folder 4, Britta C. Dwyer Papers, Detre Library and Archives, Senator John Heinz History Center, Pittsburgh. For a middle-class child's memories of the Western Pennsylvania Exposition, see Spencer, *Spencers of Amberson Avenue*, 101–2.

9. Schlereth, *Victorian America*, 19, 77. Weber and Stearns, introduction to Spencer, *Spencers of Amberson Avenue*, xxviii. For the importance of rail travel to young middle-class women and the "See America First" movement of tourism, see Kitch, "'Piazza from Which the View,'" 505–27.

10. This is a conservative estimate based on the published lists reviewed by the author. Given the amount of issues that were unable to be reviewed or illegible, the total number of published names is likely closer to ten thousand.

11. "The People's Store," *Pittsburgh Press*, April 27, 1893. "Jos. Horne & Co.'s," *Pittsburgh Post*, May 1, 1893. "Colossal Columbian Clothing Sale," *Pittsburgh Press*, May 1, 1893. "B. & B.," *Pittsburgh Press*, May 2, 1893. "Fine French Crushed Hats," *Pittsburgh Press*, August 11, 1893.

12. Spencer, *Spencers of Amberson Avenue*, 31. As was often the case in middle-class households, young domestic servants spent a few years with a family to assimilate to life in America before finding a husband and leaving to start a family of her own.

13. Spencer, *Spencers of Amberson Avenue*, 113.

14. William J. Holland to Francis R. Holland, July 1, 1893, box 24, folder 9, Holland Family Papers, Detre Library and Archives, Senator John Heinz History Center.

15. Holland to Francis R. and Eliza A. Holland, July 3, 1893, box 24, folder 9, Holland Family Papers.

16. These prices are based on advertisements appearing in the *Pittsburgh Press*, *Pittsburgh Post*, and *Commercial Gazette*.

17. "Westinghouse Fair Excursions," *Pittsburgh Press*, July 1, 1893.

18. "Being Given Vacations," *Pittsburgh Press*, August 11, 1893.

19. "Pittsburg's Protest," *Pittsburgh Press*, August 17, 1893. In the article, Pittsburgh mayor Bernard McKenna credits the chamber of commerce with being the driving force in promoting Pittsburgh's interest during the fair.

20. "Ready for Guests," *Commercial Gazette*, June 2, 1893. Much like the lists of Western Pennsylvanians attending the Columbian Exposition that appeared in local newspapers, they also printed lists of foreign visitors staying in Pittsburgh hotels.

21. "Visiting Engineers," *Pittsburgh Press*, October 17, 1893. The Homestead works provided steel plating for US naval ships and held many government contracts.

22. "Foreign Guests," *Pittsburgh Press*, July 1, 1893. "Scotch Artisans," *Pittsburgh Press*, July 17, 1893. "Advertising Pittsburg," *Pittsburgh Press*, August 6, 1893. "A Japanese Visitor," *Pittsburgh Press*, August 9, 1893. Newspapers also took the opportunity to report on visitors' reasons for stopping in the area and firsthand accounts of their sentiments on issues facing their home countries.

23. "Lost His Teeth," *Pittsburgh Press*, August 29, 1893.

24. *Pennsylvania Railroad to the Columbian Exposition*, 34.

25. Margaret Mitchell to Elizabeth Louise Magee, June 11, 1893, box 4, folder 8, Magee Family Papers, Archives and Special Collections, University of Pittsburgh Library System (hereafter Magee Papers). Mitchell's journey to the fairgrounds began at the Great Eastern Hotel at the corner of Saint Lawrence Ave. and 60th Street, just west of the Midway Plaisance. Maps of the fairgrounds do not show an entrance on 61st Street, which terminated behind the greenhouse of the Horticultural Building. There were entrances at both 60th and 62nd Streets.

26. Invoice Books, vol. 6, 181, Henry Clay Frick Papers, Frick Collection, Frick Art Reference Library Archives, New York, NY. A July 3, 1893, expense report from Frick's secretary states that from June 1 to July 3 Mrs. Frick and three others spent more than forty-three dollars on "Fair admissions etc." and more than sixty-nine dollars on chair hires.

27. Margaret Mitchell to Christopher Magee, June 9, 1893, box 4, folder 8, Magee Papers. The Horticultural Building, with its glass dome, and the Transportation Building, with its colorful Golden Doorway, would have stood out among the other monotone buildings of the White City. Based on Mitchell's description of how she traveled to the fair, these were also likely to be the first major buildings she encountered there.

28. Margaret Mitchell to Elizabeth Louise Magee, June 11, 1893, box 4, folder 8, Magee Papers.

29. Mitchell to Christopher Magee, June 9, 1893, box 4, folder 8, Magee Papers.

30. Mitchell to Louise Mitchell, June 13, 1893, box 4, folder 8, Magee Papers.

31. Mitchell to Elizabeth Louise Magee, June 13, 1893, box 4, folder 8, Magee Papers. Mitchell also noted the wheel's main competitor, the captive balloon.

32. "Uses of the World's Fair," *Pittsburgh Post*, June 19, 1893.

33. H. J. Heinz diary transcript, 204, box 4, folder 1, Papers of Robert C. Alberts, Detre Library and Archives, Senator John Heinz History Center, Pittsburgh. Heinz had attended and exhibited at several local exhibitions and world's fairs by this time and so his commendation of the Chicago Fair is high praise.

34. "Hayti and the World's Fair," *Christian Recorder*, January 19, 1893.

35. Blight, *Frederick Douglass*, 734. Wells et al., *Reason Why the Colored American*, xxv. Several transcriptions of newspaper articles found in Glasco, *WPA History of the Negro in Pittsburgh*, 391–97, indicate that Loudin was an active leader in 1870s Pittsburgh Black politics.

36. I. Garland Penn, "The Progress of the Afro-American Since Emancipation," in Wells et al., *Reason Why the Colored American*, 61.

37. Carnegie, "Value of the World's Fair," 421. John R. Dunlap to Andrew Carnegie, October 30, 1893, Andrew Carnegie Papers, Manuscript Division, Library of Congress, Washington, DC.

38. Carnegie, "Value of the World's Fair," 421.

39. Gruen, *Manifest Destinations*, 100–101.

40. Margaret Mitchell to Elizabeth Louise Magee, June 7, 1893, box 4, folder 8, Magee Papers.

41. Margaret Mitchell to Christopher Magee, June 9, 1893, box 4, folder 8, Magee Papers.

42. The Pittsburgh councils approved paying to send two policemen to Chicago. See April 17, 1893, *Municipal Record: Minutes of the Proceedings of the Select Council of the City of Pittsburgh for the Year 1893–4*, 35–36, and April 24, 1893, *Municipal Record: Minutes of the Proceedings of the Common Council of the City of Pittsburgh for the Year 1893–4*, 100.

43. "A Pennsylvanian Injured," *Commercial Gazette*, September 22, 1893. "World's Fair Visitor Hurt," *Commercial Gazette*, October 18, 1893.

44. "A Westinghouse Foreman," *Pittsburgh Press*, September 24, 1893.

45. "Made Himself at Home," *Pittsburgh Press*, October 29, 1893.

46. Couvares, *Remaking of Pittsburgh*, 75–76.

47. Johnson, "From Sabbath to Weekend," 178. Johnson, *History of the World's Columbian Exposition*, 1:359–60.

48. "Where They Will Preach," *Pittsburgh Press*, October 7, 1890. "Close of the U.P. Synod," *Pittsburgh Post*, October 24, 1890.

49. "Sabbatarians' Council," *Pittsburgh Press*, November 18, 1890. The Western Pennsylvania Sabbath Association was established in 1888 as an auxiliary to the National Sabbath Union. See *Canonsburg Weekly Notes*, December 7, 1888.

50. "Opposed to Opening," *Commercial Gazette*, January 2, 1893. For an overview of sabbatarianism in Pittsburgh, see Couvares, *Remaking of Pittsburgh*, 75–79.

51. Johnson, "From Sabbath to Weekend," 179. In chapter 6 of his dissertation, Johnson explores the role of the Columbian Exposition within the greater transition of Sundays moving from a day of worship to a day of leisure and the many arguments of sabbatarians fighting against that change.

52. Johnson, "From Sabbath to Weekend," 1. Couvares, *Remaking of Pittsburgh*, 37–50, notes that theater, sports, and music were favorite pastimes of working-class Pittsburghers in the age of iron once the mills closed on Saturday afternoons, but sabbatarianism still reigned. Once Irish, English, and German immigrants gave way to the Eastern European immigrants of the steel industry the workforce's desire for amusement on Sunday, their only day off, became stronger.

53. McCrossen, *Holy Day, Holiday*, 73. Both McCrossen and Johnson, *History of the World's Columbian Exposition*, 1:360, make the case that a Sunday opening would provide a better opportunity for the working class to improve themselves by taking in the exhibits at the exposition, the same argument used in Pittsburgh to justify the Carnegie Institute and Schenley Park. Johnson also notes that the exposition board of directors feared that if the fair were closed on Sundays the crowds of idle visitors would turn to crime throughout Chicago. Johnson, "From Sabbath to Weekend," 186, posits that the Sunday question divided the working class because some saw the fight for the Sabbath as a victory over capitalism and their only check on long hours, while others simply craved leisure time and did not really care which day of the week was made available to them.

54. "The Sunday Question," *Pittsburgh Press*, May 17, 1893. This sentiment would prove influential in Western Pennsylvania as opportunities for amusement and leisure increased at the turn of the century with the rise of trolley parks.

55. Minutes of the Meeting of the Board of Trustees of the Western University of Pennsylvania, June 5, 1893, Western University of Pennsylvania. Board of Trustees Minutes, Archives and Special Collections, University of Pittsburgh Library System. Western University was closely tied to the Presbyterian Church and so its decision to close its exhibit on Sundays is not surprising. For an overview of how the exposition's board of directors came to open the fair on Sundays, see Johnson, *History of the World's Columbian Exposition*, 1:361–62.

56. "Is Not Boycotted," *Commercial Gazette*, June 24, 1893.

57. "The Close of the Fair," *Commercial Gazette*, October 31, 1893. This take is counter to the argument presented in the competing *Pittsburgh Press* newspaper in May stating that Sunday openings were not to make money but for the betterment of visitors.

58. "The Reason of It," *Pittsburgh Press*, July 15, 1893. Johnson, *History of the World's Columbian Exposition*, 1:362–67.

59. "They Do Not Want It," *Pittsburgh Press*, July 31, 1893. Interestingly, this statement is counter to what is reported in Johnson, *History of the World's Columbian Exposition*, 1:363, 365, which states that even the Midway was not profitable on Sundays.

60. McCrossen, *Holy Day, Holiday*, 76. McCrossen also notes that the admission price of fifty cents would have been prohibitive during the Panic of 1893 for many of the working class who were at least nominally the intended beneficiaries of Sunday openings. Johnson, *History of the World's Columbian Exposition*, 1:364.

61. McCrossen, *Holy Day, Holiday*, 77, states that ending religious services in the fairgrounds on Sundays would have discouraged more liberal sabbatarians from attending. Johnson, *History of the World's Columbian Exposition*, 1:364, also notes that the plethora of court decisions relating to Sunday closures confused people as to whether the gates were actually opened on the Sabbath.

62. "Filed under Allegheny," *Pittsburgh Press*, July 11, 1893. Order and categorization were an important part of the exposition, particularly when classifying exhibits, and so it is unsurprising that even the newspapers in the state buildings were organized in a hierarchical manner.

63. *Pittsburgh Press*, September 21, 1893, 2. This particular editorial appeared in the society column and was written for a female audience. The inclusion of Pittsburgh's female contributions to the fair, though, is as significant as those of their male counterparts when considering the influential role women would play in the city's civic activism in the decades to come.

64. "Pittsburg's Protest," *Pittsburgh Press*, August 17, 1893. The article's subheadline, "Greedy Philadelphia," implies that, at least in the minds of those writing for the *Press*, the City of Brotherly Love was somehow influencing the programming of the Pennsylvania Building, despite the fact that several Western Pennsylvanians served on the Pennsylvania Board of World's Fair Managers.

65. "Pittsburg's Protest," *Pittsburgh Press*, August 17, 1893. For information on the various ceremonial days, see Johnson, *History of the World's Columbian Exposition*, 1:406–63, and for Pennsylvania Day specifically, 439. For information on Colored People's Day and African Americans at the Columbian Exposition, see Reed, *"All the World*

Is Here!"; Paddon and Turner, "African Americans and the World's Columbian Exposition"; and Wells et al., *Reason Why the Colored American.*

66. "Pittsburg's Protest," *Pittsburgh Press*, August 17, 1893.

67. "Twin City Day," *Commercial Gazette*, August 26, 1893. "The Twin City Day," *Pittsburgh Press*, August 25, 1893. The planning of Twin City Day is an excellent example of how Pittsburgh and Allegheny operated as two distinct cities, but also with each other's interests in mind.

68. August 28, 1893, *Municipal Record: Minutes of the Proceedings of the Select Council of the City of Pittsburgh for the Year 1893–4*, 223–24. "Our Day at Chicago," *Pittsburgh Press*, August 26, and August 28, 1893. The *Pittsburgh Press* used the "Our Day at Chicago" headline throughout late August to keep readers apprised of the organization of the rapidly approaching event.

69. "Our Day at Chicago," *Pittsburgh Press*, August 30, 1893. The article notes that Allegheny's committee representatives were angrier at the railroad companies' unwillingness to compromise because they had recently granted them several favors, while Pittsburgh's councilmen planned revenge by passing laws to impede the industry's progress in the city.

70. "A Railroad Roast," *Pittsburgh Post*, August 30, 1893. It is clear that McKenna and the newspapers were both hoping to build bad publicity against the railroads in an effort to shame them into conceding to the desired reduced rates.

71. "A Railroad Roast," *Pittsburgh Post*, August 30, 1893.

72. "Our Day at Chicago," *Pittsburgh Press*, August 30, 1893.

73. "McKenna Declares It Off," *Pittsburgh Post*, September 2, 1893. In McKenna's outrage at the failure of Twin City Day, he cited several reasons why he felt the railroads owed the city a reduced rate, including the fact that Pittsburgh provided more freight tonnage than any other city in the nation. He even went so far as to proclaim that the Pennsylvania Railroad was successful solely because of Western Pennsylvania.

74. *Pittsburgh Press*, October 17, 1893. In addition to the model, the Eden Musée on Fifth Avenue also included various musical and theatrical performances. Davis, who had a nose for entertainment, would go on to manage the Schenley Park Casino and open the first nickelodeon in Pittsburgh. "Harry Davis, Film Pioneer, Dies at Home," *Pittsburgh Post-Gazette*, January 3, 1940.

75. *Pittsburgh Press*, October 29, 1893, 11.

76. "Gone for a Year," *Pittsburgh Press*, October 22, 1893. Once the Western Pennsylvania Exposition began in September, Pittsburgh newspapers require a close reading to distinguish articles about the local exhibition and the Columbian Exposition as articles often refer to both attractions as "The Fair."

77. "The Pittsburg Exposition," *National Labor Tribune*, August 24, 1893. The

endorsement of the Western Pennsylvania Exposition by this newspaper is particularly interesting as its primary readers were skilled unionized workers, mostly tradesmen, thus providing insight into that population's early views on the developing Panic of 1893 and its long-term implications.

78. "Our Exposition," *Pittsburgh Press*, August 27, 1893.

79. *Pittsburg and Its Fifth Annual Exposition*, 15. This language echoed the sentiments that the chamber of commerce strove to promote at the Chicago fair, making it clear that organizers intended the Pittsburgh exposition for outside visitors as well as local citizens.

80. "Can't Hurt the Fairs," *Pittsburgh Press*, August 29, 1893. Editors of the *Press* were confident that those who attended the Columbian Exposition would also partake in the local attraction and those who could not afford to travel to Chicago would consider the Pittsburgh exposition a suitable surrogate, "A Great Opening," *Pittsburgh Press*, September 7, 1893.

81. *Pittsburg and Its Fifth Annual Exposition*, 23. "Booming the Exposition," *Pittsburgh Post*, July 12, 1893.

82. "Our Own Show," *Pittsburgh Press*, August 27, 1893. "The Exposition Opening," *Pittsburgh Post*, September 3, 1893. "Splendid Beginning," *Pittsburgh Press*, September 10, 1893.

83. "The Evolution," *Pittsburgh Press*, September 7, 1893. For a list of entertainment see *Pittsburg and Its Fifth Annual Exposition*, 27–41.

84. "Splendid Beginning," *Pittsburgh Press*, September 10, 1893. For details of several exhibits see "With Booming Cannon," *Pittsburgh Press*, September 3, 1893.

85. "Gone for a Year," *Pittsburgh Press*, October 22, 1893. "The Show Closed," *Pittsburgh Press*, October 22, 1893.

86. "A Prosperous Fair," *Pittsburgh Press*, October 16, 1893.

87. For an overview of the closing of the exposition, see Johnson, *History of the World's Columbian Exposition*, 1:485–92. For more on the assassination of Mayor Harrison, see Larson, *Devil in the White City*, 328–33.

88. "Memories of the Fair," *Pittsburgh Press*, October 22, 1893.

6: BRINGING THE EXPOSITION HOME

1. Jonnes, *Empires of Light*, 274. Leupp, *George Westinghouse*, 170. Leupp also states that when banks would not cash checks due to a lack of funds, the exposition's treasurer would send cash to Pittsburgh so the company could pay its workmen.

2. "The Westinghouse World's Fair Plant Sold," *Electrical Engineer*, December 27, 1893, 560.

3. Jonnes, *Empires of Light*, 283. For an overview of efforts to harness hydroelectric

power from Niagara Falls prior to the Cataract Construction Company, see 279–83 and Belfield, "Niagara Frontier," chapter I.

4. Lubar, "Transmitting the Power of Niagara," 13. In addition to Edison and Westinghouse, the Cataract Company also consulted with Stevens Institute of Technology president Henry Morton, Johns Hopkins University physicist Henry Rowland, and hydraulic engineer Clemens Herschel. Jonnes, *Empires of Light*, 283–88, describes the international search for the best means of transmitting electricity from the falls.

5. Jonnes, *Empires of Light*, 288, 291. Leupp, *George Westinghouse*, 174.

6. Lubar, "Transmitting the Power of Niagara," 15–16. Hughes, *Networks of Power*, 125.

7. Lubar, "Transmitting the Power of Niagara," 11–12.

8. Lubar, "Transmitting the Power of Niagara," 15. Jonnes, *Empires of Light*, 296. Cheney, *Tesla*, 119.

9. "The Great Conspiracy," *Pittsburgh Press*, May 9, 1893. "The Alleged Theft of Westinghouse Blueprints," *Electrical Engineer*, June 14, 1893, 587. "The Blue Print Conspiracy," *Pittsburgh Press*, August 4, 1893. "The Theft of the Westinghouse Blue Prints—Important Evidence Given at Pittsburgh," *Electrical Engineer*, September 13, 1893, 251. "Criminal Court," *Pittsburgh Press*, September 4, 1893. Jonnes, *Empires of Light*, 296–97. "Exposed the Whole Plot," *Pittsburgh Post*, September 9, 1893.

10. "The Blue Prints," *Pittsburgh Press*, September 6, 1893.

11. "The Blue Prints," *Pittsburgh Press*, September 6, 1893. "Mead is Given an Inning," *Pittsburgh Post*, September 6, 1893. "Mr. Clark Tells His Story," *Pittsburgh Post*, September 7, 1893. "With the Jury," *Pittsburgh Press*, September 8, 1893.

12. Jonnes, *Empires of Light*, 309, explains that it was a matter of science, business, and finances that influenced the Cataract investors to support Westinghouse over GE. It was the more stable company that held most of the patents and experience working with AC at a large scale.

13. Jonnes, *Empires of Light*, 303, 305.

14. Jonnes, *Empires of Light*, 303–5. Blalock and Woodworth, "25-Hz at Niagara Falls," 86.

15. Prout, *Life of George Westinghouse*, 151. Jonnes, *Empires of Light*, 319.

16. Prout, *Life of George Westinghouse*, 156. Jonnes, *Empires of Light*, 318–21. Cheney, *Tesla*, 120, notes that the success of the Pittsburgh Reduction Company at Niagara Falls and the resulting aluminum industry allowed Tesla's prediction of the aircraft industry to come to fruition.

17. Lubar, "Transmitting the Power of Niagara," 16. Jonnes, *Empires of Light*, 308.

18. Skrabec, *H. J. Heinz*, 126. Alberts, *Good Provider*, 119.

19. Skrabec, *H. J. Heinz*, 128. "H. J. Heinz Company Sales Consolidated and by

Company," box 2, folder 13, H. J. Heinz Company Records, Detre Library and Archives, Senator John Heinz History Center, Pittsburgh.

20. Skrabec, *H. J. Heinz*, 134. Alberts, *Good Provider*, 132. *H. J. Heinz Company*, 26–28.

21. Skrabec, *H. J. Heinz*, 227.

22. Skrabec, *H. J. Heinz*, 95, 211. Butko, "Heinz," 29. Schlereth, *Victorian America*, 46.

23. Skrabec, *H. J. Heinz*, 114. Butko, "Heinz," 30.

24. Skrabec, *H. J. Heinz*, 201, 208.

25. Anderson, *Ferris Wheels*, 71, notes that Ferris's control over and certification of official wheel merchandise, including the selling of rights to others to produce said goods, may have been an inspiration for Walt Disney and his management of the rights of his cartoon characters. Incidentally, Disney's father worked at the Columbian Exposition and the fair's influence can be seen throughout the Disney parks today. The Ferris wheel was also commemorated in pieces of music and literature featuring scenes at the exposition. Fincher, "George Ferris Jr.," 115.

26. Anderson, *Ferris Wheels*, 71–72. Anderson shows that the Ferris wheel sold more than twenty-six thousand tickets the week after the exposition formally closed. The lawsuit against the exposition was not decided until 1897, in favor of the fair. "World's Fair Wins," *Commercial Gazette*, January 23, 1897.

27. Anderson, *Ferris Wheels*, 75. Fincher, "George Ferris Jr.," 117. Petroski, "Ferris Wheel on the Occasion," 220. In addition, a December 1893 letter sought permission to build a duplicate of the Columbian Exposition wheel in London. Charles M. Jacobs to G. W. G. Ferris, December 9, 1893, George Washington Gale Ferris Papers, Chicago Historical Society.

28. Anderson, *Ferris Wheels*, 72. Petroski, "Ferris Wheel on the Occasion," 220. An 1896 prospectus of the company while at the North Clark Street location claims a $4,000-per-month profit, but the proactive solicitation of investors indicates that it was in financial trouble. See "Prospectus," Ferris Papers.

29. "Ferris Dead," *Commercial Gazette*, November 23, 1896. "G. W. G. Ferris' Estate," *Commercial Gazette*, December 31, 1896. "Ashes of George W. G. Ferris," *New York Times*, March 8, 1898. Anderson, *Ferris Wheels*, 75, 77.

30. Anderson, *Ferris Wheels*, 78. Petroski, "Ferris Wheel on the Occasion," 220.

31. Anderson, *Ferris Wheels*, 80–81. The Ferris wheel generated a $215,000 profit during its time in St. Louis.

32. Anderson, *Ferris Wheels*, 84. The story relayed by Anderson is that the C. Pardee Company of Perth Amboy, New Jersey, was in possession of the engine from 1906 to 1927.

33. Nasaw, *Going Out*, 67, explains that fair organizers recognized that amusements would be an important part of the exposition but segregated them from the formal exhibits to maintain the latter's seriousness. Lewis, *Early Encounter with Tomorrow*, 181. Schlereth, *Victorian America*, 233–34, 237. Cotkin, *Reluctant Modernism*, 122. For an overview of how Ferris wheels evolved with carnivals and amusement parks see Anderson, *Ferris Wheels*, 146–212.

34. "The Useful Sideshow," *Pittsburgh Press*, October 30, 1893.

35. "The Useful Sideshow," *Pittsburgh Press*, October 30, 1893.

36. Johnson, "From Sabbath to Weekend," 194.

37. Johnson, "From Sabbath to Weekend," 197.

38. Schlereth, *Victorian America*, 239.

39. Butko, *Luna*, 37–42. Butko is the leading expert on the history of Kennywood and has also published *Kennywood: Behind the Screams* (Pittsburgh: Senator John Heinz History Center, 2016).

40. Schlereth, *Victorian America*, 171, recognizes the importance of goods in identifying social classes and the role the exposition played in shaping middle-class tastes, as well as serving as a marketplace to distribute those goods throughout the country.

41. Receipts, box 7, folder 12, Magee Family Papers, Archives and Special Collections, University of Pittsburgh Library System.

42. Butera, "Settlement House and the Urban Challenge," 26. Spain, *How Women Saved the City*, 226–27. For an early overview of the settlement movement, see Learned, "Social Settlements in the United States," 102–12.

43. Knight, *Citizen*, 270–75. For more on the Congress of Social Settlements see Johnson, *History of the World's Columbian Exposition*, 4:219–20, and Learned, "Social Settlements in the United States," 108–11.

44. Bauman and Muller, *Before Renaissance*, 38–39. Matthews, *Meaning of the Social Settlement Movement*, 33. Zahniser, *Steel City Gospel*, 66–67.

45. *First Annual Report of the Kingsley House Association*, 9. Butera, "Settlement House and the Urban Challenge," 25. Metzger, "Study of Social Settlement Workers," 19.

46. *First Annual Report of the Kingsley House Association*, 13. Greenwald, "Women and Class in Pittsburgh, 1850–1920," 57, notes that while the Kingsley House relied on the work of women, it did not groom female leaders like at Hull House.

47. Butera, "Settlement House and the Urban Challenge," 33. *First Annual Report of the Kingsley House Association*, 7.

48. Lubove, "Pittsburgh and the Uses," 307. Butera, "Settlement House and the Urban Challenge," 38.

49. Spain, *How Women Saved the City*, 239. Lubove, "Pittsburgh and the Uses," 310.

50. *Papers of the Jewish Women's Congress*, 264–65. Selavan, "Founding of Columbian Council," 24.

51. *Papers of the Jewish Women's Congress*, 267.

52. Selavan, "Founding of Columbian Council," 24. Feldman, *Jewish Experience in Western Pennsylvania*, 124–25. Burstin, *Steel City Jews*, 182. "History of Pittsburgh Section Council of Jewish Women," box 1, folder 1, National Council of Jewish Women, Pittsburgh Section Records, Archives and Special Collections, University of Pittsburgh Library System.

53. Selavan, "Founding of Columbian Council," 28–29. Feldman, *Jewish Experience in Western Pennsylvania*, 125. Burstin, *Steel City Jews*, 197.

54. Selavan, "Founding of Columbian Council," 33. Feldman, *Jewish Experience in Western Pennsylvania*, 125.

55. Burstin, *Steel City Jews*, 188. In addition to noting that the activities of the school were guided by the Jewish faith and goodwill, Burstin also acknowledges that the established Jewish community may have acted quickly to assimilate Eastern European Jews to dissuade a rise of antisemitism in Pittsburgh.

56. Selavan, "Founding of Columbian Council," 38, 41. Metzger, "Study of Social Settlement Workers," 29.

57. Selavan, "Founding of Columbian Council," 41.

58. Metzger, "Study of Social Settlement Workers," 29.

59. Greenwald and Anderson, *Pittsburgh Surveyed*, 1–2. The volumes of the Pittsburgh Survey include *Women and the Trades*; *Work-Accidents and the Law*; *The Steel Workers*; *Homestead: The Households of a Mill Town*; *The Pittsburgh District: Civic Frontage*; and *Wage-Earning Pittsburgh*.

60. "Twentieth Century Club Passes Another Milestone," *Bulletin Index*, November 6, 1930, 10, 20.

61. Muccigrosso, *Celebrating the New World*, 64. Tselos, "Chicago Fair and the Myth," 263.

62. Tselos, "Chicago Fair and the Myth," 263.

63. Burg, *Chicago's White City of 1893*, 312–13. Hines, *Burnham of Chicago*, 138.

64. Perrin, "Wisconsin Architecture," 119–20. Muller and Bauman, "Olmsteds in Pittsburgh," 128.

65. For an examination of the use of temporary material to build the Columbian Exposition, see Graff, "Dream City, Plaster City," 705–9.

66. Tarr, "Infrastructure and City-Building," 231. Gruen, *Manifest Destinations*, 114, 121.

67. Kidney, *Landmark Architecture*, 62.

68. Kidney, *Landmark Architecture*, 73. Schlereth, *Victorian America*, 133.

69. Hines, *Burnham of Chicago*, 371–83, contains a list of all buildings associated with Burnham.

70. Hines, *Burnham of Chicago*, 221. The Henry Clay Frick Business Records, Archives and Special Collections, University of Pittsburgh Library System, contains the enormous amount of correspondence relating to the building projects, particularly the Frick Building.

71. Toker, *Pittsburgh: A New Portrait*: Park Building, 65–66; Arrott Building, 58–59; and Buhl Building, 67.

72. Bauman and Muller, *Before Renaissance*, 7, 10, 37.

73. Muller and Bauman, "Olmsteds in Pittsburgh," 132. Lubove, "City Beautiful, City Banal," 28.

74. Judd, "Edward M. Bigelow," 53. Bauman and Muller, *Before Renaissance*, 6. Bernstein, "Pittsburgh's Benevolent Tyrant," 39.

75. Toker, *Pittsburgh: A New Portrait*, 237.

76. Bauman and Muller, "Olmsteds in Pittsburgh," 195. Olmsted, *Pittsburgh, Main Thoroughfares*.

7: OAKLAND

1. Burnham, "White City and Capital City," 619. For information on early City Beautiful city plans, see, for Washington, DC, Hines, "Imperial Mall"; for Cleveland, Simpson, "Civic Center and Cultural Center," 127–35; and for Chicago, Smith, *Plan of Chicago*.

2. For analysis of Olmsted's downtown proposal, see Simpson, "Civic Center and Cultural Center," 55–56, and Oakland proposal, 88–89.

3. Simpson, "Civic Center and Cultural Center," 96–97, argues that Oakland developed into a model cultural center for other cities before coming to terms with its own status as such.

4. Toker, *Pittsburgh: A New Portrait*, 320. Couvares, *Remaking of Pittsburgh*, 107. For more on Mary Croghan Schenley, see Oresick, "What's in a Namesake?," 22–35.

5. Judd, "Edward M. Bigelow," 54. Bauman and Muller, *Before Renaissance*, 37.

6. Judd, "Edward M. Bigelow," 66. Couvares, *Remaking of Pittsburgh*, 106–8.

7. Guttenberg, *Botanical Guide through the Phipps Conservatories*, 9.

8. Guttenberg, *Botanical Guide through the Phipps Conservatories*, 10. "Big Plants for the Park," *Pittsburgh Post*, September 23, 1893.

9. Judd, "Edward M. Bigelow," 60.

10. For evidence of the proposed relocation of the Pennsylvania State Building, see

"Will Not Be Purchased," *Pittsburgh Press*, October 14, 1893. Simpson, "Civic Center and Cultural Center," 70–71. Butko, *Luna*, 16.

11. Evert and Gay, *Discovering Pittsburgh's Sculpture*, 191. Toker, *Pittsburgh: A New Portrait*, 350.

12. Muller and Bauman, "Olmsteds in Pittsburgh," 132. Simpson, "Civic Center and Cultural Center," 73–81, recounts the events surrounding the transition from a park entry to the Schenley fountain.

13. Gangewere, *Palace of Culture*, 17. Toker, *Pittsburgh: A New Portrait*, 320–21. Simpson, "Civic Center and Cultural Center," 65–68.

14. Neal, *Wise Extravagance*, 12, 14. Gangewere, *Palace of Culture*, 30. Toker, *Pittsburgh: A New Portrait*, 339.

15. Toker, *Pittsburgh: A New Portrait*, 338, 342. Couvares, *Remaking of Pittsburgh*, 105.

16. For information about early exhibits, see the Carnegie Museum Annual Reports of the Director. For more on the *Diplodocus* casts, see Nieuwland, *American Dinosaur Abroad*.

17. Schloetzer, "Andrew Carnegie's Original Reproductions," 38. Toker, *Pittsburgh: A New Portrait*, 347.

18. Saint-Gaudens, "Carnegie Institute," 297.

19. Schloetzer, "Andrew Carnegie's Original Reproductions," 46. For more information about the use of casts in museums, see Jacknis, "Refracting Images," 274–75.

20. Rhor, "Mural Painting and Public Schools," 62–70. Rhor also notes the absence of labor unrest, a subject Alexander documented for *Harper's Weekly*, and African Americans in the mural, which offers commentary on the beliefs of Carnegie and industrialists like him. Alexander, "A Description of John W. Alexander's Mural Decorations Entitled 'The Crowning of Labor,'" box 1, folder 1, John White Alexander Papers, Archives of American Art, Smithsonian Institution, Washington, DC.

21. L. G. Laureau to Andrew Carnegie, October 3, 1893, box 22, 4123–26, Andrew Carnegie Papers, Manuscript Division, Library of Congress, Washington, DC.

22. Neal, *Wise Extravagance*, 14. Gangewere, *Palace of Culture*, 132. Clark, *International Encounters*, 42.

23. Clark, *International Encounters*, 44.

24. Gangewere, *Palace of Culture*, 135. Clark, *International Encounters*, 50.

25. Clark, *International Encounters*, 18, 42.

26. Clark, *International Encounters*, 148, 151.

27. For more on Western Pennsylvanian art collecting at the end of the nineteenth century, see Weisberg, McIntosh, and McQueen, *Guide to Collecting in the Gilded Age*.

28. Muller and Bauman, "Olmsteds in Pittsburgh," 132. For more on Nicola's life,

see "Death Takes F. F. Nicola, Civic Leader," *Pittsburgh Post-Gazette*, August 19, 1938, I, 11.

29. Lubove, "City Beautiful, City Banal," 29. Toker, *Pittsburgh: A New Portrait*, 321. Simpson, "Civic Center and Cultural Center," 72.

30. Aurand, *Spectator and the Topographical City*, 152. For more on Hornbostel and the École des Beaux-Arts, see Rosenblum, "Architecture of Henry Hornbostel," 32–47.

31. Aurand, *Spectator and the Topographical City*, 139–40. Toker, *Pittsburgh: A New Portrait*, 355, 358. Rosenblum, "Architecture of Henry Hornbostel," 164.

32. Aurand, *Spectator and the Topographical City*, 151. Rosenblum, "Architecture of Henry Hornbostel," 168–74, 180, argues that the buildings reflect modern French design.

33. Aurand, *Spectator and the Topographical City*, 154.

34. Aurand, *Spectator and the Topographical City*, 152. For more on these buildings, see Rosenblum, "Architecture of Henry Hornbostel," 177–87.

35. Rosenblum, "Architecture of Henry Hornbostel," 207–9. Toker, *Pittsburgh: A New Portrait*, 323.

36. "List of material donated to the Western University from Worlds Fair Exhibits," box 2, folder 10, Chancellor William Holland Papers, Archives and Special Collections, University of Pittsburgh Library System.

37. Fessenden, *Fessenden*, 62–72. Starrett, *Through One Hundred and Fifty Years*, 193–94.

38. "Report of the Committee on the Change of Name of the University," March 4, 1908, Minutes of the Meeting of the Board of Trustees of the Western University of Pennsylvania, Western University of Pennsylvania. Board of Trustees Minutes, Archives and Special Collections, University of Pittsburgh Library System.

39. Aurand, *Spectator and the Topographical City*, 179–89. Rosenblum, "Architecture of Henry Hornbostel," 210, references six constructed buildings as being part of Hornbostel's Acropolis Plan, possibly incorrectly including the Old Mellon Institute and Alumni Hall in his count.

40. Rosenblum, "Architecture of Henry Hornbostel," 189–92. Toker, *Pittsburgh: A New Portrait*, 283–85.

41. Rosenblum, "Architecture of Henry Hornbostel," 203. Toker, *Pittsburgh: A New Portrait*, 371–73.

42. For information on Benno Janssen's Oakland buildings, see Miller, *Architecture of Benno Janssen*, and Toker, *Pittsburgh: A New Portrait*, 330–31, 373–74.

43. Skrabec, *World's Richest Neighborhood*. Couvares, *Remaking of Pittsburgh*, 103, 107.

44. Butko, *Luna*, 16–17. The author defers to Butko's extensive review of local newspaper coverage concerning early attractions in Oakland.

45. For more on Forbes Field, see Bonk, "Ballpark Figures," 53–70.

46. Butko, *Luna*, 34. Marylynne Pitz, "Luna Park's Luminary: Entrepreneur/Roller Coaster Designer Deserves His Due," *Pittsburgh Post-Gazette*, September 1, 2008.

47. Butko, *Luna*, 28–29. Warren, "City as Theme Park," 85–87.

48. Butko, *Luna*, 43.

49. Butko, *Luna*, 47–48. "Pittsburg Luna Park," *Street Railway Review*, May 15, 1905, 311.

50. Butko, *Luna*, 57. "Pittsburg Luna Park," 312.

51. Butko, *Luna*, 56.

52. Butko, *Luna*, 62. "Pittsburg Luna Park," 312.

53. Butko, *Luna*, 69. The target audience for the park is evident in the amount of ink expended by the *Pittsburgh Bulletin*, a newspaper targeted toward the middle and upper classes of the East End, while promoting its attractions.

54. Florence Larrabee Lattimore, "Skunk Hollow: The Squatter," in Kellogg, *Pittsburgh District Civic Frontage*, 130. Tarr, "Pittsburgh Survey as an Environmental Statement," 175–76.

55. Butko, *Luna*, 48–49.

56. Butko, *Luna*, 97. During the local Sabbath debate during the Columbian Exposition, the fact that Phipps Conservatory was successfully opened on Sundays was a reason many Pittsburghers supported the Chicago fair being open seven days a week. That Kennywood came under fire for Sunday openings thus resulting in Luna's closure demonstrates the region's, or at least the ruling class's, conservative bent in the early twentieth century.

57. Butko, *Luna*, 9–10, 83–84.

58. "Pittsburgh's Civic Center," *Builder*, October 1912, 36.

59. Bauman and Muller, *Before Renaissance*, 48.

EPILOGUE

1. *Official Book of the Fair*, 8–9.

2. Chicago World's Fair Centennial Celebration, H.R. Doc. No. 293-73 (1934), 1–5.

3. *Official Book of the Fair*, 93–97.

4. Schrenk, *Building a Century of Progress*, 213–26.

5. Schiavo, "Modern Design Goes Public," 81, 89–90. Ganz, *1933 Chicago World's Fair*, 63.

6. Schrenk, *Building a Century of Progress*, 227–41. Schiavo, "Modern Design Goes Public," 90.

7. Couvares, *Remaking of Pittsburgh*, 81. Table 16, "Population of the 100 Largest Urban Places: 1930," found in Campbell Gibson, "Population of the 100 Largest Cities and Other Urban Places in the United States: 1790–1990," U.S. Bureau of the Census, Working Paper No. POP-WP027, June 1998.

8. Miller, *Architecture of Benno Janssen*, 140–51.

Bibliography

ARCHIVAL COLLECTIONS

Alberts, Robert C. Papers, 1812–1988, MSS 37. Detre Library and Archives, Senator John Heinz History Center, Pittsburgh

Alexander, John White. Papers, 1775–1968, AAA.alexjohn. Archives of American Art, Smithsonian Institution, Washington, DC

Aluminum Company of America. Records, 1857–1992, MSS 282. Detre Library and Archives, Senator John Heinz History Center, Pittsburgh

Burnham, Daniel H. Collection, 1836–1946, 1943.1. Art Institute of Chicago

Carnegie, Andrew. Papers, 1803–1935, MSS 15107. Manuscript Division, Library of Congress, Washington, DC

Carnegie Steel Corporation. Records, 1853–1912, MSS 315. Detre Library and Archives, Senator John Heinz History Center, Pittsburgh

Dwyer, Britta C. Papers, 1985, MSS 760. Detre Library and Archives, Senator John Heinz History Center, Pittsburgh

Ferris, George Washington Gale. Papers, 1892–1896. Chicago Historical Society

Frick, Henry Clay. Business Records, 1892–1987, AIS.2002.06. Archives and Special Collections, University of Pittsburgh Library System

Frick, Henry Clay. Papers. Frick Collection, Frick Art Reference Library Archives, New York, NY

George Westinghouse Museum Collection, c.1864–2007, MSS 920. Detre Library and Archives, Senator John Heinz History Center, Pittsburgh

Greater Pittsburgh Chamber of Commerce. Records, 1874–1996, MSS 284. Detre Library and Archives, Senator John Heinz History Center, Pittsburgh

H. J. Heinz Company. Records, 1850s–1996, MSS 57. Detre Library and Archives, Senator John Heinz History Center, Pittsburgh

Holland, Chancellor William. Papers, 1891–1901, UA.2.10.1891. Archives and Special Collections, University of Pittsburgh Library System

Holland Family Papers, 1747–1933, MSS 168. Detre Library and Archives, Senator John Heinz History Center, Pittsburgh

Kingsley Association. Records, 1894–1980, AIS.1970.05. Archives and Special Collections, University of Pittsburgh Library System

Magee Family Papers, 1790–1952, DAR.1968.01. Archives and Special Collections, University of Pittsburgh Library System

National Council of Jewish Women. Pittsburgh Section Records, 1894–2011, AIS.1964.40. Archives and Special Collections, University of Pittsburgh Library System

Starrett, Agnes Lynch. Research Files, 1787–1962, UA.0.3.1. Archives and Special Collections, University of Pittsburgh Library System

Western University of Pennsylvania. Board of Trustees Minutes, UA.1.4. Archives and Special Collections, University of Pittsburgh Library System

Westinghouse Electric Corporation. Records, 1865–2000, MSS 424. Detre Library and Archives, Senator John Heinz History Center, Pittsburgh

World's Columbian Exposition Records, 1890–1904. Chicago Historical Society

PERIODICALS

Bulletin and *Bulletin Index* (Pittsburgh)
Canonsburg Weekly Notes
Chicago Journal of Commerce and Metal Industries
Christian Recorder
Commercial Gazette (Pittsburgh)
Daily Commercial (Pittsburgh)
Electrical Engineer
Engineering Magazine
Engineering News
Frank Leslie's Illustrated
Iron Age
National Labor Tribune
New York Times
News-Herald (Franklin, PA)
Pittsburg Dispatch
Pittsburgh Gazette
Pittsburgh Post
Pittsburgh Post-Gazette
Pittsburgh Press
Scientific American

Scientific Machinist

Washington Post

Western Electrician

World's Columbian Exposition Illustrated

PRIMARY AND SECONDARY SOURCES

Addresses Delivered before the World's Railway Commerce Congress. Chicago: Railway Age and Northwestern Railroaders, 1893.

Alberts, Robert C. *The Good Provider: H. J. Heinz and His 57 Varieties.* Boston: Houghton Mifflin, 1973.

Anderson, Norman D. *Ferris Wheels: An Illustrated History.* Bowling Green, OH: Bowling Green State University Popular Press, 1992.

Appelbaum, Stanley. *Spectacle in the White City: The Chicago 1893 World's Fair.* Mineola, NY: Calla Editions, 2009.

Aurand, Martin. *The Spectator and the Topographical City.* Pittsburgh: University of Pittsburgh Press, 2006.

Bancroft, Hubert Howe. *The Book of the Fair: An Historical and Descriptive Presentation of the World's Science, Art, and Industry, as Viewed through the Columbian Exposition at Chicago in 1893.* 5 vols. Chicago: Bancroft, 1893.

Bauman, John F., and Edward K. Muller. *Before Renaissance: Planning in Pittsburgh, 1889–1943.* Pittsburgh: University of Pittsburgh Press, 2006.

Bauman, John F., and Edward K. Muller. "The Olmsteds in Pittsburgh: (Part II) Shaping the Progressive City." *Pittsburgh History,* Winter 1993/1994, 191–205.

Belfield, Robert B. "Niagara Frontier: The Evolution of Electric Power Systems in New York and Ontario, 1880–1935." PhD diss., University of Pennsylvania, 1981.

Bernstein, Steven. "Pittsburgh's Benevolent Tyrant: Christopher Lyman Magee." *Western Pennsylvania History,* Summer 2003, 24–40.

Blalock, Thomas J., and Craig A. Woodworth. "25-Hz at Niagara Falls: End of an Era on the Niagara Frontier, Part I." *IEEE Power & Energy Magazine,* January/February 2008, 84–90.

Blight, David W. *Frederick Douglass: Prophet of Freedom.* New York: Simon and Schuster, 2018.

Bonk, Daniel L. "Ballpark Figures: The Story of Forbes Field." *Pittsburgh History,* Summer 1993, 53–70.

Bonney, Charles C. "Bibliography of World's Congress Publications." *Dial,* January 1, 1896, 7–10.

Brain, David. "Discipline & Style: The Ecole des Beaux-Arts and the Social Production of an American Architecture." *Theory and Society* 18, no. 6 (1989): 807–68.

Brands, H. W. *The Reckless Decade: America in the 1890s*. Chicago: University of Chicago Press, 2002.

Bridge, James Howard. *The Inside History of the Carnegie Steel Company: A Romance of Millions*. New York: Aldine Book Company, 1903.

Brownell, W. C. "The Paris Exposition: Notes and Impressions." *Scribner's Magazine*, January 1890, 18–35.

Brownfield, Robert L. *Pennsylvania Art Contributions: State Building, Art Gallery and Women's Building*. Harrisburg: Edwin K. Meyers, 1893.

Burg, David F. *Chicago's White City of 1893*. Lexington: University Press of Kentucky, 2015.

Burgoyne, Arthur G. *All Sorts of Pittsburghers*. Pittsburgh: Leader All Sorts, 1892.

Burnham, Daniel H. "White City and Capital City." *Century Illustrated Magazine*, February 1902, 619–20.

Burnham, Daniel Hudson, Joan E. Draper, and Thomas S. Hines. *The Final Official Report of the Director of Works of the World's Columbian Exposition*. 2 vols. New York: Garland, 1989.

Burstin, Barbara Stern. *Steel City Jews: A History of Pittsburgh and Its Jewish Community*. Pittsburgh: Barbara S. Burstin, 2008.

Butera, Ronald J. "A Settlement House and the Urban Challenge: Kingsley House in Pittsburgh, Pennsylvania, 1893–1920." *Western Pennsylvania Historical Magazine*, January 1983, 25–48.

Butko, Brian. "Heinz: Much More than 57 Varieties." *Western Pennsylvania History*, Fall 2014, 20–33.

Butko, Brian. *Luna: Pittsburgh's Original Lost Kennywood*. Pittsburgh: Senator John Heinz History Center, 2017.

Calhoun, Charles W., ed. *The Gilded Age: Perspectives on the Origins of Modern America*. 2nd ed. Lanham, MD: Rowman and Littlefield, 2007.

Campbell, John A., ed. *A Biographical History with Portraits of Prominent Men of the Great West*. Chicago: Western Biographical and Engraving Company, 1902.

Carnegie, Andrew. *The Gospel of Wealth and Other Timely Essays*. New York: Century, 1901.

Carnegie, Andrew. "A Look Ahead." *North American Review* 156, no. 439 (June 1893): 685–710.

Carnegie, Andrew. "Value of the World's Fair." *Engineering Magazine*, January 1894, 417–22.

Catalogue: Catholic Educational Exhibit. Chicago: La Monte-O'Donnell, 1893.

Catalogue of the Exhibit of the Pennsylvania Railroad Company at the World's Columbian Exposition. Chicago: n.p., 1893.

Catalogue of the Exhibits of the State of Pennsylvania and of Pennsylvanians at the World's Columbian Exposition. Harrisburg, PA: C. M. Busch, 1893.

Centennial Exhibition Philadelphia, Pa., United States Centennial Commission. *International Exhibition, 1876: Official Catalogue.* 5th and rev. ed. Philadelphia: John R. Nagle, 1876.

Chamber of Commerce of Pittsburgh. *Guide to All Points of Interest in and about Pittsburgh.* Pittsburgh: Chamber of Commerce, 1893.

Cheney, Margaret. *Tesla: Man Out of Time.* New York: Touchstone, 2001.

Clark, Vicky A. *International Encounters: The Carnegie International and Contemporary Art, 1896–1996.* Pittsburgh: Carnegie Museum of Art, 1996.

Committee for the International Exposition of 1892 of the City of New York. *Address to the Senate and House of Representatives of the United States of America.* New York: Committee for the International Exposition, 1890.

Corn, Wanda M. *Women Building History: Public Art at the 1893 Columbian Exposition.* Berkeley: University of California Press, 2011.

Cotkin, George. *Reluctant Modernism: American Thought and Culture, 1880–1900.* New York: Twayne, 1992.

Couvares, Francis G. *The Remaking of Pittsburgh: Class and Culture in an Industrializing City, 1877–1919.* Albany: State University of New York Press, 1984.

Crow, James E. "Report of the Chief Engineer of the Fire Department." In *Annual Report of the Comptroller and the Various Officers and Standing Committees of the City Government, City of Allegheny, for the Fiscal Year Ending December 31, 1883, by Order of Councils,* 235–63. Pittsburgh: Best, 1884.

Dahlinger, Charles W. "The Pittsburgh Sanitary Fair." *Western Pennsylvania Historical Magazine,* April 1929, 97–101.

Daniel, Dorothy. "The Sanitary Fair." *Western Pennsylvania Historical Magazine,* Summer 1958, 145–62.

Davis, George L. "Pittsburgh's Industrial Representation in Fairs and Expositions, 1852–1900." *Western Pennsylvania Historical Magazine,* Fall 1956, 175–85.

Davis, Kathleen. "Tycoon Medievalism, Corporate Philanthropy, and American Pedagogy." *American Literary History* 22, no. 4 (2010): 781–800.

Description of the Westinghouse Air Brake Co's Exhibits at the Centennial Exhibition, Philadelphia, PA. Pittsburgh: S. R. Johnston, 1876.

Doenecke, Justus D. "Myths, Machines and Markets: The Columbian Exposition of 1893." *Journal of Popular Culture* 6, no. 3 (1973): 535–49.

Downey, Dennis B. "The Congress on Labor at the 1893 World's Columbian Exposition." *Journal of the Illinois State Historical Society* 76, no. 2 (1983): 131–38.

Downey, Dennis B. *A Season of Renewal: The Columbian Exposition and Victorian America*. Westport, CT: Praeger, 2002.

Dudley, Pemberton. *Transactions of the World's Congress of Homoeopathic Physicians and Surgeons*. Philadelphia: Sherman, 1894.

Eagle, Mary Kavanaugh Oldham, ed. *The Congress of Women Held in the Woman's Building, World's Columbian Exposition*. Chicago: S. I. Bell, 1894.

Edison Electric Light Company. *A Warning from the Edison Electric Light Co.* [New York, NY?]: Edison Electric Light, [1887?].

Evert, Marilyn, and Vernon Gay. *Discovering Pittsburgh's Sculpture*. Pittsburgh: University of Pittsburgh Press, 1983.

Feldman, Jacob S. *The Jewish Experience in Western Pennsylvania: A History, 1755–1945*. Pittsburgh: Historical Society of Western Pennsylvania, 1986.

Fessenden, Helen M. *Fessenden: Builder of Tomorrows*. New York: Coward-McCann, 1940.

Fincher, Jack. "George Ferris Jr. and the Great Wheel of Fortune." *Smithsonian*, July 1983, 108–18.

First Annual Report of the Kingsley House Association, June 20, 1894, No. 1707 Penn Avenue, Pittsburgh, Pa. Pittsburgh: William G. Johnston, 1894.

Fleming, George Thornton. *History of Pittsburgh and Environs*. 5 vols. New York: American Historical Society, 1922.

Flinn, John J. *Official Guide to Midway Plaisance*. Chicago: Columbian Guide, 1893.

Gangewere, Robert J. *Palace of Culture: Andrew Carnegie's Museums and Library in Pittsburgh*. Pittsburgh: University of Pittsburgh Press, 2011.

Ganz, Cheryl R. *The 1933 Chicago World's Fair: A Century of Progress*. Urbana: University of Illinois Press, 2008.

Glasco, Laurence. "Double Burden: The Black Experience in Pittsburgh." In Hays, *City at the Point*, 69–109.

Glasco, Laurence A., ed. *The WPA History of the Negro in Pittsburgh*. Pittsburgh: University of Pittsburgh Press, 2004.

Graff, Rebecca S. "Dream City, Plaster City: Worlds' Fairs and the Gilding of American Material Culture." *International Journal of Historical Archaeology* 16, no. 4 (2012): 696–716.

Greenwald, Maurine W. "Women and Class in Pittsburgh, 1850–1920." In Hays, *City at the Point*, 33–68.

Greenwald, Maurine W., and Margo Anderson, ed. *Pittsburgh Surveyed: Social Science and Social Reform in the Early Twentieth Century*. Pittsburgh: University of Pittsburgh Press, 1996.

Griggs, Frank, Jr. "George S. Morison: Pontifex Maximus." *STRUCTURE Magazine*, February 2008, 54–57.

Grom, Robert M. *Physician-Soldiers at the Forks: The Impact of the Military on Medical Care in Pittsburgh (1754–1900)*. Charleston, SC: America through Time, 2019.

Gruen, J. Philip. *Manifest Destinations: Cities and Tourists in the Nineteenth-Century American West*. Norman: University of Oklahoma Press, 2014.

Guttenberg, Gustave. *Botanical Guide through the Phipps Conservatories in Pittsburg and Allegheny*. Pittsburg: Foster, Dick, 1894.

H. J. Heinz Company: Producers, Manufacturers and Distributors. Pittsburgh: H. J. Heinz, 1910.

Hall, J. Morton. *America's Industrial Centre: Pittsburgh's Great Industries, and Its Enormous Development in the Leading Products of the World*. Pittsburgh: Wm. G. Johnston, 1891.

Handy, Moses P., ed. *The Official Directory of the World's Columbian Exposition*. Chicago: W. B. Conkey, 1893.

Hanson, J. W. *The World's Congress of Religions; the Addresses and Papers Delivered before the Parliament, and an Abstract of the Congresses*. Chicago: Monarch, 1894.

Harlan, A. W., ed. *Transactions of the World's Columbian Dental Congress*. 2 vols. Chicago: Knight, Leonard, 1894.

Harvey, George. *Henry Clay Frick: The Man*. New York: C. Scribner's Sons, 1928.

Hays, Samuel P., ed. *City at the Point: Essays on the Social History of Pittsburgh*. Pittsburgh: University of Pittsburgh Press, 1989.

Hays, Samuel P. "The Development of Pittsburgh as a Social Order." *Western Pennsylvania Historical Magazine*, October 1974, 431–48.

Higinbotham, Harlow N. *The Report of the President to the Board of Directors of the World's Columbian Exposition, 1892–1893*. Chicago: Rand, McNally, 1898.

Hines, Thomas S. *Burnham of Chicago: Architect and Planner*. New York: Oxford University Press, 1974.

Hines, Thomas S. "The Imperial Mall: The City Beautiful Movement and the Washington Plan of 1901–1902." *Studies in the History of Art* 30 (1991): 78–99.

Hogg, J. Bernard. "The Homestead Strike of 1892." PhD diss., University of Chicago, 1943.

Holland, William J. *Abstract of the Report of the Chancellor of the Western University of Pennsylvania, June 5, 1893*. Pittsburgh: Western University of Pennsylvania, 1893.

Holland, William J. *The Carnegie Museum Pittsburgh Annual Report of the Director for the Year Ending March 31, 1898*. Pittsburgh: Murdoch-Kerr, 1898.

Holland, William J. *The Carnegie Museum Pittsburgh Annual Report of the Director for the Year Ending March 31, 1899*. Pittsburgh: Murdoch-Kerr, 1899.

Holland, William J. *The Carnegie Museum Pittsburgh Annual Report of the Director for the Year Ending March 31, 1900*. Pittsburgh: Murdoch-Kerr, 1900.

Holland, William J. *The Carnegie Museum Pittsburgh Annual Report of the Director for the Year Ending March 31, 1901*. Pittsburgh: Murdoch-Kerr, 1901.

Hughes, Thomas P. *Networks of Power: Electrification in Western Society, 1880–1930*. Baltimore, MD: Johns Hopkins University Press, 1983.

Hutton, John. "Picking Fruit: Mary Cassatt's 'Modern Woman' and the Woman's Building of 1893." *Feminist Studies* 20, no. 2 (1994): 318–48.

Industries and Wealth of Pittsburgh and Environs. New York: American Publishing and Engraving, 1890.

Ingham, John N. "Steel City Aristocrats." In Hays, *City at the Point*, 265–94.

Ingram, J. S. *Centennial Exposition Described and Illustrated*. Philadelphia: Hubbard Bros., 1876.

Jacknis, Ira. "Refracting Images: Anthropological Display at the Chicago World's Fair, 1893." In *Coming of Age in Chicago: The 1893 World's Fair and the Coalescence of American Anthropology*, edited by Curtis M. Hinsley and David R. Wilcox, 261–336. Lincoln: University of Nebraska Press, 2016.

Jay, Robert. "Taller than Eiffel's Tower: The London and Chicago Tower Projects, 1889–1894." *Journal of the Society of Architectural Historians* 46, no. 2 (1987): 145–56.

Johnson, Karl E. "From Sabbath to Weekend: Recreation, Sabbatarianism, and the Emergence of the Weekend." PhD diss., Cornell University, 2011.

Johnson, Rossiter, ed. *A History of the World's Columbian Exposition*. 4 vols. New York: D. Appleton, 1897.

Jonnes, Jill. *Empires of Light: Edison, Tesla, Westinghouse, and the Race to Electrify the World*. New York: Random House, 2003.

Jucha, Robert John. "The Anatomy of a Streetcar Suburb: A Development and Architectural History of Pittsburgh's Shadyside District, 1860–1920." PhD diss., George Washington University, 1980.

Judd, Barbara. "Edward M. Bigelow: Creator of Pittsburgh's Arcadian Parks." *Western Pennsylvania Historical Magazine*, January 1975, 53–67.

Karlowicz, Titus M. "American Expositions and Architecture." Summary in "Proceedings of Thematic Sessions of the Twenty-Ninth Annual Meeting of the Society of Architectural Historians." *Journal of the Society of Architectural Historians* 35, no. 4 (1976): 272–79.

Karlowicz, Titus M. "D. H. Burnham's Role in the Selection of Architects for the

World's Columbian Exposition." *Journal of the Society of Architectural Historians* 29, no. 3 (1970): 247–54.

Keeler, James E. "The Wave-Lengths of the Two Brightest Lines in the Spectrum of the Nebulae." *Astronomy and Astrophysics* 12 (1893): 733–36.

Kellogg, Paul Underwood, ed. *The Pittsburgh District Civic Frontage*. New York: Survey Associates, 1914.

Kidney, Walter C. *Landmark Architecture: Pittsburgh and Allegheny County*. Pittsburgh: Pittsburgh History and Landmarks Foundation, 1985.

Kitch, Carolyn. "'A Piazza from Which the View Is Constantly Changing': The Promise of Class and Gender Mobility on the Pennsylvania Railroad's Cross-Country Tours." *Pennsylvania History* 72, no. 4 (Autumn 2005): 505–27.

Kleinberg, Susan J. "Technology and Women's Work: The Lives of Working Class Women in Pittsburgh, 1870–1900." *Labor History* 17, no. 1 (1976): 58–72.

Knight, Louise W. *Citizen: Jane Addams and the Struggle for Democracy*. Chicago: University of Chicago Press, 2005.

Krause, Paul. *The Battle for Homestead, 1880–1892: Politics, Culture, and Steel*. Pittsburgh: University of Pittsburgh Press, 1992.

Larson, Erik. *The Devil in the White City: Murder, Magic and Madness at the Fair That Changed America*. New York: Crown, 2002.

Learned, Henry Barrett. "Social Settlements in the United States." *University Extension World* 3, no. 4 (April 1894): 102–12.

Lederer, Francis L., II. "Competition for the World's Columbian Exposition: The Chicago Campaign." *Journal of the Illinois State Historical Society* 65, no. 4 (1972): 382–94.

Leupp, Francis E. *George Westinghouse: His Life and Achievements*. Boston: Little, Brown, 1918.

Lewis, Arnold. *An Early Encounter with Tomorrow: Europeans, Chicago's Loop, and the World's Columbian Exposition*. Urbana: University of Illinois Press, 1997.

List of World's Congress Departments, Divisions and Chairmen of Committees as contained in the Preliminary Publications of the Auxiliary; to January, 1892. Chicago: World's Congress Auxiliary, 1892.

Litwicki, Ellen M. "The Influence of Commerce, Technology, and Race on Popular Culture in the Gilded Age." In Calhoun, *Gilded Age*, 187–209.

Livesay, Harold C. *Andrew Carnegie and the Rise of Big Business*. New York: Longman, 2000.

Locomotives Exhibited by the Pittsburgh Locomotive Works. Allegheny, PA: Office and Works, 1893.

Lubar, Steven. "Transmitting the Power of Niagara: Scientific, Technological, and

Cultural Contexts of an Engineering Decision." *IEEE Technology and Society Magazine*, March 1989, 11–18.

Lubove, Roy. "City Beautiful, City Banal: Design Advocacy and Historic Preservation in Pittsburgh." *Pittsburgh History*, Spring 1992, 26–36.

Lubove, Roy. "Pittsburgh and the Uses of Social Welfare History." In Hays, *City at the Point*, 295–325.

Masich, Andrew E. "Rodman's Big Gun." *Western Pennsylvania History*, Winter 2015–2016, 20–31.

Mathews, Nancy Mowll. *Mary Cassatt: A Life*. New York: Villard Books, 1994.

Matthews, William H. *The Meaning of the Social Settlement Movement, Together with a Chronological Sketch of the Development of the Work of Kingsley House, Pittsburgh, Pa*. Pittsburgh: Kingsley House, 1909.

McCabe, James D. *The Illustrated History of the Centennial Exhibition, Held in Commemoration of the One Hundredth Anniversary of American Independence*. Philadelphia: National Publishing, 1876.

McCrossen, Alexis. *Holy Day, Holiday: The American Sunday*. Ithaca, NY: Cornell University Press, 2000.

Mercer, L. P. *Review of the World's Religious Congresses of the World's Congress Auxiliary of the World's Columbian Exposition*. Chicago: Rand, McNally, 1893.

Metzger, Elizabeth A. "A Study of Social Settlement Workers in Pittsburgh, 1893–1927." Seminar paper, Department of History, University of Pittsburgh, 1974.

Miller, Donald. *The Architecture of Benno Janssen*. Pittsburgh: Carnegie Mellon University, 1997.

Miller, Ernest C. "Pennsylvania's Petroleum Industry." *Pennsylvania History* 49, no. 3 (1982): 201–17.

Minutes of the Board of World's Fair Managers of Pennsylvania. Harrisburg, PA: n.p., 1894.

Minutes of the Executive Committee of the Board of World's Fair Managers of Pennsylvania. Harrisburg, PA: n.p., 1894.

Morris, Charles R. *The Tycoons: How Andrew Carnegie, John D. Rockefeller, Jay Gould, and J. P. Morgan Invented the American Supereconomy*. New York: Henry Holt, 2005.

Muccigrosso, Robert. *Celebrating the New World: Chicago's Columbian Exposition of 1893*. Chicago: Ivan R. Dee, 1993.

Muller, Edward K. "Industrial Suburbs and the Growth of Metropolitan Pittsburgh, 1870–1920." *Journal of Historical Geography* 27, no. 1 (2001): 58–73.

Muller, Edward K., and John F. Bauman. "The Olmsteds in Pittsburgh: (Part I) Landscaping the Private City." *Pittsburgh History*, Fall 1993, 122–40.

Municipal Record: Minutes of the Proceedings of the Common Council of the City of Pittsburgh for the Year 1893–4. Pittsburgh: Devine, 1894.

Municipal Record: Minutes of the Proceedings of the Select Council of the City of Pittsburgh for the Year 1891–2. Pittsburgh: Devine, 1892.

Municipal Record: Minutes of the Proceedings of the Select Council of the City of Pittsburgh for the Year 1893–4. Pittsburgh: Devine, 1894.

Nasaw, David. *Andrew Carnegie*. New York: Penguin, 2006.

Nasaw, David. *Going Out: The Rise and Fall of Public Amusements*. New York: Basic Books, 1993.

Neal, Kenneth. *A Wise Extravagance: The Founding of the Carnegie International Exhibitions, 1895–1901*. Pittsburgh: University of Pittsburgh Press, 1996.

Nieuwland, Ilja. *American Dinosaur Abroad: A Cultural History of Carnegie's Plaster Diplodocus*. Pittsburgh: University of Pittsburgh Press, 2019.

Norton, Frank H. *Frank Leslie's Illustrated Historical Register of the Centennial Exposition, 1876*. New York: Frank Leslie, 1876.

Official Book of the Fair: An Introduction to a Century of Progress International Exposition. Chicago: A Century of Progress, 1933.

Official Manual of the Board of Lady Managers of the World's Columbian Commission. Chicago: Rand, McNally, 1891.

Official Report of the Fifth Universal Peace Congress. Boston: American Peace Society, 1893.

Olmsted, Frederick Law. *Pittsburgh, Main Thoroughfares and the Down Town District: Improvements Necessary to Meet the City's Present and Future Needs*. Pittsburgh: Committee on City Planning, 1911.

Oresick, Jake. "What's in a Namesake? Mary Schenley." *Western Pennsylvania History*, Fall 2015, 22–35.

Osman, Jay, and Tim Klinger. "'Susquehanna,' Pride of the Fish Commission." *Pennsylvania Angler and Boater*, September–October 1998, 35–36.

Osterberg, Max, ed. *Proceedings of the International Electrical Congress*. New York: American Institute of Electrical Engineers, 1894.

Paddon, Anna R., and Sally Turner. "African Americans and the World's Columbian Exposition." *Illinois Historical Journal* 88, no. 1 (1995): 19–36.

Papers of the Jewish Women's Congress. Philadelphia: Jewish Publication Society of America, 1894.

Parke, John E. *Recollections of Seventy Years and Historical Gleanings of Allegheny, Pennsylvania*. Boston: Rand, Avery, 1886.

Parmet, Robert D. "Competition for the World's Columbian Exposition: The New

York Campaign." *Journal of the Illinois State Historical Society* 65, no. 4 (1972): 365–81.

Patton, Phil. "'Sell the Cookstove If Necessary, but Come to the Fair.'" *Smithsonian*, June 1993, 38–51.

Peebles, Sheila Elaine. "A History of the Pittsburgh Stage, 1871–1896." Master's thesis, Kent State University, 1973.

Pennsylvania and the World's Columbian Exposition. Harrisburg: E. K. Meyers, 1893.

Pennsylvania Railroad to the Columbian Exposition. 2nd ed. Philadelphia: Allen, Lane and Scott, 1893.

Perrin, Richard W. E. "Wisconsin Architecture in the Wake of the Columbian Exposition." *Wisconsin Magazine of History*, Winter 1962/1963, 118–23.

Petroski, Henry. "The Ferris Wheel on the Occasion of Its Centennial." *American Scientist*, May–June 1993, 216–21.

Pittsburg and Its Fifth Annual Exposition. Pittsburg: Press of Pittsburg Printing Company, 1893.

"Pittsburg Luna Park." *Street Railway Review*, May 15, 1905, 311–12.

"Pittsburgh's Civic Center." *Builder*, October 1912, 36.

Proceedings of the International Congress on Aerial Navigation. New York: American Engineer and Railroad Journal, 1894.

Programme of the World's Religious Congresses of 1893. Chicago: Rand, McNally, 1893.

Prout, Henry G. *A Life of George Westinghouse.* New York: American Society of Mechanical Engineers, 1921.

Reed, Christopher Robert. *"All the World Is Here!": The Black Presence at White City.* Bloomington: Indiana University Press, 2000.

Reed, George Irving. *Century Cyclopedia of History and Biography of Pennsylvania.* Vol. 2. Chicago: Century Publishing and Engraving, 1904.

"Report of the Secretary: Inception and Organization Minutes of the Meetings and List of Members." In *The World's Columbian Water Commerce Congress.* Boston: Damrell and Upham, 1893.

Report of the Committee on Awards of the World's Columbian Commission: Special Reports upon Special Subjects or Groups. 2 vols. Washington, DC: Government Printing Office, 1901.

Report of the Proceedings of the International Congress of Charities, Correction and Philanthropy. Baltimore, MD: Friedenwald, 1894.

Reports of the United States Commissioners to the Universal Exposition of 1889 at Paris. 4 vols. Washington, DC: Government Printing Office, 1890.

Rhor, Sylvia Christina. "Mural Painting and Public Schools in Chicago, 1905–1941." PhD diss., University of Pittsburgh, 2004.

Rice, Luther V. "Ferris Wheel." In *Report of the Committee on Awards*, 473–80.

Roberts, Thomas P. *Address of Thomas P. Roberts on the Commercial Outlets of the Great Lakes, with Special Reference to the Proposed Lake Erie and Ohio River Ship Canal*. Pittsburgh: Chamber of Commerce of Pittsburgh, 1893.

Roberts, Thomas P. "The Projected Lake Erie and Ohio River Ship Canal." In *The World's Columbian Water Commerce Congress*. Boston: Damrell and Upham, 1893.

Rosenblum, Charles Loren. "The Architecture of Henry Hornbostel: Progressive and Traditional Design in the American Beaux-Arts Movement." PhD diss., University of Virginia, 2009.

Rotenstein, David S. "Model for the Nation: Sale, Slaughter, and Processing at the East Liberty Stockyards." *Western Pennsylvania History*, Winter 2010–2011, 36–47.

Rydell, Robert W. *All the World's a Fair: Visions of Empire at American International Expositions, 1876–1916*. Chicago: University of Chicago Press, 1984.

Rydell, Robert W., and Laura Burd Schiavo, eds. *Designing Tomorrow: America's World's Fairs of the 1930s*. New Haven, CT: Yale University Press, 2010.

Saint-Gaudens, Homer. "Carnegie Institute." *Art and Archaeology*, November–December 1922, 287–300.

Samber, Mark David. "Networks of Capital: Creating and Maintaining a Regional Industrial Economy in Pittsburgh, 1865–1919." PhD diss., Carnegie Mellon University, 1995.

Schiavo, Laura Burd. "Modern Design Goes Public: A Photo Essay." In Rydell and Schiavo, *Designing Tomorrow*, 77–139.

Schlereth, Thomas J. *Victorian America: Transformations in Everyday Life, 1876–1915*. New York: HarperCollins, 1991.

Schloetzer, Mattie. "Andrew Carnegie's Original Reproductions: The Hall of Architecture at 100." *Western Pennsylvania History*, Fall 2007, 36–47.

Schrenk, Lisa D. *Building a Century of Progress: The Architecture of Chicago's 1933–34 World's Fair*. Minneapolis: University of Minnesota Press, 2007.

Selavan, Ida Cohen. "The Columbian Council of Pittsburgh, 1894–1909: A Case Study of Adult Immigrant Education." PhD diss., University of Pittsburgh, 1976.

Selavan, Ida Cohen. "The Founding of Columbian Council." *American Jewish Archives*, April 1978, 24–42.

Seventh Annual Pittsburgh Exposition, 1883. Pittsburgh: Office of the Pittsburgh Exposition Society, 1883.

Silkenat, David. "Workers in the White City: Working Class Culture at the World's

Columbian Exposition of 1893." *Journal of the Illinois State Historical Society* 104, no. 4 (2011): 266–300.

Simpson, Donald E. "Civic Center and Cultural Center: The Grouping of Public Buildings in Pittsburgh, Cleveland, and Detroit and the Emergence of the City Monumental in the Modern Metropolis." PhD diss., University of Pittsburgh, 2013.

Skrabec, Quentin R., Jr. *H. J. Heinz: A Biography.* Jefferson, NC: McFarland, 2009.

Skrabec, Quentin R., Jr. *The World's Richest Neighborhood: How Pittsburgh's East Enders Forged American Industry.* New York: Algora, 2010.

Smith, Carl. *The Plan of Chicago: Daniel Burnham and the Remaking of the American City.* Chicago: University of Chicago Press, 2006.

Smith, Frank H. *Art, History, Midway Plaisance and World's Columbian Exposition.* Chicago: Foster, 1893.

Spain, Daphne. *How Women Saved the City.* Minneapolis: University of Minnesota Press, 2001.

Spencer, Ethel. *The Spencers of Amberson Avenue: A Turn-of-the-Century Memoir.* Pittsburgh: University of Pittsburgh Press, 1983.

Standiford, Les. *Meet You in Hell: Andrew Carnegie, Henry Clay Frick, and the Bitter Partnership That Changed America.* New York: Crown, 2005.

Starrett, Agnes Lynch. *Through One Hundred and Fifty Years: The University of Pittsburgh.* Pittsburgh: University of Pittsburgh Press, 1937.

Stearns, John Newton. *Temperance in All Nations: History of the Cause in All Countries of the Globe Together with the Papers, Essays, Addresses, and Discussions of the World's Temperance Congress.* New York: National Temperance Society and Publication House, 1893.

Steffens, Lincoln. *The Shame of the Cities.* New York: McClure, Phillips, 1904.

Steeples, Douglas, and David O. Whitten. *Democracy in Desperation: The Depression of 1893.* Westport, CT: Greenwood, 1998.

Tarr, Joel A. "Infrastructure and City-Building in the Nineteenth and Twentieth Centuries." In Hays, *City at the Point*, 213–63.

Tarr, Joel A. "The Pittsburgh Survey as an Environmental Statement," In Greenwald and Anderson, *Pittsburgh Surveyed*, 170–89.

Toker, Franklin. *Pittsburgh: A New Portrait.* Pittsburgh: University of Pittsburgh Press, 2009.

Toker, Franklin. *Pittsburgh: An Urban Portrait.* University Park: Pennsylvania State University Press, 1986.

Tome, Vanessa Priscilla. "The Western Pennsylvania Exposition, 1889–1916: A Microcosm of American Musical Life." PhD diss., University of Georgia, 2012.

Trachtenberg, Alan. *The Incorporation of America: Culture and Society in the Gilded Age.* New York: Hill and Wang, 1982.

Tselos, Dimitri. "The Chicago Fair and the Myth of the 'Lost Cause.'" *Journal of the Society of Architectural Historians* 26, no. 4 (1967): 259–68.

Universal Exhibition, Paris, 1889: Practical Guide. Paris: C. H. Bertels et Florent, 1889.

Vivian, Cassandra. *Hidden History of the Laurel Highlands.* Charleston, SC: History Press, 2014.

Warren, Stacy. "The City as Theme Park and the Theme Park as City: Amusement Space, Urban Form, and Cultural Change." PhD diss., University of British Columbia, 1993.

Weingardt, Richard. *Circles in the Sky: The Life and Times of George Ferris.* Reston, VA: American Society of Civil Engineers, 2009.

Weisberg, Gabriel P., DeCourcy E. McIntosh, and Alison McQueen. *A Guide to Collecting in the Gilded Age: Art Patronage in Pittsburgh, 1890–1910: An Exhibition at the Frick Art Museum, Pittsburgh, April 6–June 29, 1997.* Pittsburgh: Frick Art and Historical Center, 1997.

Wells, Ida B., Frederick Douglass, Irvine Garland Penn, and Ferdinand L. Barnett. *The Reason Why the Colored American is not in the World's Columbian Exposition: The Afro-American's Contribution to Columbian Literature.* Edited by Robert W. Rydell. Urbana: University of Illinois Press, 1999.

Wolmar, Christian. *Blood, Iron, and Gold: How the Railways Transformed the World.* New York: Public Affairs, 2010.

World's Congress of Bankers and Financiers Comprising Addresses upon Selected Financial Subjects, and Also a Series of Papers on Banking in the Several States and Territories, Prepared by Delegates Specially Appointed by the Governor. Chicago: Rand, McNally, 1893.

Zahniser, Keith A. *Steel City Gospel: Protestant Laity and Reform in Progressive-Era Pittsburgh.* New York: Routledge, 2005.

Index

Note: Page references in *italics* refer to figures.